1982

Critical Observations

A
Joan Kahn
B O O K

by the same author

THE THIRTIES
A Dream Revolved

THE TELL-TALE HEART
The Life and Works of Edgar Allan Poe

Critical Observations

JULIAN SYMONS

TICKNOR & FIELDS

New Haven and New York

1981

Library of Congress Cataloging in Publication Data

Symons, Julian, 1912-
    Critical observations.

    "A Joan Kahn book."
    1. Literature, Modern—20th century—History and criticism—Addresses, essays, lectures. I. Title.
PN771.S93   809′.04   81-8904
ISBN 0-89919-055-3   AACR2

Printed in the United States of America

s 10 9 8 7 6 5 4 3 2 1

Contents

Contents

PERSONAL MEETINGS

FOR ROBERT CONQUEST

Preface

These essays, articles and reviews are a selection from a much larger number written over the past fifteen years. They have appeared in the *London Magazine*, the *New York Review of Books*, *The Times* and the *Times Literary Supplement*. The articles on Raymond Chandler and Dashiell Hammett were first printed in *The World of Raymond Chandler* and *The Crime Writers* respectively. My thanks are due to all the editors and publications concerned for permission to reprint.

The pieces appear as they were first printed, with a very few minor textual amendments to take account of errors pointed out to me, and of the change from magazine to book publication. Only two of them seem to need comment. The article on Edith Sitwell had been in the hands of Alan Ross at the *London Magazine* for some time before he finally decided to print it. Edith Sitwell died very soon after its publication, and the article caused much offence, a number of readers cancelling their subscriptions. That reason for offence has long since faded, and the piece seemed worth reprinting. The single exception in which I have added materially to an article is in the case of 'The Little Magazine and *The Review*', where a postscript seemed necessary for reasons which will be obvious.

JULIAN SYMONS
1981

Poets, Novelists, Critics

Something About a Namesake

I was looking in the London Library for one of my own books when I noticed next door to me the Collected Works of Arthur Symons. There are nine volumes of these very incomplete Collected Works, which appeared under Martin Secker's imprint in 1924. The production is done with Secker's customary taste, but although the edition was limited to 650 copies, sales were more limited still, and the projected last seven volumes were never published.

The last time I had seen these nine volumes was when, as an adolescent, I poked about in the large Nineties library of my brother AJ. I then actually read them, or in them, as I read a lot of other Nineties writers, from Aubrey Beardsley to Theodore Wratislaw. I don't suppose I shall look again at the poems of Eugene Lee-Hamilton, Victor Plarr, Wratislaw or most of the others, but the accident of contiguity and a slight uncertainty about what had happened to my namesake led me to take a couple of these volumes off the shelves, and after that to go on reading. Arthur Symons was hardly a great critic as Edith Sitwell suggested, and he was certainly not a great poet, yet he does not deserve the oblivion into which he has fallen. The image he offers us is of that outmoded but honourable figure, the Man of Letters.

But Symons's career has another interest, of a slightly melancholy kind. If he is remembered at all today it is as a figure of the Nineties, and he is indeed the super-typical literary man of the decade. If one were looking for a single writer to exemplify the spirit of the period it is Symons who should be chosen, rather than more obvious names like Wilde and Dowson. In an obituary of Millais he wrote:

> The burial of Millais in St Paul's should have been an honour done to a great painter who died at the age of thirty-five, the painter of 'The Eve of St Agnes', of 'Ophelia', of 'The Vale of Rest'; it was but an honour done to a popular painter, the painter of 'Bubbles', and other coloured supplements to Christmas numbers, who died at the age of sixty-seven. In the eulogies that have been justly given to the late President of the Royal Academy, I have looked in vain for this

sentence, which should have had its place in them all: he did not make the 'great refusal'. Instead of this, I have seen only: he was so English, and so fond of salmon-fishing.

In 1900 Symons too was 35. He had already published the poems he wrote of any lasting interest, and his most valuable work of criticism, *The Symbolist Movement in Literature*. He was to live for another forty-five years, and to publish many more books, but he truly existed as a writer only during a single decade, and his mental breakdown in 1908 symbolized the acknowledgement that his time was over.

Few can have dedicated themselves to a writer's career so early. Symons's family was Cornish, his father a narrow-minded Wesleyan preacher from St Columb Minor, his mother the daughter of a Cornish yeoman. Part of his childhood was passed in St Ives, part in Devon, where the family shifted frequently from one place to another, so that he had no settled home. From his early teens he seems to have wanted to escape from the poverty and enforced pieties of family life. His schooling ended when he was seventeen, and he was so ignorant of many things that there was never any question of his passing an examination. On the other hand he picked up French and Latin easily, Greek with more difficulty, and at a later stage learned in a couple of weeks enough Italian to be able to read it. He learned to play the piano without tuition. And above all he read, mostly modern poets and Elizabethan dramatists. The letters he wrote to Churchill Osborne, a teacher who advised him and lent him books, discuss poetry and music at length, and hammer away continually at the possibility of going to London, and making a living as a writer and reviewer. He also wrote hundreds of poems. 'My most prolific day was last Saturday, when I wrote three poems during a walk in the morning, eight triolets during a walk in the evening and a Ballade when I came in.' With a dozen pieces printed he had earned only a guinea, but when he was nineteen the *National Review* accepted a twenty-page article on Mistral ('Do you know the *National* pays as much as the *Contemporary*, a pound a page?'). Less than two years later his first book, a study of Browning, was published, and received a friendly review from Walter Pater. Editors gave him work to do, on the Mermaid series of dramatists and on the Henry Irving edition of Shakespeare.

He moved to London and found a place to live, temporarily at first and then permanently, in the Temple's Fountain Court. George Moore, who also lived in the Temple, had advised him to look at notices in the window of the local barber's shop. There he found news of a top flat to let, a flat with 'a stone balcony from which I looked down on a wide open court, with a stone fountain in the middle'. He took it in March 1891, and lived there for ten years. Always inclined to romanticize his own life, he wrote that 'I was born, "like a fiend hid in a cloud"', never quite human, never quite normal,' and he believed that lack of a stable home in his childhood had cut him off from 'whatever is stable, of long growth in the world'. Now, for the first time, he felt that he had a home.

He had come home also, in a different sense, in coming to London, for his interests at this time were wholly urban. In 'A Prelude to Life', written much later, he put down what he called the intoxication of the city, a feeling that only other urbanites can fully understand.

When I found myself alone, and in the midst of a crowd, I began to be astonishingly happy. I needed so little at the beginning of that time. I have never been able to stay long under a roof without restlessness, and I used to go out into the streets, many times a day, for the pleasure of finding myself in the open air and in the streets. I had never cared greatly for the open air in the country, the real open air, because everything in the country, except the sea, bored me; but here, in the motley Strand, among these hurrying people, under the smoky sky, I could walk and yet watch.

This sense of being an observer rather than a participant stayed with him through most of his life.

The young man who had entered London literary life was, according to one view, big, blond and very English; by another, that of Ernest Rhys, he was 'almost pretty to look upon—rosy cheeks, light-brown hair, blue eyes, and peculiarly white skin.' He quickly met and became friendly with several Nineties writers, including Yeats and Dowson. Yeats said that Symons was better able than any man he had ever known to 'slip as it were into the mind of another, and my thoughts gained in richness and in clearness from his sympathy, nor shall I ever know how much my practice and theory owe to the passages that he read me from Catullus and Verlaine and Mallarmé.' He was the interpreter of the French symbolist poets, and the expositor of the new literature which he called decadent, because it showed 'an intense self-consciousness, a restless curiosity in

15

research, an over-subtilising refinement upon refinement, a spiritual
and moral perversity'. This interesting and beautiful new literature
was, he said, 'really a new and beautiful and interesting disease'.

In Symons's eyes the time itself was decadent, and the most
sensitive people in it were bound to pursue the pleasures of instant
sensation distantly recommended by Pater. He moved in a whirl of
excitement about the new ideas, the new art, the new life, that some
found repellent or ridiculous. Wilde, who seems to have regarded
Symons as a sort of cheerleader for better writers, made evident his
dislike by mispronouncing his name, giving it a long, instead of a
short '*i*'. When rebuked he said: 'How can you be so childish? It is
perfectly clear that Symons doesn't know how to pronounce his own
name.' George Moore made jokes about his passionate faith in
symbolism and his passionate attachment to the dancers at the
Empire and Alhambra:

> Symons came in, tired after long symbolistic studies at the Empire,
> and so hungry that he began to eat bread and butter. . . .[Symons]
> is intelligent and well versed in literature, French and English; a
> man of somewhat yellowish temperament, whom a wicked fairy
> had cast for a parson; but there was a good fairy on the sill at the
> time, and when the wicked fairy had disappeared up the chimney
> she came in through the window, and bending over the cradle, said:
> 'I bestow upon thee extraordinary gifts.'

The gifts may have been extraordinary, as they were certainly
multifold, but very often the expression was not. Wilde also remarked
of Symons that he was a sad example of an egoist without an ego, and
there is an impression often in his poems of a writer trying to express
an intensity of emotion that he does not actually feel. Yet there are
some exceptions. The virtues of his best poems spring from his love of
urban life. With only a little exaggeration he said that he could not
distinguish oats from barley, an oak from a maple, a blackbird from a
thrush. The city was more real to him than the country, and his feeling
for the life of cities was much greater than his feeling for people, who
existed for him as part of cities, and in particular for the night life
associated with music halls and the ballet, dancers and amateur or
professional prostitutes.

Silhouettes (1892) and *London Nights* (1895) contain most of his
best poems, and they express again and again his obsession with the
city, its singers and dancers, a world of sex made more attractive by its

artificiality and its evanescence. Nocturnes and vignettes follow each other, poems celebrate Peppina at the Empire, Flo at the Foresters, Minnie in the primrose dance at the Tivoli, among a stream of Renées, Noras and Violets. A poem about a violet in an orchid house, which takes on an orchid's colouring, is constructed with typically urbane elegance:

> The orchid mostly is the flower I love,
> And violets, the mere violets of the wood,
> For all their sweetness, have not power to move
> The curiosity that stirs my blood.
>
> Yet here, in this spice-laden atmosphere,
> Where only nature is a thing unreal,
> I found in just a violet, planted here,
> The artificial flower of my ideal.

Poem after poem is written with a driving sexuality that has its own obsessive power. The best-known is 'Stella Maris', an assertion of the pleasure to be found in a one-night stand, a pleasure derived partly from the fact that nothing permanent is involved. Again Symons puts it with epigrammatic neatness:

> The Juliet of a night? I know
> Your heart holds many a Romeo . . .
> Why should I grieve, though I forget
> How many another Juliet?
> Let us be glad to have forgot
> That roses fade, and loves are not,
> As dreams, immortal, though they seem
> Almost as real as a dream.

The poem was famous in its period, and *Punch* parodied its author in the line:

> Yes, I am, I know,
> The devil of a Romeo!

The suggestion that these affairs were imaginary is more or less endorsed by Symons's biographer, Roger Lhombreaud, but this seems unlikely. Symons himself admitted in old age to the 'immorality' of his life as a young man, and there is no doubt about his love affair with a nineteen-year-old dancer at the Empire. He called her Bianca in poems, Lydia in autobiographical reflections published in 1940, near the end of his life. She clung about him, he said, like a poisonous atmosphere, though she was also virtuous. At times his writing about her is so vague that it is difficult to know exactly what he means. Often he writes about the pleasures of pretended innocence, sometimes the innocence seems partly real:

> It is your ambiguity
> That speaks to me and conquers me,
> Your capturing heats of captive bliss,
> Under my hands, under my kiss,
> And your strange reticences, strange
> Concessions, your elusive change,
> The strangeness of your smile, the faint
> Corruption of your gaze, a saint
> Such as Luini loved to paint.

The sonnet sequence in *Amoris Victima* (1897), which records the end of the affair, expresses anguish that comes through as genuine, although the Shakespearean sonnet is not the happiest form for it. Although Symons went on writing poems for many years, their spring of sexual feeling wound down at some time near the end of the nineteenth century, leaving him with nothing more than a facility unaccompanied by any particular power or originality of image.

As a critic he possessed an immense fund of sympathy, understanding and goodwill for all writers who could be brought under the umbrella of the modern, and his emotional antennae sensed almost unerringly what was most interesting in the art of the time. *The Symbolist Movement in Literature* (1899) was an immensely influential book. Eliot, reading it in 1908, was moved to his first interest in Laforgue, and it served for a whole generation of poets as their introduction to Rimbaud, Verlaine and Mallarmé. A characteristic essay gives essential facts, which for most readers were fresh and valuable, a few quotations to give the flavour, a brief but always generous appreciation, mostly with a few shrewd comments. An introductory source book of this kind, however, is inevitably outdistanced by time. Modern scholarship and modern critical values have made much of this pioneer work appear elementary.

The other criticism of Symons that I have read—the studies of Wilde, Hardy and Conrad, the pieces about the drama and music— all have a feet-on-the-ground shrewdness. A sensibility is in operation, but always in the service of common sense. 'I have never reasoned deeply on deep questions,' he wrote towards the end of his life. 'I have generally hated logic. And I have imagined more than I have thought.' Yet the qualities that come through in his criticism are pre-eminently those of a rational, logical man. He shows the ability discerned by Yeats to enter into the minds of other writers, he makes an effort—or more strikingly, does not have to make an effort—to understand their artistic ends, yet there is still a core of coolness at the centre of his sympathy. One is often brought up sharply, as in the course of a piece in praise of William Morris, when he comments: 'It is curious, in an art so addressed to the senses, that Morris is so unsensuous in his writing, so modest and temperate.' There is no easy eclecticism, but rather a struggle to appreciate the worth of a writer like Hardy, whose work does not obviously fit in with Symons's theories.

The chief limitation of his admirable criticism is, indeed, a tendency to refer any actual work back to theory, at first to theories about symbolism and decadence, later to what he called a 'universal science of beauty', towards which he thought all art should aim. Art is referred to other art, rather than to life, and it is in Symons rather than in Wilde, Yeats or Beardsley, that art for art's sake becomes a doctrine rather than a phrase.

The magazine he edited, the *Savoy*, is the most characteristic, and by far the most intelligently edited, production of the period. The *Yellow Book* has this reputation but, as Holbrook Jackson has remarked, after the Wilde case and the sacking of Beardsley it 'was hardly to be distinguished from any high-class magazine in book form'. The *Savoy* was a different matter, and it would not be easy to exaggerate the shock and offence it caused in its time. Beardsley had been sacked from the *Yellow Book* because of protests made by the best-selling novelist Mrs Humphrey Ward, and that archetypally respectable Victorian poet, Sir William Watson. When Symons was offered the editorship, he accepted on condition that Beardsley should be art editor. Beardsley's influence is predominant in the art work, as that of Symons is in the whole magazine, to which he contributed editorial notes and a monthly causerie, as well as poems, stories and essays.

His editorial talent is shown in the list of contributors to the magazine's eight numbers, which reads like a roll-call not only of the writers, but also of the ideas, associated with the Nineties movement:

Poets, Novelists, Critics

Yeats writing on Blake; Havelock Ellis on Nietzsche (then almost unknown in England) and on *Jude the Obscure*; Verlaine on the visit to London partly organized by Symons; stories and articles by Conrad, Shaw, Beerbohm; drawings by Beardsley, Rothenstein, Conder, Sickert. Symons found the publisher for the magazine, or perhaps it would be truer to say that the publisher found him. This publisher was Leonard Smithers, a pasty-faced solicitor from Sheffield, who lost by backing the period's poets and artists the money that he made by publishing high-class pornography. Yeats at this time shared Symons's apartments in Fountain Court, occupying part of them that opened through a passage into Symons's rooms, so that if anybody rang at either door, one or other would look through a window in a connecting passage and report, so that they could decide which, if either, of them should answer the door. He remembered Smithers's visit, and Symons's insistence on Beardsley.

It was not a recommendation to have Smithers as a publisher. Yeats was asked by his hostess at a party why he sent poems to the *Savoy* and not to the *Spectator*. When he said that his friends read the monthly review but not the weekly periodical, his answer was not approved. Nor was disapproval confined to hostesses. The Irish poet AE wrote to Yeats that he never saw the magazine, 'nor do I intend to touch it. It is all mud from a muddy spring.' Yeats himself had refused to meet Smithers, although he was eventually persuaded by Symons to attend a celebratory supper party at the publisher's house, on condition that he would never have to go there again. It was after this party that Beardsley entertained himself by asking Smithers to play a hurdy-gurdy. The publisher, 'perspiration pouring from his face, was turning the handle', while Beardsley urged him to play on and on, saying that it was perfect music and that the tone was beautiful. But soon there was little to celebrate. The combination of Smithers's name, and what was thought to be the scandalous nature of the magazine's contents, was fatal. Perhaps the final blow was the banning of the *Savoy* from Smith's bookstalls, after they had objected to the reproduction of a Blake drawing. In his bitter final causerie, Symons kept the art for art's sake banner flying high: 'Comparatively few people care for art at all, and most of these care for it because they mistake it for something else.' In the last issue all of the drawings were by Beardsley, all of the writing by Symons. The variety of the writing shows his remarkable fecundity and range: a fourteen-page poem, a

Something About a Namesake

translation from Mallarmé, an essay on Pater and a piece about visiting the Isles of Aran, a short story—in all nearly eighty large pages. Beardsley's mournful cover shows pierrot, the period's emblem, with hands in pockets, down in the dumps.

When Symons reviewed 'The Ballad of Reading Gaol', generously making a particular request that his article should be signed, Wilde's opinion of him changed: 'I have written to my solicitor to inquire about shares in Symons Limited,' he said. 'Naturally in mass productions of that kind you can never be certain of the quality. But I think one might risk some shares in Symons.' He must have seemed a safe investment at this time, a poet and particularly a critic, whose fame could only grow. But Wilde would have lost his money, as he did so often.

In 1901 Symons married Rhoda Bowser, the daughter of a Newcastle ship-owner, a woman nine years younger than himself. It seems to have been a desperate move on the part of a man who had always maintained that the nomadic life was ideal for an artist, who had managed to do a remarkable amount of travelling on extremely little money, and who had casually shared his London rooms with Havelock Ellis and Yeats among others. His gloomy proposal of marriage suggests the desperation:

> I am writing to you very deliberately and collectedly. I am not carried away by any excitement . . . I have lived a certain life of my own: it has been marvellously interesting, but it remains incomplete and it left me in the end miserable. You brought me the one possibility of happiness that I have ever had. Shall we join two discontents, and see if they will not make one happiness?

So there were to be no more London nights, no more Minnies and Noras, and of course no poems about them. Rhoda had warned him that she was extravagant, and although she did her best not to spend money, and he gave up gold-tipped cigarettes and stopped taking cabs, they were never free of money worries. Where writing had been a pleasure it became something like drudgery, as he tried by reviews, articles, and books done to order, to support them both in flats at Maida Vale and St John's Wood, and then in a cottage at Wittersham in Kent. He contracted debts, and travelling became out of the question, until in 1908 they visited Italy. There, in Venice, he suddenly vanished, went to Bologna and then to Ferrara, and was

21

arrested by the police for no apparent reason. He spent some days in prison, manacled hand and foot, before he was freed and put in an asylum. A little later he was brought back to England.

In the *Confessions* that he wrote several years later, Symons talks about himself as being mad. There seems no doubt that he was suffering from acute depression, with some of the delusions that may accompany it. This, however, was not the diagnosis made. His doctors agreed that he was in the early stages of GPI, General Paralysis of the Insane, which can be caused by syphilis. He was quickly whisked off to a mental home at Crowborough, from which he escaped to have dinner at a neighbouring hotel, where he told the management that his doctor would pay the bill. Rhoda was practically without money, and even to maintain him in a cheaper London mental home was beyond her means. Friends provided funds for this, and she was assured by Dr Risien Russell that she was doing the right thing in keeping him in a home, and that he would probably die without having a lucid interval. Three months later, when he continued to improve in spite of the appalling sanitary and other conditions in the home, Dr Russell was still reassuring. 'As far as one can judge of your husband's condition the probabilities are that he would live for about eighteen months or so, but . . . he may live two years, or even a little longer.'

In 1909 he began to write again, and in April 1910 he was allowed to leave the home and return to Wittersham. There he lived for another thirty-five years, making occasional visits to London and three brief trips to France. He and Rhoda had six guineas a week to live on, provided by friends and the Royal Literary Fund, and he maintained himself by writing books and articles. From 1913 to 1940, his biographer says, he produced twenty-three books 'based on manuscripts written before the crisis', nineteen new volumes and ten translations. Few of them were much noticed, none had a considerable sale. His later work shows only the ghost of his talent, as John's portrait or the later photographs of him show the ghost of a man, a full beard completely concealing what a woman interviewer in the past had called the 'full but firm, sweet mouth', the eyes remote or empty. The literature produced after the war was almost wholly alien to him. He knew Joyce, had helped to place some of his poems in magazines, and had written the first review of *Chamber Music*, remarking that the poems had an occasional 'sharp prose touch, as in Rochester, which gives a kind of malice to sentiment', but all that had

Something About a Namesake

been long ago, and although he wrote a postscript to a 'Joyce Book', he cannot possibly have cared for *Ulysses*.

In 1936 Rhoda died in London. Her husband, M. Lhombreaud says, showed no sign of emotion, but 'set out alone for the Café Royal'. Occasionally he revisited these shades, still wearing his Inverness cape and wide-brimmed black hat, artistic trappings of the past. There John Betjeman saw him, and wrote in the manager's autograph book:

> I saw him in the Café Royal,
> Very old and very grand . . .
> Where is Oscar? Where is Bosie?
> Have I seen that man before?
> And the old one in the corner,
> Is it really Wratislaw?

Yeats said of Symons that he had always had a longing to commit great sin, but had never been able to get beyond ballet girls. Perhaps that is literally true, and in a way it is a fair critical comment on the poems; but in a personal sense it was more important that he hoped for some mystical experience, as he suggested when dedicating to Yeats *The Symbolist Movement in Literature*, but found only humdrum respectableness and then the spindrift of madness. When he slipped out of life on 22 January 1945, he was one of the forgotten men of English letters. The artificial flower of his ideal flourished for only a decade, and he might now be better remembered if he had died with his friends and fellow-artists, Dowson, Beardsley and Wilde, nearly half a century before.

(1973)

Miss Edith Sitwell Have and Had and Heard

Introduces.
This is for her and not for Mabel Weeks.
She could not keep it out.
Introduces have and heard.
Miss Edith Sitwell have and heard.
Introduces have and had.
Miss Edith Sitwell have and had.
Introduces have and had introduces have and had and heard.
Miss Edith Sitwell have and had and heard.

GERTRUDE STEIN

I LEGEND

I don't think anybody has noticed how closely the graph of Edith
Sitwell's reputation resembles that of a stock once very much fancied
by speculators, Icelandic Herpetologicals. Issued during the 1914–18
war, the stock rose steadily during the boom years of the twenties. Its
decline during the decade before World War II was perhaps
signalized rather than prompted by a strongly adverse verdict from
investigator Leavis. It will be remembered that after examining the
company's advertised claims, Leavis came to the conclusion that they
bore little relation to reality. Those who bought during this slump
period felt themselves justified when, during and after the war,
Icelandic Herpetologicals were quoted at something like a thousand
per cent above pre-war par. About ten years ago, however, the
reports of young post-Leavisite field-workers began to filter through,
and Icelandics suffered a decline from which they have never
recovered. These reports bore out the view that had been maintained
all along by those bearing the market: there are no snakes in
Iceland.

This is not, of course, a view of the matter that would be accepted
by Dame Edith. There is a legend, which she has done nothing to
discourage, that her genius was immediately acknowledged and has
never since been seriously questioned. It is my object here to question
the legend, and to suggest that her reputation has always been based

24

Miss Edith Sitwell Have and Had and Heard

on the movement of social and literary fashion. What is attempted is less literary criticism than the history of a reputation.

Let me begin by providing evidence from a reliable source, the *New Statesman*. The word *reliable* is used in the sense that the *New Statesman* is an excellent guide to conventional highbrow feeling at any given time. Contrary to general belief it has not often immediately acclaimed new literary talent—Eliot, Wyndham Lewis, Auden, were all sniffed at cautiously in its pages before approval was given. The paper is, however, a champion endorser of reputations just established, and its collected volumes are a reference book to who is intellectually in or out at a given time. More perceptive criticism of early Edith Sitwell (as of early Auden) appeared in *The Times Literary Supplement*, but her treatment in the *New Statesman* reflects very well the vagaries of her reputation.

The first book of her maturity, *Bucolic Comedies* (1923), was not reviewed—and this was by no means juvenilia like *The Mother* (published in 1915), but included 'Façade' and other poems later much anthologized. The first reference to her that I have found is in 1925, when 'Affable Hawk' (Desmond MacCarthy) rebuked her for praising the work of Gertrude Stein and for 'frequently using words regardless of their sense'. Two years later there was a cautiously friendly review of her *Rustic Elegies* ('No detractor is likely to deny her verse an individual quality' is a phrase that sets the characteristic tone), but other small volumes like *Troy Park* (1925), *The Sleeping Beauty* (1929) and *Gold Coast Customs* (1929) stayed unreviewed. In 1930 the publication of her *Collected Poems* was the occasion of a long, hostile review by Edward Shanks. What did she mean, he asked, by saying that 'technique is very largely a matter of physique'? Would not the reverse be equally true? He attacked the clumsiness of her own technique. 'There are lines crammed with heavy syllables, lines awkwardly too long or too short for the metrical pattern, and many, too many, in which she arrives gasping at the rhyme word as though only by main force had she been able to put it in its proper place.'

A chance of reversing this unfavourable verdict came in 1936, when her *Selected Poems* appeared, with a long introduction specially written to explain her approach to poetry. The book was ignored. Two years earlier G. W. Stonier, in a review of her *Aspects of Modern Poetry*, had struck a blow at her reputation that to many people appeared final and decisive. Stonier pointed out in his review the remarkable similarities between passages in her book and F. R.

Leavis's *New Bearings in English Poetry*. One, or even half a dozen, of these similarities might be thought accidental, but after Stonier's review a correspondent pointed out nineteen parallels between her book and Leavis's, and Geoffrey Grigson joined in with the discovery of parallels between her work and Herbert Read's *Form in Modern Poetry*. Miss Sitwell pleaded that because Leavis had been accurate about facts, she surely need not be inaccurate about them (but she evaded the point, which rested in such things as that both she and Leavis had begun their discussions of Yeats by examining the same sonnet of Andrew Lang's), and defended herself also by the facetiousness that with her has always passed for humour. 'It is right and natural that Mr Stonier should admire Dr Leavis. It reminds me of Miss Nellie Wallace's appeal to her slightly denuded feather boa: "For God's sake, hold together, boys." ' After this affray, which lasted for weeks in the *New Statesman* and spilled over into *The Times Literary Supplement*, where the many inaccuracies in her quotations from Hopkins were pointed out, did anybody take Edith Sitwell seriously? It was to appear afterwards that many people did, but in the years before the war their voices were not loudly raised.

II ZENITH AND DECLINE

It was not until the war that legend turned into fact. The change began with the first book of poems Edith Sitwell published during the war, *Street Songs* (1942). In the *New Statesman* the book received a solus review from Stephen Spender which was critical of her early work, but enthusiastic about these poems. 'This volume shows an astonishing development of Miss Sitwell's talent as a technician, as well as in her material. . . . A fascinating book, at moments tragic, and always full of charm.' The new note was to sound again and again during the next decade, in reviews of the books that came from her during these years—*Green Song* (1944), *The Song of the Cold* (1945), *The Shadow of Cain* (1949) and others. It was now discovered that her early verse was almost on a level with her later achievement. Henry Reed, reviewing *The Song of the Cold*, had been re-reading her early poetry and had found 'that it anticipates more of her later grandeur than one had thought'. More than this, her poetry as a whole was 'more flowingly musical than almost any other kind of English verse', and beyond grandeur and flowing music there was warmth. 'Always

Miss Edith Sitwell Have and Had and Heard

in these poems there is a hard core, a flaming centre, which appears with a sudden amazing vividness, and which, as one re-reads, irradiates its surroundings from end to end.' Her total achievement was of a kind that 'one may not casually assess'.

Those who wish to see the peak of critical esteem reached by Miss Sitwell just after the end of the war should look for a little book called *A Celebration for Edith Sitwell*, published in 1948 on the occasion of a visit she made to the United States. Here her admirers, respected and some of them surprising names, are collected to do her honour. There is Sir Maurice Bowra acclaiming her tragic power and prophetic fury, and the 'great flowering of her genius' which is 'her reward for years of devoted and patient labour at her art'. Here again is Stephen Spender, still battling with his feeling that those early poems are in a sense 'fashionable' and so may go out of fashion, but becoming lyrical about 'the light, the ripeness, the death and the anguish' of her war poems, those 'prodigious hymns'. Here is John Piper ('full ripe words . . . evil in the late poems is cold . . . is the poet heartless, like the Snow Queen?') and Sir Kenneth Clark ('this was not merely exquisite poetry: it was great poetry . . . reminds us of Crashaw . . . Traherne's rapture at created things, and Vaughan's sense of eternity') and John Lehmann ('Among all modern poets she seems to me to be supreme in seeing the tragedy of our age in the perspective not only of all the history and all the thought and art that began for us so long ago in the lands of the Eastern Mediterranean, but also of the undateable antiquity of the universe beyond that'). Here too is the Marxist Jack Lindsay—the wheel of admiration covered the full political circle—offering an explanation, which may be found not painfully simple, of her poem 'The Shadow of Cain':

> Since this poem has been found difficult of comprehension, perhaps I may be permitted to give an outline of its theme.
>
> It opens with a broad statement (in Hegelian terms) of this issue from the focus of physics, which is linked with the picture of geologic phases of convulsive movement—we are at the molecular level as well as in a dream-space. Man emerges (as in a primitive myth such as that of the Zuni). Man in his primitive ritual finds his precarious unity with the vast forces; and through the imagery of the birth-trauma relates his own experience to his intuitions of elemental change.

And here are other offerings, 'Some Notes On' and 'Trends in the

Poets, Novelists, Critics

Poetry Of' and 'Her Infinite Variety'. Miss Sitwell became Doctor Sitwell as universities competed to do her honour, and Doctor Sitwell turned into Dame Edith. In these plenteous years the earth brought forth by handfuls.

Just as the *New Statesman* review in 1942 may be taken as marking the beginning of the era in which Edith Sitwell was thought of as a great poet, so a piece in the periodical marked its end. In January 1954, there appeared in its pages a profile of Edith Sitwell. These profiles are anonymous, and although interior evidence suggests that it was written by G. W. Stonier, that is no more than a guess. What is interesting in a paper so sensitive to the prevailing cultural wind, is that the writing of the profile was given to somebody by no means inclined to accept Edith Sitwell at her own poetic valuation.

The title, 'Queen Edith', was ironic, for it was suggested that she wore the crown as personality, not as poet. She had created a legend, like Byron or Baudelaire, but whereas their poetry projected the image of a personality, 'not so with Queen Edith . . . not what she writes, but what she is, exerts the real fascination'. Some of the battles of the past were recalled, and it was suggested that from each defeat 'she herself emerged, more majestic, more unaccountably "modern" than ever.' After the affair in 1934 she had sent the editor a stuffed puppy, a 'touch of magic' which 'presumably disposed of the whole thing'. At this distance of time the profile, which placed her poetic talent roughly on a level with Christina Rossetti's, seems rather amiable, but that was not the feeling of Sitwellians. Mr Tom Driberg wrote an indignant letter expressing their feelings. 'One merit of a catcall, from gallery or gutter, is usually that it is brief.' This cad must be somebody who had been deservedly snubbed by Doctor Sitwell. Or, worse, perhaps she had once done him a kindness, 'an offence which persons of his quality often find it hard to forgive'. But Mr Driberg's suggestion that the profile writer was just no account trash was unavailing. For the *New Statesman* the days of Sitwellian glory were over. In the week following the profile there appeared a far from enthusiastic review of her new book, *Gardeners and Astronomers*, a review that discovered in her work 'uncomfortable imprecision, and a certain occasional monotony'. In 1957 her *Collected Poems* were granted some merit, but the famous war poems were dismissed as 'spineless and Swinburnian in argument'. To couple her name with those of Yeats and T. S. Eliot was to place her out of her class. In 1962

28

Miss Edith Sitwell Have and Had and Heard

her latest book of poems, *The Outcasts*, was dismissed in six contemptuous lines.

III   THE HUB OF WHEELS

To understand the fluctuations of Edith Sitwell's reputation one must look back to the yearly anthology *Wheels*, the six cycles of which she edited. (The first appeared in 1916 and the last in 1921.) *Wheels* is part of the legend. It figures, in the minds of those who have never seen it, as a daring and even outrageous periodical, part of the 'revolution of the word' that was effected in poetry primarily by Eliot and Pound during the first twenty years of this century. 'Fifty years hence the publication of *Wheels* will be remembered as a notable event in the inner history of English literature,' the *Morning Post* critic said on its first appearance, and elsewhere the poets who contributed to it were attacked for their gloom, squalor, rebelliousness. 'Every page shouts defiance of poetic conventions,' said the *Observer*. Now that we are nearly fifty years on, it is hard to understand why anybody was either excited or infuriated by *Wheels*.

On the title page the names of the contributors shoot out from the hub like the spokes of a bicycle. At the centre, the hub, appears after the first two cycles the name of Edith Sitwell. Until the last volume there were no more than eight or nine contributors, and certain names recur: Osbert and Sacheverell Sitwell naturally, and from the second issue onwards Aldous Huxley. These are known names, but even those concerned with the literary minutiae of the period are not likely to have examined the work of E. Wyndham Tennant, Victor Tait Perowne, Arnold James, Iris Tree, Sherard Vines. What was there that defied poetic convention in such lines as those of one much-praised contributor:

> How shall I tell you of the roads that stretch away
> Like streamers from a dancing pole in the tripsome month of May,
> For what care you for aught beside your porto and tokay,
> How shall I tell you?

Or in the lines with which another contributor's poem begins:

> I look into your eyes
> And see Eternity.

Poets, Novelists, Critics

Or in the 'Ballad' of a third:

> Many things I'd find to charm you,
> Books and scarves and silken socks,
> All the seven rainbow colours
> Black and white with 'broidered clocks.

The characteristic poetry of *Wheels* bears no resemblance at all to the truly original work of the time, and it must be looked at in a context less literary than social. *Wheels* was primarily a protest by a group of upper-class young men and women against the jingoism of current attitudes during the war. Of those now remembered as the 'war poets', Siegfried Sassoon, Robert Graves, Isaac Rosenberg, Wilfred Owen, only Owen was a contributor and that posthumously, but the spirit of *Wheels* was very much that of these anti-war poets. Osbert Sitwell's savage 'Corpse-Day', written in 1919, is not a good poem but it is a powerful piece of anti-war propaganda, and there are other poems, in particular some curious ones by Sherard Vines, that break through the barrier of rather Ninetyish literary language which is on the whole the prevailing tone of the periodical. *Wheels* caused indignation not because of its literary Bolshevism (to use a phrase then current) but because of the subject matter of some poems, and the attitude of those who wrote them towards the war.

Edith Sitwell's own verses in *Wheels* are another matter. They include some of the poems later printed in *Façade*, and alone among the principal *Wheels* contributors she showed an interest in language, not merely in the sound of the poem but in the original use of words:

> By the blue wooden sea—
> Curling laboriously,
> Coral and amber grots
> (Cherries and apricots)
> Ribbons of noisy heat
> Binding them head and feet,
> Horses as fat as plums
> Snort as each bumpkin comes.

Such language does not look very exciting or important if it is compared with the passionate force behind Owen's best work, or with Graves's continual search for new forms of expression, but it was unquestionably novel, and one does not have to make a great effort of historical imagination to see that this verse seemed in 1918 new, exhilarating and outrageous, that it was both an expression of and a sort of parallel to the 'Jazz Age' and the Russian Ballet. Edith Sitwell was at this time part of a 'movement' which was in revolt against established orthodoxies in painting, music and poetry, and in particular against the Squirearchy.

It is not easy to realize how far the writ of J. C. Squire and his friends ran in the early 1920s. 'The tone of the *New Statesman* literary pages from the beginning under Squire until after Ellis Roberts's time (the beginning of the thirties) was, to borrow an adjective which has a clear, received meaning when applied to a school of poetry, Georgian,' Edward Hyams says in his history of the paper, adding justly enough that 'no widely read weekly had any other style.' There is a lively lampoon on Squire by Augustine Rivers (Osbert Sitwell?) in the last cycle of *Wheels*:

'Praise Squire, praise Squire,' we hear the swift refrain
That leaps like fire from every school and college,
From stately London home or Cotswold cottage,
Wherever poet meets a poet brother
(Or makes an income by reviewing each other).
The echo alters to 'We never tire
Of hearing Squire on Shanks and Shanks on Squire'.

The Sitwells revolted against the rule of the Squirearchy more noisily than anybody else, and any reader sympathetic to what was then called the modern movement would have been on Edith Sitwell's side rather than on that of Desmond MacCarthy when reading MacCarthy's attack upon her for praising (in *Vogue*) the 'rubbish' of Gertrude Stein. Modernists at this time needed all the allies they could find, and the Sitwells were welcomed rather in the way that Britain welcomed the entry of the Soviet Union into World War II, in the spirit that whatever might be said against them they were on the right side. That their self-professed modernity was so noisy and so closely allied with the fashion magazines, that Cecil Beaton photographed Miss Sitwell with hands joined among the lilies, and as Saint Cecilia with fingers on the harp strings, all this was forgiven and even thought, in a word of the time, amusing. And to be amusing was, in the twenties, fashionable.

Fashion: any future historian of the Sitwells can hardly fail to note their emotional reaction to the importance of being fashionable. On this point they have always been deeply sensitive, a sensitivity curiously manifested in a libel action brought by them in 1941 against *Reynolds News*.

In a short review of Edith Sitwell's anthology, *The Pleasure of Poetry*, it had been suggested that oblivion had claimed these lively characters of the twenties, and that they were remembered 'with a kindly, if slightly cynical, smile'. Harmless words? They might seem so to ninety-nine in every hundred writers, but the suggestion of neglect was to the Sitwells more offensive than detailed strictures upon their actual writing. Flanked by Charles Morgan and Arthur Waley, they entered the witness box to testify that they were not neglected. 'It was utterly untrue to say that she had passed into oblivion,' Edith Sitwell said in her evidence. 'She knew of no facts upon which such a statement could be based.' Like the character in Edgell Rickword's poem, she

> Had championed Epstein, Gertrude and *Parade*,
> and even now was nothing of a die-hard.

How was it possible that somebody always so conscientiously modern could be out of date? She was asked in cross-examination whether a perfectly fair critic might not think that she and her brothers did not figure so prominently now as they had done in the 1920s. Her answer has a certain poignancy: 'I do not agree. We are not out of fashion.'

The jury awarded damages of £350 to each of the Sitwells. Honour was satisfied, oblivion pressed back. Pressed back, it may have seemed, for ever. In the following year came the first of her wartime volumes of poems, and the time of glory began.

IV   REALITY: CRITICAL SPECIMENS

I said that literary criticism as such was not my primary purpose, but still it seems in place to comment briefly on a few samples of Edith Sitwell's work both critical and poetic.

Her critical writing has two sides to it, the first her general view of a writer or a work of art, and the second her detailed technical criticism of lines or verses. Some of her general comments on modern writers are memorable for their imperceptiveness. Two that have stayed in my mind are: 'Mr MacNeice's poems are very dull and seem coated with chocolate,' and a review of Laura Riding's *Poet: A Lying Word*:

Miss Edith Sitwell Have and Had and Heard

'And it certainly is in her case.' But when she looks back and is not concerned with the present day her comments are respectful and even reverential, and they have the merit that it is possible to play a fairly difficult 'spot the subject' game with them. For instance, identify these two English poets:

(i) 'In the veins of this innocent and childlike, yet earthly saint, a Seraphic light ran instead of blood.'
(ii) 'This strange and lovely archangel who had taken on flesh, lived in the piercing white radiance of the sun that angels know, and that is not known by mortal man.'

Say what is being referred to here:

(iii) 'To this (ancestral) memory is added the wisdom of all the thousands of springs that have budded since the first Spring, and all the complex character and strangeness of the heart of Man.'

And finally, what is it that

(iv) 'Has a strange hive-humming music, like that of shepherds' pipes, and this changes, sometimes, to a dark drumming sound, like that of great drops of water falling over the rocks of a forest cavern.'

(Answers at bottom of page)*

What do these statements tell us that is interesting or valuable? How often has Dame Edith heard drops of water falling in a forest cavern? But such a rational approach is out of place, for these remarks are really revelations of their writer and not of her nominal subjects.

Her technical criticism, which has caused admirers to call her a 'mistress of technique', is of the same order. Here are four quotations:

(i) 'I would like to call the reader's attention to the fact that in the line:

"The Cowslippes tall her pensioners bee"

the three-syllabled word "pensioners" has a little trembling sound, like that of dew being shaken from a flower.'

(ii)   ' "I sought my death and found it in my womb.
I looked for life and saw it was a shade,
I trod the earth and knew it was my tomb,
And now I die, and now I was but made." '

---

* *Answers:* (i) Blake, (ii) Shelley, (iii) *Hamlet*, (iv) Sidney's 'Strephon and Kaius'

'The lovely balance of these lines is built on the variation of vowel sounds. "Sought", "found" and "womb" are all *long* dissonances, and the second line is made up of a series of *short* vowels with two long ones—first the abruptness of "life" and then the darkness and sadness of "shade". In the third line "trod" and "tomb" are again contrasted, and this prepares us for the way in which the whole fourth line swells sonorously like some great organ sound.'

(iii) 'In these lines Milton has made a lively use of all sunny, warm, dark, or dewy mixtures of 'O's, 'U's, 'AU's, 'OU's, 'EW's and 'OW's, with the result that we find ourselves walking in a warm and sunny garden, where shadow seems only a passing air of perfume—a garden which is full of the bee winged lights of afternoon, and where sight is hardly distinguishable from sound.'

(iv) 'Through these clouds of 'S's (in Keats's "The Dark Lady's Song") beauty is glimpsed occasionally, refulgent as the moon, and is then obscured again by storms of hard consonants, 'T's and 'V's predominating. But note the emergence of the 'S' theme again in

"Cheated by shadowy wooer from the clouds,
         But hides and shrouds
Beneath dark palm trees by a river side." '

It is impossible to parody Edith Sitwell's criticism, but two of these extracts were written by me in ten minutes, while the others are genuine Sitwell. It may be said that parody proves nothing, but in Dame Edith's case does it not show that her critical opinions are so wholly arbitrary and personal as to be valueless? If we accept that 'pensioners' has a 'little trembling sound', that 'life' is abrupt and 'shade' is dark and sad, that 'AU's' and 'OW's' may help to make warm, dark and dewy mixtures, that beauty may be glimpsed through clouds of 'S's' (and it would easily be possible to maintain the contrary of all these things, for instance that the sound of 'pensioners' is long and sleepy), have we learned anything at all that helps us to evaluate or appreciate the poems? How can a writer who offers such remarks as criticism, and presents them in such language, be called a mistress of technique?

V REALITY: POETIC SPECIMENS

A defence of Edith Sitwell's poetry that may still be encountered nowadays runs like this: 'Certainly she is not a good critic, no doubt

Miss Edith Sitwell Have and Had and Heard

her public utterances are sometimes vain and silly, but to say this is not to criticize her poetry, which expresses an utterly distinctive and fresh enjoyment in the handling of words. Her critical feelings can't be justified, but her poetic practice can.' There is some truth in this. Poetry begins, poets begin, by pleasure in the use of words. Original poets do something fresh with the language they use, and the early Edith Sitwell was an original poet. The verbal frolics of *Façade* can be enjoyed very much as we enjoy the typographical tricks of e. e. cummings. Much of *Façade* and *Bucolic Comedies* is agreeably ingenious nonsense verse:

> The Wind's bastinado
> Whipt on the calico
> Skin of the Macroon
> And the black Picaroon
> Beneath the ga''oon
> Of the midnight sky.
> Came the great Soldan
> In his sedan
> Floating his fan—
> Saw what the sly
> Shadow's cocoon
> In the barracoon
> Held. Out they fly.

This sort of poem shows the best, because the least pretentious, Edith Sitwell. She plays with words and rhythms cleverly and charmingly within the limits of very light verse. The total effect resembles the formal artificiality of one of Picasso's guitars, or better still one of Severini's clowns. But what is noticeable also about these early poems is that they almost exclude reference to the world of natural objects. In one sense original, they are in another sense extremely literary. When fruits are mentioned they seem made of wax, when Edith Sitwell writes of flowers they have no roots in earthly soil. Like other objects, flowers are named by words, and for her it is the words and not the objects that exist, coloured literary counters to be played with. So when she says that Skelton's poems 'have the sharpness and coldness of an early spring flower's petals', it is plain that she has truly encountered neither the poem nor the 'early spring flower' (what flower?). It is this inability to see and hear what is around her that is Edith Sitwell's deepest limitation as a poet. The area within which her kind of originality works successfully is an extremely limited one. Just as cummings when he abandoned typographical tricks wrote distressingly sentimental sonnets, so Edith Sitwell when she gave up levity and became serious offered us extravagance of language in place of deep feeling. 'My tears were Orion's splendour with sextuple suns and the million/Flowers in the fields of the heaven,' she wrote early in the war. Does anybody believe that these are real tears?

Such a comment is uncomfortably literal, but it makes the point that it is the view taken of such verbal extravagance that most deeply separates Edith Sitwell's admirers from her denigrators. For her admirers the poetry she wrote during and after the war, and after a decade of poetic silence, expresses the agony of a generation and of an individual, and into it 'the whole inner personality of the poet and a lifetime of experience has entered', as one of them says. To me it seems that this later verse is bedded utterly in other literature, not in reality. It is the verse of somebody who has not felt deeply, but has felt how important it is to feel deeply, and has expressed her awareness of this importance by crying out continually at the top of her voice. The language has changed, certainly, but it has changed for the worse. These later poems seem to be the product of almost continuous verbal intoxication, with *thee* and *thou* and *doth* and *sere* and *drops of dew fall'n*, and a hundred other tropes that one had thought (after Eliot, after Auden) could never again be used seriously in poetry. To look at the language in which a poem has been written is a test that should always be made when we are in danger of being swept away simply by a feeling about the subject matter, a feeling basically as sentimental as that induced by a popular song or a bad epic film. Big events—the Spanish Civil War, war-time bombing, Hiroshima—generate lots of bad verse (some good verse too, of course) but the pressure of the events may conceal it at the time. Look first at the *language* of Edith Sitwell's poems. Is it not a variation on the evasive rhetoric of her much-admired Swinburne, or worse still, of Dante Gabriel Rossetti? Something of the strain in the poetry is expressed by a rash of capital letters, which are used for the Starved Man, the Rain, the Field of Blood, the Bone, the Ape and the Fiery Chariot. It is as though the writer is afraid that we might not realize the importance of the things she is saying if she did not use capital letters to tell us. And when the symbols she uses are examined, they are seen often to be inappropriate for the uses to which she puts them.

Miss Edith Sitwell Have and Had and Heard

Consider the first verse of one of the most famous of these war poems, 'Still Falls the Rain':

> Still falls the Rain—
> Dark as the world of man, black as our loss—
> Blind as the nineteen hundred and forty nails
> Upon the Cross.

Is it merely pernickety to point out that rain is itself not black nor even dark, and that even in its symbolic meaning (Rain=bombs) black does not seem a right or powerful word? Is it impermissible to ask why the nails on the cross are called blind, and to wonder how they could possibly see? There can be no doubt, at least, of the vulgar and too-timely smartness that equates the number of nails upon the cross with the year in which the poem was written.

These later poems are full of symbols used with similar arbitrariness. The Bone is the intellect, the Sun is the heart or the emotions, and often there seems no reason why the symbols should not be interchanged. I don't mean to attack highly personal symbols, any more than to attack a romantic use of language: it is the use made of them, the truth with which they are felt, the human reality seen through them, that matter. Nobody could have used synbols more wilfully than Yeats, yet he shows us that any symbols may be used to make powerful and beautiful poems. This does not happen in Edith Sitwell's work because there is no reference through the symbols to reality as there is in Yeats, there are few memorable and exact images, there is nothing but an endless Swinburnian flow of would-be evocative words. Another poem, 'Heart and Mind', ends:

> Said the Sun to the Moon—'When you are but a lonely white crone,
> And I, a dead King in my golden armour somewhere in a dark wood,
> Remember only this of our hopeless love
> That never till Time is done
> Will the fire of the heart and the fire of the mind be one'.

How much really is evoked for us by the image of the moon as a lonely white crone, and of her love affair with the sun, or earlier in the poem by the Lion and the Lioness? Why are these synbols relevant to the poem's subject, the irreconcilability of heart and mind, feeling and intellect? Compare this imagery with that in an equally visionary poem by Yeats, 'The Second Coming':

Poets, Novelists, Critics

> Somewhere in sands of the desert
> A shape with lion body and the head of a man,
> A gaze blank and pitiless as the sun,
> Is moving its slow thighs, while all about it
> Reel shadows of the indignant desert birds.

Yeats's terrible figure is real because it is something that the poet conceived, understood, *saw*, and put down with the finest and tightest control. Edith Sitwell's rhetoric is the product merely of words ringing like bells in her head. Those who thought otherwise for a few years were deceived by the experience of war, war the most powerful blurrer of intelligence, the arch-nurse of empty phrases. At no other time than during the war could poems which reverted in their language to Victorian archaism and rhetoric, poems so lacking in coherent thought and so determined to ignore the world of objects in which we live, have deceived so many intelligent critics.

After the verdict in the 1941 libel case, *The Times* published an ironical editorial on the Sitwells:

> They will not claim to be exempt from the sentence of Holy Writ: 'Our names shall be forgotten in time, and no man shall have our works in remembrance.' But, if Sainte-Beuve rightly defines a critic as one whose watch is five minutes ahead of other people's, yesterday's judgement is a salutary warning that that habit may be expensive.

Are not the five minutes now up?

(1964)

Hart Crane's Letters

Hart Crane's poetry has never found many admirers in Britain. The editors of the *Calendar* introduced his work here in 1926, and the *Criterion* later printed a section of 'The Bridge', but by the time his collected poems appeared in 1938, six years after his suicide, the poetic climate was unfavourable both to Crane's broad Whitmanesque optimism and to the particular extravagances of his style:

> Bind us in time, O Seasons clear, and awe.
> O minstrel galleons of Carib fire,
> Bequeath us to no earthly shore until
> Is answered in the vortex of our grave
> The seal's wide spindrift gaze toward paradise.

Such unabashedly romantic rhetoric is deeply uncongenial to most English tastes, and this has caused Crane to be written off over here as another breast-beating Roy Campbell, or an American Flecker. Yet any serious reading of his work will show this verdict to be wrong and obtuse. Flecker and Campbell both used rhetoric to conceal the fact that they had little to say, although it was said with much fluency. Crane was always trying to struggle through rhetoric to some absolute truths about the modern world, the human spirit, America. An English reader is bound to be struck by the American character of Crane's imagery. It is not merely that he is intensely concerned with his own country, but that he was profoundly excited by the total identification he made between America and the 'modern'. He was fascinated by automats, the cinema, skyscrapers, radio antennae, subways, dandruff advertisements, traffic lights.

The difficulties in Crane's poems, which were found almost incomprehensible by many critics in the early twenties, sprang from the fact that he incorporated this apparatus of modernity in what was thought to be irrelevantly neo-Elizabethan language, and used contemporary images to illustrate the past. So the early 'Chaplinesque' sprang from an enthusiasm for Chaplin in *The Kid* which moved him to identify the film actor as a man trying to preserve poetic feelings in 'the mechanical scramble of today', and 'For the Marriage of Faustus and Helen' interpreted the legend, with Crane himself as

Poets, Novelists, Critics

Faustus and Helen embodying the abstract idea of beauty, in terms of street cars and a scene on the roof garden of a hotel where the rhythm caught the quality and tone of the new jazz. Crane does not seem to be claiming too much when he says that his achievement here was 'something entirely new in English poetry'. His first book, *White Buildings*, had a mixed reception when it appeared in 1926, but after its publication even hostile critics treated him with respect.

Crane was fascinated above all by bridges. They were emblems of city life, they linked the present and the past, they joined Columbus and Pocahontas to twentieth-century Manhattan. His long poem 'The Bridge' was designed as 'a mystical synthesis of America' in which 'history and fact, location, etc.', would 'all have to be transfigured into abstract form that would almost function independently of its subject matter'. The introductory 'To Brooklyn Bridge' conveyed his feeling about 'the most beautiful bridge in the world':

> How many dawns, chill from his rippling rest
> The seagull's wings shall dip and pivot him,
> Shedding white rings of tumult, building high
> Over the chained bay waters Liberty . . .
>
> Down Wall, from girder into street noon leaks,
> A rip-tooth of the sky's acetylene,
> All afternoon the cloud-flown derricks turn . . .
> Thy cables breathe the North Atlantic still.

The poem was conceived in 1923. Crane talked about it for years, and several sections appeared in magazines. By the time it appeared in 1930 he was sliding fast down the slope to self-destruction. His homosexuality had moved from an idealistic search for the perfect companion to brutal encounters with sailors, his drinking had become compulsive, he had quarrelled with most of his friends, he was conscious of failing powers. Even admirers like Allen Tate, who regarded Crane as the greatest modern American poet, were disappointed by the way in which the poem split into parts which did not fit the grand design, and Yvor Winters's review was so hostile that Crane burst into tears after reading it.

His last two years were spent in Mexico, drinking and quarrelling with everybody, looking for young men. In April 1932 he decided to return to America by sea, after an attempt to commit suicide by drinking first iodine and then mercurochrome. He was accompanied on the voyage by a woman friend with whom he had established an affectionate but inevitably unstable relationship. After a violent argument with her he went down drunk into the sailors' quarters and was there beaten and robbed. He made an attempt to jump overboard that night, but was restrained by the night watch. About noon on the following day, 16 April, he vaulted over the rail into the boiling wake at the stern of the ship.

In Dylan Thomas's letters he suggests to Henry Treece, after reading a short article of mine on Crane, that Treece should look at Crane's poems for resemblances between them. There are obvious similarities, not only between the rhetoric of their writing, but in their unhappy fates. Both drank obsessively, lived from hand to mouth, believed that they were finished as poets. But the differences are more important than the similarities, as a comparison between a recent reissue of Crane's *Letters, 1916–1932** with Thomas's letters makes clear. Thomas was a fine letter writer, with a splendid comic sense, but he does not seem to have had a capacity for deep personal feeling. About his personality, even in times of great distress, there was always something clownish. About Crane's, even in such comic passages of his life as his quarrel with Allen Tate and his wife about how many times he passed through their kitchen to use the communal pump in the house they were sharing, there was often something tragic. The course of his life is shown painfully through letters that move from the vivid optimism of his youth into periods of doubt, desperate attempts at self-adjustment, and moods in which he saw everything that was wrong with 'The Bridge' ('intellectually judged the whole theme and project seems more and more absurd'), to final abandonment of everything except drink and sex:

A paean from Venusberg! Oy-oy-oy! I have just had my ninth snifter of Scotch . . . O André Gide! no Paris ever yielded such as this—away with all your counterfeiters! Just walk down Hollywood Boulevard someday—if you must have something *out* of uniform. Here are little fairies who can quote Rimbaud before they are 18—and here are women who must have the tiniest fay to tickle them the one and only way! You ought to see B.C. shake her tits— and cry *apples* for a bite!

---

* *The Letters of Hart Crane, 1916–1932*, edited by Brom Weber, Cambridge University Press, 40s.

41

Poets, Novelists, Critics

Crane's character was shaped by the dissension between his father and mother which began in his childhood and ended in their separation and divorce while he was still in his teens. 'I don't want to fling accusations, etc., at anybody, but I think it's time you realized that for the last eight years my youth has been a rather bloody background for yours and father's sex life and troubles,' he wrote to his mother in 1919, when he was 20 years old. Crane took his mother's side but tried hard to stay on good terms with his father, and the remarkable thing about these family letters is the maturity they show, and their demand that he should be treated not as a boy but as an equal adult. Everybody in this tragic triangle felt goodwill, and made intermittent attempts to understand the positions of the others. Clarence Crane, a prosperous candy manufacturer in Ohio, had little education, but he tried hard to induce his son to enter college so that he could obtain what seemed to the father the right background and knowledge for a writer. When Hart refused, his father, as Mr Weber says, 'recognized no realistic alternative other than adjustment to the business world and development of his poetic life as an adjunct to his mercantile life'. Crane tried to make such an adjustment and worked in one of his father's stores for some time before the inevitable quarrel drove him away. In a long letter written in 1924 refusing finally the offer of a job as travelling salesman with eventual control of the wholesale side of the business, he acknowledged his father's generosity and made a plea for understanding:

> In closing I would like to just ask you to think some time—try to imagine working for the pure love of simply making something beautiful—something that maybe can't be sold or used to help sell anything else, but that is simply a communication between man and man, a bond of understanding and human enlightenment.

The plea did not go unanswered. Clarence Crane responded sympathetically, sent a cheque and continued to provide intermittent financial assistance. In New York Crane worked in advertising ('it is quite a stylish and almost snobbish set of educated people at J. Walter Thompson's'), writing copy for hot water heaters, car tyres, and a paint christened Barrelled Sunshine. He either left or was dismissed from several jobs, and in the last six years of his life lived through the generosity of friends, buttressed by a bequest he received after his grandmother's death and a gift from the millionaire Otto Kahn. Crane's letter to Kahn in 1925 asking 'to borrow the sum of a thousand dollars at any rate of interest within 6 per cent', to enable him to finish 'The Bridge', brought him an interview with the great man, a gift of $2,000, and a further small sum when this was exhausted. 'I hope,' Kahn wrote, 'that you will prove yourself a master builder in constructing "The Bridge" of your dreams, thoughts and emotions.' Typically, Crane, again very unlike Thomas, was haunted by deep guilt-feelings because he did not finish the poem within the time laid down. His last period in Mexico was made financially possible by a Guggenheim Fellowship, given to provide leisure for the production of work embodying 'the emergent features of a distinctive American poetic consciousness'.

His letters of the early twenties show the effect of post-war modernity upon an untutored, immensely responsive mind. He was overwhelmed by the discovery of Donne, Webster, Jonson, Marlowe—in drunken moments he would reel down the street shouting 'I am Christopher Marlowe'—and dazed by the problem of relating their language to modern themes. The photography of Alfred Stieglitz evoked a comparison with Blake, modern music was a revelation that drove him 'almost crazy'. *Ulysses*, partly read in the *Little Review* and then smuggled in from Paris, seemed to him 'the epic of the age', with *Tarr* not far behind it. There is a very touching freshness about these letters, and about the openness with which Crane gave himself to his friends. These friends, Gorham B. Munson, Waldo Frank, Matthew Josephson, were among the little magazine editors, participants in running such periodicals as *Severn Arts*, *Broom* and *Secession*. Most of them were respectable figures— Munson was particularly valued by the others for his 'imposing, waxed handlebar moustaches'—and their early passion for 'writers preoccupied with researches for new forms' in many cases quickly faded. None of them is well known here, and English readers could do with some explanatory notes.

Crane was typically open about his homosexuality. In 1919 he wrote to Munson: 'This "affair" that I have been having has been the most intense and satisfactory one of my whole life, and I am all broken up at the thought of leaving him. Yes, the last word will jolt you.'

Crane later quarrelled with Munson, as he did with almost all of his friends, but at this time and a little later he had his place as the 'wild man' in a group of rather solemn characters, whose excesses were mostly verbal. Later, his 'chronic need to love and to be loved', as Mr

Weber puts it, drove him to different friends, and to deliberate crudity in the search for sexual satisfaction. His chief passion was for sailors, and in addition to keeping an address book full of names, he subscribed to a navy bulletin which reported the movements of the fleet, so that he could telephone sailors when they were in New York. The increasing brutality of his sexual encounters accompanied his extinction as a poet. An indication of what his friends were asked to endure is given by the collapse of his relations with Katherine Ann Porter, another Guggenheim Fellow, who rashly invited him to stay at her house in a Mexico City suburb. Friendly and charming in the mornings, Crane would drink hard every night, returning at midnight, often with a boy he had picked up, sometimes brawling with a taxi driver. After one incident he left, sending her a note: 'Have gone to the Mancera [a hotel] . . . . Excuse my wakefulness, please.

'PS. No. Haven't been busy with "lovers". Just yeowls and fleas. Lysol isn't necessary in the bathtub. Haven't got "anything" yet.'

Unfortunately for Miss Porter the house next door to her was vacant. Crane rented this, and the drinking and violence continued. When sober he told her that he was no longer capable of feeling anything except under the most violent and brutal shocks, 'and I can't even then deceive myself that I really feel anything'. He talked of suicide almost every day. . . .

As a poet, Crane was a magnificent failure. 'The Bridge', which was to have been the crown of his achievement, emerged as a collection of lyrics, some brilliantly devised, others over-written and incoherent. Yet he was much more than another exponent of the great flatulent American dream. Some of the early poems, like 'Praise for an Urn', are masterly in their control of style and feeling:

> It was a kind and northern face
> That mingled in such exile guise
> The everlasting eyes of Pierrot
> And, of Gargantua, the laughter.

> His thoughts, delivered to me
> From the white coverlet and pillow
> I see now, were inheritances—
> Delicate riders of the storm.

Hart Crane's Letters

The slant moon on the slanting hill
Once moved us toward presentiments
Of what the dead keep, living still,
And such assessments of the soul

As, perched in the crematory lobby,
The insistent clock commented on,
Touching as well upon our praise
Of glories proper to the time.

But in the end he could not be satisfied with such simplicity. There will always be people who feel that Crane's passionate identification with the 'modernity' of the twenties was vulgar, and that a phrase like 'a rip-tooth of the sky's acetylene' is ridiculous, although it is not more absurd than a conceit of Donne's. Certainly the pieces which get nearest to reaching the total expression of modernity he sought, 'For the Marriage of Faustus and Helen' and the sequence of 'Voyages', are among the most extraordinary poems of the century. He put down what he hoped to achieve, at a time when he still believed in his own capacity to become 'a suitable Pindar for the dawn of the machine age', in a comment on music:

I went to hear D'Indy's *II Symphony* last night and my hair stood on end at its revelations. To get those . . . into *words*, one needs to *ransack* the vocabularies of Shakespeare, Jonson, Webster (for theirs were the richest) and add our scientific, street and counter, and psychological terms, etc. Yet, I claim that such things can be done!

(1967)

45

About Frances Newman

You will not find Frances Newman's name in Walter Allen's survey of modern English and American fiction, *Tradition and Dream*. Look back to the early forties, at Alfred Kazin's almost encyclopaedic interpretation of modern American prose literature, *On Native Grounds*, and she stays unmentioned. Even Edmund Wilson's chronicle of the twenties and thirties, *The Shores of Light*, does not find space for her name to put beside those of Zona Gale and Carl van Vechten and Thornton Wilder and Elinor Wylie. Yet the two novels she wrote, *The Hard-Boiled Virgin* and *Dead Lovers are Faithful Lovers*, are the product of a remarkable talent and an original mind. She has been so totally forgotten because she was a representative of that shiny American aestheticism of the 1920s which tarnished so quickly that all its works have been thrown out into the dustbin. Yet along with the rubbish some things were discarded, like Elinor Wylie's books and Frances Newman's, which were truly small works of art.

Some biographical background is necessary. Frances Newman was born in Atlanta in 1888, the fifth child of a district judge who had lost an arm fighting for the Confederacy, and who had become city attorney of Atlanta when he was only twenty-eight. She was very much a product of the American South, and most of her life was spent in Atlanta, although she made several trips to Europe and at one time spent some months in Paris, where she read and wrote only in French. She also tried unsuccessfully to acclimatize herself to the pace and temper of life in New York. The first of her visits to Europe was made in 1910, when the Newmans sent their daughter on a European tour. Many of the observations in her journal pay a due and almost automatic tribute to culture, but she remarked also that St Paul's was dirty and not very beautiful, and found Westminster Abbey 'the worst arranged church in the world, full of horrible tombs of very nice people'. Back in Atlanta she became a librarian, and in 1914 was appointed head of the lending department in the Carnegie Library there.

Her name first became publicly known six years later when she began to contribute 'Library Literary Notes' to the *Atlanta Sunday*

Constitution. These became a series of longish introductions to a very mixed bag of writers including Aldous Huxley, Rose Macaulay, James Branch Cabell, Eugene O'Neill, Georg Kaiser, Sinclair Lewis, Ezra Pound, H. L. Mencken, Ronald Firbank and Scott Fitzgerald. In looking at this list of names it should be remembered that Huxley had only just written his first novel, *Crome Yellow*, that Fitzgerald was merely the author of *This Side of Paradise*, and that few people even in England knew Ronald Firbank's name. The articles were written in a sinuous, extremely intricate and fully developed style. The style will be fully displayed later on, as it appeared in her novels, and here it will be enough to quote a description of it as 'the most amazing prose style in America . . . crammed with allusions to the work of almost every notable writer in the three major modern languages'. Her introductions were rather too obviously based on enormously wide reading, and although they were often passionately appreciative they were almost as often vitriolically wounding. She called the one on *This Side of Paradise* 'assault with intent to murder', and it provoked a reply from the author which made her comment, 'I feel as if I had pulled a spoiled baby's curls.' Hugh Walpole was horrified by a review she wrote of *The Cathedral*. 'My God!' he said 'What have I done to the woman? It was the only really vicious review the book got.'

She had become by this time a home-grown Georgia exquisite, in her person as well as in her writing. She had a passion for a colour variously described as violet, lavender, fuchsia, heliotrope and purple. She always wore some shade of violet, used lavender-coloured writing paper, and was delighted when she was able to obtain lavender-coloured painted furniture for her bedroom. The personality behind this fuchsia façade was engagingly enthusiastic. Her entry into a room, a woman friend said, 'was, beyond that of any other person I have ever seen, a floating incarnation of eagerness. In spite of her frailness, her startling thinness of face and figure and voice, her immense psychic vitality informed every sentence and gesture.' Another friend remarked in her the survival of a timid, rebuffed but headstrong child who played 'in a kind of enforced braggadocio seasoned everywhere with a bit of uneasiness, at being grown up'. She was always acutely aware of what she feared to be her own physical unattractiveness, observing in thoughts she attributed to her heroine Katharine Faraday that 'the stupidest girl with a short upper lip and curly golden hair is born to a social situation much pleasanter than the social situation of the cleverest girl with a long upper lip and straight black hair,' an observation based upon the fact that her own upper lip was long, and her hair straight and black.

After the death of her parents she lived in an apartment with a young nephew whom she cared for, and the Negro mammy who had presided over her birth. 'Marriage is an institution created for human beings in a primitive state of society and of intelligence,' she wrote, and she never married, although her letters mention a number of love affairs, most of them with men younger than herself. By the early nineteen-twenties she was accepted as a member of the dominant school of American aesthetes. It was a period when Cabell's *Jurgen* was compared to *Tristram Shandy*, when Elinor Wylie's *Jennifer Lorn* was called the first truly civilized American novel, when Carl van Vechten wrote books which blended Firbank and Nineties diabolism, and daringly gave mixed parties for whites and Negroes. Frances Newman never quite belonged to this world, but she adhered to most of its judgements and their implications. She deplored all prophetic inspiration as ridiculous, and all moral dogmatism as uncivilized. Like Katharine Faraday again, 'she abandoned John Ruskin after his first morning in Florence, and Samuel Johnson after his first cup of tea, and all the major and minor prophets in their turn', and she abandoned religion because 'beliefs of any kind would certainly ruin her style.' When she referred to 'the immortal Joseph' she meant Joseph Hergesheimer, and although *Candide* was her ideal novel she regarded James Branch Cabell as 'the most delightful and the most important living prose writer'. But if some of her judgements look as absurd to us as (say) current critical illusions about the genius of William Carlos Williams will look in thirty years' time, many more were finely perceptive and firmly based. Her *coda*, written in 1927, is not unacceptable today:

> I want a book to have wit and profundity, and I don't like dull, solemn, pompous writers like Hardy and Dreiser and O'Neill and Willa Cather, or thin dull writers like Blomfield . . . I have a grand passion for Max Beerbohm, Aldous Huxley, Joyce and Lawrence, and I like Rose Macaulay and Virginia Woolf. I like Morand and Giraudoux and Madame Colette and a dozen other French writers, and I bow whenever I mention Pirandello's name . . . And I nearly forgot to say that I am speaking only of living writers and not even of admirations so lately dead as Proust and Katharine Mansfield,

and that I read every word Ring Lardner writes. In short, I like writers who know how to write, and I don't like writers who don't know the meaning of all the words they use, and who don't know how to put them together. Which is why I don't like Carl van Vechten and Scott Fitzgerald.

From the appearance of her first literary notes she was urged to write a novel by influential friends, including H. L. Mencken and Cabell, who acted to some extent as her adviser and arbiter. As an aspiring novelist she started with two conflicting ideas, the first that a writer should deal with the life he knew, and the second that 'American life is as unsuited to literature as modern trousers are to sculpture.' She felt that deliberate stylization was thus forced on her, and thought of writing a novel which should unwind its theme in a single paragraph of several hundred pages. This was an intention that she never fulfilled, but in 1922 she began to write the book which four years later appeared—with, of course, a fuchsia binding and with the Oxford spelling which she insisted on—as *The Hard-Boiled Virgin*. She rarely wrote more than one page a day, constantly revised what she had done, and at one time despaired of finishing the book. She meant to call it *Parthenos* because it was 'about a hard-boiled virgin', but was persuaded by a publisher that the misleadingly sensational title finally chosen was appropriate. Although it was not written in a single paragraph, the stylization she settled on was strange enough. The book is a series of episodes in the life of a girl born and brought up in Atlanta. Each episode is from two to eight pages in length, and consists of a single paragraph. Dialogue was necessarily excluded by such a plan, and there is not a line of conversation. It is not easy to show the style's effect by quotation, because it is necessarily cumulative, but the first episode—given here in its entirety—will give an idea of the flavour:

Though her father and mother would not have accounted for her in just that way, Katharine Faraday was the sixth pledge of their love. They had not much curiosity concerning the stars or the arts, and they would have been as unlikely to say that she was born under the sign of Virgo and in the earlier Beardsley period. But when she was eight years old, the spirit of that age was still unknown in cities far more worldly wise than Atlanta. The prestige of double beds and double standards was not seriously diminished, and society still called upon husbands to be as faithful as nature requires to tangent wives neatly buttoned into white cambric which flowed to their ankles, and upon wives to be as faithful as nature required to tangent husbands buttoned into white cambric which flowed only to their knees. Katharine Faraday's mother had no reason for suspecting that the Atlantic Ocean and the German language were concealing the opinions of Sigmund Freud from Georgia, or for suspecting that some women can be mothers only by day and wives only by night, and when Katharine Faraday had a sore throat which would almost certainly become measles before next morning, her little walnut bed was moved into the carefully curtained off bay-window of her mother's room. But if Katharine Faraday had dared to risk escaping over its creaking rail, she would not have been lying in her bed when morning came, and her ears would not have been vainly stopped against her mother's reproaches and against her father's stumbling steps and his stumbling excuses. She did not like to feel the emotion she did not know was called pity, and she did not understand how her father could have reached such age and such eminence without learning that all mothers are as infallible as any pope and more righteous than any saint. Neither did she understand why he had never learned that wise husbands and children acknowledge their sins immediately, and acknowledge them with such despair and such moving lamentations that virtue is likely to relent, and that unless she relents she finds herself unable to compete with the repentant sinner's self-abasement. She had already discovered the awkwardness of quarrels between partners of a bed, but if she had known that she was beginning to walk in the holy footprints of Saint Katharine of Alexandria, she could not have wept longer when she discovered that the horrifying felicities of the holy bonds of matrimony sometimes follow the horrors of connubial fury, and when she discovered that a father and a mother are a man and a woman—that they are not only one flesh, but two.

Such a style might be no more than a clever trick, but in her case it was one beautifully suited both to her literary character and to her subject. To her character because, as she said, 'I like inferences, not flat-footed declarations, and of course that requires a protasis and an apodosis.' To her subject, because the ironic view of Southern social mores in the early years of the century, and of the way in which Katharine Faraday gradually emancipates herself from them and loses her virginity, could have been shown successfully only by indirection. Through the style she obtained an effect of distance and detachment in dealing with material that was potentially shocking to readers, and in giving general value to what was essentially her personal story. Katharine Faraday shared a great many tastes with her creator, including a liking for various shades of violet, and her progression from acceptance of her society's code of values about love and marriage to a recognition that love was in fact sexual fulfilment was no doubt Frances Newman's own, yet the identification is never so close that it mars a wonderfully witty and original comedy of manners. The book might have been sub-titled 'The Education of a Southern Lady', and it emphasizes the fact that the great difference between Frances Newman and most of the other American literary dandies was that she had something real and interesting to write about.

Katharine Faraday's mother prepares for her daughter's future marriage when she is fifteen by providing her with

> several intimate friends whose great-grandfathers had given their names to the counties of the more distinguished southern states, whose fathers knew on Wednesday what the price of cotton would be on Thursday, whose brothers were members of the Piedmont Driving Club, and whose mothers would be arranging careful dinners and dances and lunches in another four years.

She is sent to school in Washington so that she may observe the ladies of the diplomatic corps and come back 'with a more ingenious method of doing her hair and with some information concerning methods of arousing ardent but honourable passions in young gentlemen'. Katharine does her best, but is extraordinarily unsuccessful in arousing honourable passion among the young lieutenants and captains she meets at dances. She is inquisitive but innocent and when Captain Cabot, with whom she decides she has fallen in love, tries to embrace her on a sand dune, taking off her hat with one hand and pressing her against his blue coat with the other, she believes that 'if Edward Cabot could offer her the insult of an unbetrothed kiss he did not love her', and sends a telegram to her mother saying that she is coming home.

Several similar incidents convince the Faradays that marrying off Katharine will be a problem. She is delighted when the death of an elder brother (she discovers after the funeral that he has died of syphilis) leaves her with the residue of his estate, amounting to some ten thousand dollars.

> Her pleasure in such a surprising proof of Arthur Faraday's surprising ability to appreciate her uncommon charms was not disturbed by any suspicion that the gift for understanding his fellow-men which had made him Fulton County's youngest commissioner had convinced him that his youngest sister would never have the kind of charms which were likely to get her a satisfactory husband, or which were likely to get her any husband at all.

Made desirable by cash, she is still unable to procure a husband. A promising young Southern politician presents her with Buckle's *History of Civilization in England* as prelude to a declaration of his intentions, but when at last his eyes become damp and he begins 'to breathe so noticeably that Katharine Faraday acquired a permanent distaste for breathing', she is not able to look at him again. She begins to write stories, one of which is published, and goes to Europe. In Paris she places black irises on Oscar Wilde's grave (Frances Newman did this too), and begins but does not finish affairs with several men. Their intentions are dishonourable and their habits disconcerting. When she smiles across a narrow Venice canal at a young man who looks like a gentleman and is singing to his guitar, he immediately drops his guitar and exposes his genitals, her romantic feeling for a surgeon ceases when he turns out to be an abortionist, and her impression that she is in love with a journalist is ended by his failure to bring a handkerchief to a picnic. Moving at last among literary people, she resists a novelist and an editor, who both assure her that her style will be greatly improved by the loss of her virginity, and has finally decided that she is a hard-boiled virgin and will never be anything else, when she allows herself to be seduced by a dramatist who has written a play which lasted seven weeks at the Forty-Third Street Theatre. She does not see him again, and in the last pages she is about to embark on a love affair with a young man in the knowledge that his also will not be lasting:

> She supposed an evening would come when she would tell him that he had tied together enough last straws to make a sheaf of wheat on the grave of their love, and she knew she would not be consoled by the opportunity of using a phrase she admired . . . And she was sure

she would tell him that he had shattered her last illusion, but she knew that she would go on discovering that one illusion had been left to her a minute before, and that she would discover it every time she heard another illusion shattering on the path behind her.

The Hard-Boiled Virgin was an immediate success, partly because of its title and its subject (Atlanta was 'shocked into convulsions'), partly because of the warmth with which the critics praised it, partly because it received the imprimatur of being banned in Boston. Against all likelihood—in view of its style and approach—it became a bestseller. In England Heinemann admired but said that they dared not publish it, and it appeared at Compton Mackenzie's instigation under the imprint of Martin Secker. Mackenzie feared that the wit would not carry across the Atlantic, and it created hardly a ripple of interest here. The American success, however, meant that after being short of money for several years—just before the book's publication the bank had returned one of her cheques because there were no funds to meet it—she was able to give up her library job and think at leisure about her next book.

She had a great many ideas for books that remained unwritten, of which the most interesting was perhaps that of a 'Peacock novel' to be called *There's a Certain Elegance about Celibacy*. A number of writers, modelled recognizably after contemporaries and including Katharine Faraday, were to be gathered under the roof of a lavishly hospitable, determinedly unmarried literary figure who had written one great novel which seemed to him so faulty that he was spending the rest of his life revising it. She did not write a line of this book, nor a line of the history of sophistication on which she had been brooding for years, nor of *Eminent Virgins, So-Called* (she had a gift for choosing unhappy titles), a series of short biographies including those of Leonardo, St Francis, Jane Austen, Cardinal Newman and Henry James. She planned a novel which was to be written under a pseudonym neither certainly male nor female, neither positively English nor American, so that the reader would not be able to tell the writer's sex or nationality. She invented the pseudonym and naturally enough kept it a secret, but she did not write the book.

There was another theme that she discussed with friends more fruitfully. 'I want to write about a woman who lets herself be entirely absorbed by love—lets it eat up everything she has in her, simply sinks down into it. I could do that myself, I feel sometimes,' she told a woman friend, and to another friend who had recently married she wrote:

> Sometimes I think of taking a husband temporarily at least, just to find out the sensations of a married woman. I would like to understand the extraordinary complacency which seems strange to me, but which must be so comfortable. But I don't suppose it exists except in what I suppose must be called bourgeois marriages, and I don't like the idea of that kind.

Eventually the original idea was transformed into the story of Evelyn Cunningham, who is so much in love with her husband that she spends the whole time dreading the day when he will love her less. He tries to escape from this stifling affection into a love affair with a librarian, but the affair is still unconsummated when he is taken ill and dies. The marriage has endured for twelve years, and in the course of it the wife's love has changed too. She has become precisely like the solid, complacent Mrs Perryman, who seemed so incomprehensible to her in the early days of her own marriage. Mrs Perryman's chief emotion when her husband dies and she attends the funeral wearing a trailing black crape veil is a 'calm consciousness that her marriage was victoriously ended, and that a husband in a black morning coat and striped grey trousers was safely waiting for her in the soil of the most aristocratic town in North Carolina.' And Evelyn Cunningham feels a similar sensation of triumph in considering her husband's death, which is revealed to us only in the book's last three words:

> When the pain rushed through every one of her nerves again as she lifted her hand to her little hat, it did not tell her that she felt herself walking at last in the green oasis of a memory over which she was dropping the victorious curtain of her very long black crape veil.

Her victory is implied in the title: *Dead Lovers are Faithful Lovers*.

This might be the summary of an ironic masterpiece, but *Dead Lovers* is far from that. Cabell had wisely suggested that her second book should avoid any suggestion of scandal and that it ought to be 'quite dialoguish' but, in fact, she used the episodic and dialogueless approach of the earlier novel, although the episodes were divided into paragraphs, and she introduced another ingenious technical device. The story is told partly by the wife and partly by the librarian, Isabel Ramsay, and what she called the modulation from one to the other is managed with wonderful skill exactly halfway through the book, when Evelyn Cunningham looks across a room at Isabel Ramsay and thinks that her beauty is too calm and quiet and cool to be encouraging to men, and Isabel Ramsay looks across and wonders if Mrs Charlton Cunningham can possibly feel as complacent as she looks. *Dead Lovers* was to have been dedicated to Cabell, 'the ex post facto justification of all Virginia's pride', as she characteristically phrased it, but he was disappointed by the novel and preferred to wait for the history of sophistication.

Dead Lovers does, indeed, show how easily literary dandyism can drop disastrously into preciosity and sentimentality. There are far too many of the detailed descriptions of clothes and colours that she derived from Hergesheimer, which give force to the remark that such prose was less like architecture than like interior decoration, and there is far too much about Charlton Cunningham's dark and Viennese head and about the forked veins which 'wave their green lines up his unburned forehead'. Frances Newman was not wrong in calling herself mentally cynical and personally sentimental. Yet her intelligence was so keen and her artistic conscientiousness so faithful that this is still a book of considerable interest. The original ironic intention is not firmly and clearly carried through, but enough of it remains to suggest what a devastating attack upon rich American bourgeois life this might have been. Many passages show her comic sense and her serpentine wit. Above all, the early part of the story conveys better than any other novel of the period an almost oppressive sense of sexual pleasure in physical contact. The preparations made by Evelyn Cunningham for sex with her husband are described over and over again like a sacred rite, and so with slight variations is her discovery that men 'drop helplessly to the bottom of their emotions as soon as they are lying in a horizontal position'. In letters she discussed in detail the exact positions in which the lovers lay in bed:

> If you imagine that the groom is lying on his right side and the bride on her left side, his hand will be turned upward across the soft upper part of her arm. And she can easily clutch what she doubtless calls her stomach without moving her arm more than two inches, from the elbow down, and turning her hand.

The effect of the physical passages is again heightened by the detachment with which they are described. Within the limits of what could be said at the time she really did convey the feeling of a woman 'drowned in love'.

In the spring of 1928, just after the publication of *Dead Lovers*, she went to Paris to work in the Bibliothèque Nationale on the history of sophistication. Just before leaving she made an appearance in court which showed that a concern for style did not preclude the possession of a social conscience. She went to make a personal plea for a Negro who had entered her home and stolen sixteen cents. ('Miss Newman wore a hat from the rue Castiglione and a frock from the rue Cambon. Both were in shades of violet,' the local press reported.) Her plea had some effect, for the man received a reduced sentence, but it was still one of three years' imprisonment, and on coming home she took to her bed 'and was ill for three days from the sight of *justice*'. She enjoyed Paris more than she had ever done before, and made plans to translate Laforgue's *Moralités Légendaires*. She had often suffered from minor illnesses and now was troubled by what was at first called a congested right eye. She returned to New York for further advice, bringing nine new frocks, six hats and five coats. 'If ever, this is the time for the grand amour,' she wrote hopefully.

In America, however, her eye condition grew steadily worse. She felt an incessant vibration behind her 'roaring and rumbling' right eye which was insusceptible to diagnosis—or rather, ten doctors and two dentists diagnosed it differently. She went from New York to Atlanta, then back to New York and to Philadelphia, in search of a cure. She was unable to read or write but refused to give up working, and translated four of the Laforgue stories by dictating passages as they were read aloud to her. She was in New York, having rejected a neurologist's advice that she should go into a sanatorium for a long rest, when she was found unconscious in her hotel. She died on 22 October 1928. A cerebral haemorrhage was at first said to have been the cause of death, but in fact she had taken an overdose of veronal.

She was forty years old when she died. It is possible that her art might have developed to include a wider area of human experience, just as possible that the chilling climate of the thirties might have withered it altogether. But what she actually wrote was greatly talented. She deserves a place, although obviously not a foremost one, in any literary history of the years between the wars. The last letter she wrote, or rather dictated, to the printer of the Laforgue translations shows the invariable fastidiousness of her talent, a fastidiousness which is often infuriating but just as often impressive, and is in any case rare enough to be worth remembrance:

To the Printer of Six Moral Tales
   This book is to be spelled and its words are to be hyphened according to the usage of the Concise Oxford Dictionary.
   Page introduction continuously with the tales.
Do not put brackets around the numbers of the pages.
   All the 'todays' and all the 'tomorrows' should be spelled without hyphens.
   Do not put 'The End' at the end.

(1966)

Wyndham Lewis's First Novel

Mrs Dukes' Million by Wyndham Lewis
Wyndham Lewis: A Descriptive Bibliography by Omar S. Pound and Philip Grover

Some quarter of a century ago the typescript of an unpublished novel by Wyndham Lewis was found in a London junk shop. It was called *Khan and Company* and had been written, Lewis told the literary agent J. B. Pinker, simply to make money. 'As the only thing of which there is question as far as this book is concerned is money-making,' Lewis wrote with his frequently disastrous candour, he would be glad to make any commercially useful changes. 'The titles of the chapters are chosen as vulgarly effective—suppose that is right? But perhaps I am going too quickly, and my miserable pot-boiler has not even any money value.' That was in fact Pinker's view. Lewis took away the manuscript and wrote: 'I shall not trouble any more about it, I think; and it is a lesson showing the futility of pot-boiling for me.'

This is the book that has now been published by a small Canadian press, from the typescript in the Lewis Collection at Cornell, with a certain amount of editing by the magazine editor Charles Davey. It would be interesting to know more about the editing. According to W. K. Rose, editor of Lewis's letters, the title *Khan and Company* appears on the typescript. Why then is the awkward *Mrs Dukes' Million* (the eye automatically reads *Mrs Duke's Millions*) preferred? Lewis told Pinker that he would use the pseudonym James Sed, but Mr Davey tells us that the typescript carries the name John Lawrence. And then there must have been at least one other version of the book, for Lewis in a letter to Pinker suggests that the first chapter may be too long, and that can hardly be said of this version, in which the chapter occupies less than three pages. It seems very likely that what we have is an early draft, and that in the typescript sent to Pinker some of the rough places had been smoothed out. Mr Davey suggests from references in the book that the present version may have been completed in 1908. Lewis did not write to Pinker for another year or more.

Lewis did himself an injustice in saying that the book was of no

58

interest. *Mrs Dukes' Million* cannot be called a successful novel on the intended pot-boiling terms, but the theme and its handling prefigure ideas about the relationship of art and reality that were one of Lewis's chief concerns in fiction. With three biographies of Lewis in hand or projected, the first serious bibliography just published and another on the way, *Mrs Dukes' Million* gives the chance of reconsidering Lewis as a writer of fiction, and of reflecting on the course of his career.

The idea that we all wear masks of one kind or another, masks behind which more or less discreditable secrets are hidden, is recurrent in Lewis's work. The Enemy, that title which he gave to a magazine and also happily accepted as a personal label, actually appears 'cloaked, masked, booted, and with gauntlets of astrakan' in the poem *One-Way Song*. The mysterious Pierpoint moving ambiguously in the background of *The Apes of God* is one kind of mask, the brawling rhetorical Bailiff in the first part of *The Childermass* another, Percy Hardcaster in *The Revenge For Love* a third. This novel is full of masks and pretences. Percy's wooden leg is not the heroic symbol it appears, Victor Stamp's occupation is the forgery of van Goghs, a conjectural load of guns turns out to be a load of bricks. Vincent Penhale's personality in *The Vulgar Streak* is built upon the forgeries he circulates and he is, as he says in a confessional moment, 'a sham from head to foot'. Lewis had throughout his life an interest in the form of the thriller, and in several novels he tried deliberately to use this form for serious ends. *Mrs Dukes' Million* is a thriller conceived without serious purpose. Its origins are in *Volpone* and *The Alchemist*, but it may owe something to Arthur Machen's Stevensonian thriller *The Three Impostors* and to Chesterton's morality in terms of a fantastic thriller, *The Man Who Was Thursday*, which appeared in 1908.

Mrs Dukes is an old Cockney who lives in a dingy bric-à-brac shop off Oxford Street, with her son Cole, who spends most of his time in the cellar chopping wood. Cole strays above ground from his subterranean habitat only to eat haddock or to help his mother with the washing-up. The shop does not provide a living, and Mrs Dukes lets rooms. She has, however, unknown to herself inherited a million pounds from the estate of the husband who deserted her thirty years earlier, and is therefore a natural victim for the Actor-Gang, who specialize in impersonations. She is spirited away and replaced by Evan Royal, an actor who has been lodging in her house so that he can study her. When the solicitors dealing with the estate come to see Mrs Dukes they meet Royal in her guise, and in case Royal should be taken ill or falter in his role, a third Mrs Dukes is in training to replace him. The Actor-Gang is ruled by the Khan, who in public life is the ambassador in England of a small central Asian country. The plot is concerned with the gang's attempt to get hold of Mrs Dukes' million, and the moves made by a rival American gang to kidnap Evan Royal and get the money themselves.

The story is preposterous, particularly in the idea that the most suitable replacement for an old woman would be a comparatively young man. Once accept it, however, and the tale is developed with tremendous verve and ingenuity. Not just one or two, but positively dozens of actors play their parts in making the scheme work. The author creates difficulties for the pleasure of solving them. All of the lodgers leave the house except for a recalcitrant curate, who insists on staying on for a few weeks. He is induced to leave by the visit of a 'portly, eupeptic, rich-voiced, oleaginous clergyman, looking rather like the skipper of a passenger steamer, who spent most of the time with the ship's guests'. The clergyman is of course a member of the gang, like the lodgers who replace the old ones, and the new charwoman. When Mr Hatchett the solicitor arrives from Liverpool he meets a brand new cast, and finds nothing to cause suspicion.

Except, of course, Cole. Is it to be supposed that a son, even so strange a son as Cole is shown to be, does not know his own mother? The treatment of this problem is masterly. Cole, on one of his visits to the upper atmosphere, says suddenly, 'Oo are you? You're not mother?' Royal responds: 'Oo am I, Cole? Whatever are ye talkin' about. What've ye got in ye 'ead now, I should like to know?' Cole repeats that this is not his mother. Is he going to blow the gaff? On the contrary Cole, who disliked his mother, positively welcomes the new regime, in particular the fact that he is now allowed to smoke his pipe in the cellar. Cole, therefore, without ever admitting that he knows Royal to be an impostor, becomes a partner in the plot. When Royal is abducted by the Americans and has to be replaced hurriedly by the third Mrs Dukes, a young man named Hercules Fane, Cole is startled into the exclamation 'Oh, I say', and immediately retires to the cellar with his pipe. There is a felicitous touch late in the book, when Cole has to make a railway journey to a new home in Liverpool. 'He had evidently enjoyed the darkness of the tunnel very much, and had been seen in the faint light thrown by the lamp overhead to smile slightly.'

Wyndham Lewis's First Novel

A new cellar has been prepared for him in Liverpool, and although at first shy of it, he soon settles down to chopping wood. The portrait of Cole, like the conception of the three Mrs Dukes, anticipates in some respects the comedy of the Marx Brothers. So does a passage in which Mr Hatchett and his clerk, when visiting Mrs Dukes, find that their chairs collapse. The clerk's chair closes up on him like a concertina, while Hatchett's immediately makes a cracking sound and starts to tilt. Such exaggerative comedy is often found in the later Lewis, but at this point in time it was markedly original.

The book's limitations are inherent in its conception. The farcical plot, which becomes very wild near the end, allows no room for development of character, so that all the people are fixed Jonsonian humours. The sleazy central London setting is well done, but it is not altogether new, and sometimes seems like a Gissingesque scene played for comedy instead of drab realism. Yet the story remains interesting for those suggestions of seriousness that Lewis could never resist even in work lightly conceived. The idea that feigning is itself a kind of reality is advanced on several occasions, in particular by the Khan. ('All my greatest feelings . . . possessed me only when I was feigning.') It is suggested that the Khan's activities are those of an alternative world order, not necessarily inferior to the one generally obeyed in Edwardian society. People in his service do not think of themselves as criminals. Royal sees himself as 'a disinterested adventurer', perhaps rather in the Raffles line. Like Raffles he is not interested in women. He is counterposed to Fane, who falls in love with another member of the gang. The three escape with a fair slice of Mrs Dukes' money, and the end finds them in the Museum Galleries of the Luxembourg. All have assumed new names, and Fane is now a successful painter and Royal a dashing early aviator. 'Take me for a fly,' Lucy says: 'And soon they were flying for all they were worth over Paris, and to the amazement and delight of the Parisian population, alighted in the open space usually given over to diabolo at the observatory side of the gardens, facing the clock of the palace.'

There is something engagingly ingenuous about such passages, and indeed about the whole book: but the fact that it was written at all is of some significance, even though Lewis made only one half-hearted attempt to achieve publication. It is hard to imagine Eliot, Joyce or Pound, the literary contemporaries with whom Lewis was most closely linked, producing a work of this kind. The contrast between *Mrs Dukes' Million* and the stories collected in *The Wild Body*, the

61

first of which was printed in 1909, is very great, both in the attitudes suggested by the stories and the texture of the prose, just as there is a marked difference between Lewis's early drawings and those produced in 1909 when he had assimilated influences leading towards abstraction.

Lewis was a late developer, especially as a writer: but there was a continuing dichotomy in both graphic and literary work, but especially in his writing, between abstraction and images of action. The extreme abstract literary works, like *The Enemy of the Stars* and the first part of *The Childermass*, are concerned with ideas about the nature of man and his place in society. The descriptive passages and shards of humour are there basically to hold our attention on the philosophical argument. The true novels, however, are built from quite complicated plots leading to violent action. The finest of them, *The Apes of God* and the books of the thirties already mentioned, are those that blend the two elements, putting the astonishing prose style fully developed by the early 1920s to ends not altogether removed from those of the Edwardian novelists Lewis despised. Like them he wished both to observe, and to change the shape of, society. *Tarr* provides the prime exception to these remarks, as a work of extreme brilliance and psychological subtlety which contains the element of violence, yet is concerned with 'art' rather than with 'society' so far as the two can be separated: but then *Tarr* stands quite on its own among Lewis's fictions.

If those fictions have never been generally appreciated it is at least in part because much of Lewis's early writing was misdirected. It was a mistake ever to think that prose could be used to obtain effects like those of abstract painting (*The Childermass* and bits of *The Apes of God*), a mistake to attempt to present philosophical arguments in semi-fictional shape. The label of an intractable highbrow was pinned to Lewis, and his more accessible later fictions were much less read than they might have been because of it. When to this label was added another saying 'Hitlerite', derived from Lewis's tentative support of Hitler before he came to power plus his unwavering opposition to the Popular Front, the result was disastrous for his reputation. Edgell Rickword once remarked that in the twenties no British writer received more critical attention than Lewis, but the bibliography produced by Omar S. Pound and Philip Grover tells some grim truths about reputation and sales. *Tarr* has been translated into Japanese, French and Italian, but the only other book translations noted are three in Germany during the time of Lewis's flirtation with Nazism, one in post-Hitler Germany and a couple of others in Japan. Lewis's American reputation collapsed when his political attitude in the thirties became known, and since that time only one book has found a large American publisher. *The Revenge for Love* had to wait fifteen years for any sort of American publication, and several books have not appeared there at all. His most successful work in this country has been, surprisingly, *Self Condemned* (1954), which went into three impressions totalling 7,000 copies. For the Tauchnitz edition of *Tarr*, in 1931, Lewis was paid £27.

The Pound and Grover bibliography is useful rather than satisfactory. It omits all writing about Lewis, and the compilers have been able to obtain very little information about the size of printings outside Britain. Elsewhere some readily accessible information has been omitted, such as the size of the advances paid on *Snooty Baronet* and *The Revenge for Love* (£300 and £400 respectively), and the sales figures of the Penguin editions of *The Apes of God* and *The Revenge for Love* (roughly 22,000 and 10,000) and other paperback editions. There is an interesting list compiled by D. G. Bridson of radio and television features concerning Lewis, including Bridson's own remarkable productions of the three parts of *The Human Age*, *Tarr* and *The Revenge for Love*. At least one radio broadcast, of a long extract from *One-Way Song*, has been omitted here.

There are several signs of revival in Lewis's literary reputation, including the foundation of a Wyndham Lewis Society many of whose members are young. It seems likely, however, that such a revival—which obviously would be helped by an intelligent biography—would be in the first place scholarly rather than general, and that it would be based on the fiction rather than on the philosophical and political books. *The Art of Being Ruled* and *Time and Western Man*, the major statements of Lewis's ideas, contain unique insights into the nature and quality of modern society, but they were written half a century ago, and have been out of print for several years without any call for a second edition. The most immediately rewarding approach to the fiction would probably be in analysing texts to show both that Lewis was not, as is often said, a careless writer, and that he was badly served by publishers. As Hugh Kenner has said, the charge of hasty writing is altogether untrue. The impression comes perhaps from the exclamatory energy of Lewis's characteristic style, but he rewrote again and again. Kenner mentions half-a-dozen stages in the opening of *The Apes of God*, and I have seen myself several versions of passages in *Hoodopip* and *Joint*, two unfinished works of the twenties.

And Lewis's punctuation, with its deliberate visual effects obtained by interjections, hyphens and exclamation marks, was not amenable to the house rules imposed by most publishers. In an unpublished thesis on *The Revenge for Love*, Linda Sandler compared passages from Lewis's typescript with the final printing by Cassell, and showed that the conformity with a standard house style was often damaging to the effects at which Lewis was aiming. One of his skills as a writer was the ability to catch on the page the random incoherent repetitious nature of conversations between groups of people, and to shape and style this incoherence into an artistic pattern. The party scene in *The Apes of God* shows this technique working perfectly, and it is present in an embryonic form in *Mrs Dukes' Million*. A full-length study of the ways in which this technique was used during his career, or a detailed examination of the changes made between the first and the fully revised editions of *Tarr*, would do more than anything else to re-establish Lewis's reputation. If a quarter of the pains had gone into analysing his fiction that have been taken in producing exegeses of Joyce and Pound, the unique nature of his literary genius would already have been recognized.

(1978)

Snow on Western Man

Last Things by C. P. Snow

> I had the idea out of the blue—in what seemed like a single moment—in Marseilles on 1 January 1935. I was walking down the Canebiere. It was a bitterly cold night, well below freezing point . . . I was extremely miserable. Everything, personal and creative, seemed to be going wrong. Suddenly I saw, or felt, or experienced, or whatever you like to call it, both the outline of the entire *Strangers and Brothers* sequence and its inner organization, that is, the response or dialectic between Lewis Eliot as observer and as the focus of direct experience.

So C. P. Snow remembered in 1962 the basic idea for the eleven books of which the first appeared in 1940 and the last is now published. But what was this basic idea? It is a help in understanding the implications of the series to look more closely at what is meant by an 'outline of the entire sequence'. Clearly, Snow could not have had in 1935 the idea of such a book as *The New Men*, which is concerned with the development of the atomic bomb during the war, or *The Sleep of Reason* which is chiefly concerned with a sex crime that bears resemblances to the Moors Murders. It was, then, the 'inner organization' that he discovered, the idea of what he calls elsewhere a resonance between what his narrator Lewis Eliot sees and what he feels. By looking meticulously at the career of a single man who typifies in himself the scientific and political ideas of many intelligent people in his generation, and by placing this man into situations through which he observes or participates in politically and socially important events, an attempt has been made to define the nature of our society. Within this framework, and obviously of lesser importance, although still essential to the texture of the whole, runs the story of Eliot's personal life. The whole concept, viewed in this way, has an unquestionable grandeur. It can be seen as nothing less than the creation of a composite portrait, in the lives of Eliot and his friends, of twentieth-century Western man.

That is how the design appears to one outsider, but it is not the way

65

in which it is seen by the insider chiefly concerned. The differences are partly a matter of emphasis, but they are important. In a prefatory note to *The Conscience of the Rich*, published in 1958 but planned to appear as the second book in the series and delayed by extra-literary reasons, Snow makes it clear that although he has looked at society in general, 'the inner design has always lain elsewhere.' Eliot was by intention much more than a filter for events, the matter of 'resonance' is all-important. 'Some of the more important emotional themes he observes through others' experience, and then finds them enter his own.' Important among them are the theme of 'possessive love', which Eliot sees and then experiences, and also that of 'the love of power and the renunciation of power'. Given the clue, one can see that these themes play a large part in *Last Things*, in which Eliot renounces both possessive love in relation to his son Charles and also the chance of exercising power when he turns down a job in the Labour government. But 'possessive love' and 'power' are abstract concepts, in themselves so vague as to be almost meaningless. If they were really the only springs of the novels, we should pay these books little more attention than is given now to the work of Charles Morgan.

Snow is not the first novelist to have produced effects which differed from his intentions. Zola's series of Rougon-Macquart novels had their origins in a crude blend of materialist psychology and mock science, and the novels were meant to demonstrate the correctness of the theories. Trollope's political novels, which give so fine a picture of deviousness and time-serving in the English social structure during part of the nineteenth century, were designed rather to show that his Prime Minister, Plantagenet Palliser, Duke of Omnium, was a perfect gentleman in a mercenary time. Few would call 'Planty Pall' one of Trollope's more successful portraits, but the novelist himself thought that if his name was remembered as a writer of fiction it would rest on his drawing of three characters, among whom he put Palliser first. In the directness of his realism and the plainness of his style, Snow bears some relation to both Zola and Trollope, and like them he is likely to find what he regards as his main theme more or less ignored and his secondary ones praised.

Before considering Eliot as a character, one has to get clear of the idea that there is any critical value in identifying him with his creator. The points of similarity in their backgrounds and careers have often been noticed, and more are provided in *Last Things*. During the course of an eye operation for the replacement of a detached retina Eliot's heart stops, as Snow's heart stopped when he had a similar operation. In some details Eliot's family life resembles Snow's, just as at several points the posts he has held are like those held by Snow. But anybody setting out on an enterprise like this novel sequence makes use of the materials to hand, and what materials are better known to a writer than those of his own life? It has clearly been Snow's conscious intention from the start to fit whatever happened to him into the pattern of the sequence when this seemed appropriate, but none of the books is to be identified as a *roman à clef* full of real characters and incidents masquerading under deceptive labels. Some of the things that happened to C. P. Snow add flavour and veracity to events in the life of Lewis Eliot, but the points of difference are far more numerous and more notable than those of correspondence.

The chief weakness of Eliot as a character is not that he can be identified with his creator, but that it is often difficult to identify him at all. He is at the centre of three books, including *Last Things*, and he is the medium by which the action of all the others is shown to us, yet he seems very often to be described rather than understood. In part this comes from a certain distancing effect created and maintained throughout the series, which is evident even in the name he is given. The ingenious suggestion that the name was derived from two writers disapproved of by Snow, Wyndham Lewis and T. S. Eliot, is hardly to be taken seriously, but nevertheless names are important in these books and this one must have been chosen with care. It is likely that the use of names which are easily interchangeable—Eliot Lewis would run just as well—was made with the purpose of achieving this sort of detachment. To call somebody 'Lewis' does not sound especially friendly, and whatever else Eliot may be, he does not come through in the early books as a friendly man. At first he seems a self-important climber, using pretentious phrases like 'I had always been a man of the Left', and pushing his nose into all sorts of affairs that have little to do with him. Yet this impression does not prevail. In the three personal novels the portrait is deepened and its colours changed. In *The Sleep of Reason* he becomes involved in a distasteful murder trial largely through adherence to an old friendship, and in *Last Things* there is something pathetic in his never fully expressed love for his son Charles, and his attempts to come to terms with the student generation. At the end of *Last Things* he has a sweet serenity quite uncharacteristic of the early Eliot, and there seems to be a suggestion in the 'Announcements' at the end of the book that another novel may be in preparation—or is the announcement of an event nowhere mentioned in the book, the death of David Schiff, an oversight related to some material first included and later excised? And yet although Eliot develops, it remains true that too much of his character is conveyed to us through his own musings, like this one at the end of *Time of Hope*:

> I had not seen enough of my life yet to perceive the full truth of what my nature needed. I could not distinguish the chance from the inevitable. But I already knew that my bondage to Sheila was no chance. Somehow I was so made that I had to reject my mother's love and all its successors. Some secret caution born of a kind of vanity made me bar my heart to any who forced their way within. I could only lose caution and vanity, bar and heart, the whole of everything I was, in the torment of loving someone like Sheila, who invaded me not at all and made me crave for a spark of feeling, who was so wrapped in herself that only the violence and suffering of such a love as mine brought the slightest glow.

The objection to such passages is that we are being told rather than shown something. At a later point in Eliot's life Margaret, who becomes his second wife, says: 'With anyone who wants you altogether you are cruel . . . With most people you're good, but in the end you'll break the heart of anyone that loves you.' This may be true, but again there is little evidence of it. In dealing with men and women together Snow shows an awkward restraint never present when he is writing about an emotional relationship between men. Sheila, Eliot's first wife, is sexually frigid (she is an enlargement of Audrey in his first serious book *The Search*), but this is never shown to us in a satisfactory way. There is no point at which we feel that sexual passion causes Lewis Eliot joy or anguish on the level at which he feels them in his relationship with the brilliant young Roy Calvert, whose pro-Nazi views do not particularly worry this man of the Left. Indeed, there is more than one occasion when one wonders whether Eliot is a sublimated homosexual.

Although Eliot is never fully seen—no touch of irony, for instance, is allowed to invade the attitude adopted towards him by other people, as surely it must have done in reality—he engages our sympathy in the end through his weakness. There is a fine balance in the gloomy opening of *Homecomings*, with its account of Sheila's breakdown and suicide, and the return at the end of Eliot and Margaret to their house, which has 'a light shining in one room . . . a homecoming such as, for years, I thought I was not to know'. Snow rarely engages in psychological speculation or analysis, but it is made clear that the need for the kind of comfort provided by this image represents something emotionally important to this apparently self-contained man. The other side of this need to be comforted appears in the irrational warning of disaster that he feels as a child in the opening pages of *Time of Hope*, a feeling that is repeated in several books. The note is struck once more on the first page of *Last Things* when, coming back after a journey, he experiences this sensation of dread and remarks that he feels it 'not only when there was something to fear in a homecoming, but when, as now, there was no cause at all'. Description of scenery is cut to a minimum, but exceptions are made for the urban life that stirs Eliot's sensibility, the appearance of a town garden, or lighted rooms in derelict squares. In his own life, as in his contacts with the lives of others, Eliot is almost always, as he is when regarding wistfully those inaccessible lighted rooms, an outsider looking in.

In this sense he is a figure perfectly suited to carry the nature of what Snow has to say. The world shown by him through the eyes of this almost invariably judicious observer is one where matters are decided by groups and committees which form and reform, change shape and character, but remain entities more important than the individuals whose lives they order. Sometimes a group may gather round a magnetic individual, like George Passant in *Strangers and Brothers*, sometimes it is a committee within institutional confines, like those groups in a Cambridge college which decide whether or not Roy Calvert shall be elected a Fellow in *The Light and the Dark*, and who shall be the next Master in *The Masters*. *The Affair*, set at a time sixteen years after *The Masters*, shows many of the same people deciding whether or not a former Fellow, who has been dismissed for committing fraud in the publication of his scientific research, shall be reinstated. In *The New Men* there are groups clashing with each other within the development scheme for the atomic bomb. *Corridors of Power*, near the end of the series, carries on the argument about the atomic weapon in the corridors of Whitehall, and decides it in the division lobbies of that very large committee, the House of Commons. Roger Quaife, an ambitious Tory Minister, decides that his policy must be abandonment of the bomb as a weapon, and is defeated by force of numbers. Numbers are always important in these struggles. Calvert gets his fellowship by eight votes to four, many pages in *The Masters* are occupied by the totting up of votes, and here the civil servant Hector Rose does his sums in advance. 'Anything under 280, and he was in great danger. Anything under 270, and it was all over.' In the end Quaife gets 271 votes for his policy. Rose looks at Eliot and says: 'I consider this unfortunate.' Although the government wins the decision, Quaife is compelled to resign.

These variations on a theme may sound monotonous. In fact they have the excitement of a good detective story and they reinforce, too, the comparison with Trollope. Like *The Last Chronicle of Barset* and *The Eustace Diamonds* these novels depend on the solution of a problem. What will happen to George Passant at his trial, will Jago or Crawford be elected Master, can Quaife survive? The narrative skill with which these questions are handled has been greatly underestimated. Snow's style is without ornament, his movement from one scene and character to another may appear arbitrary or casual, but in fact the development of his novels is done with an art as notable for its omissions as its inclusions. The concentration of material solely on matters that are relevant is remarkable. *The Masters* is set in 1937, a time of deep student concern about politics in general and about the Spanish Civil War in particular, but such matters are not mentioned in the book. It would almost be true to say that in this Cambridge there are no undergraduates but only committees. This is not because Snow is incapable of imagining the lives and attitudes of students (the theme of 'student revolt' enters *Last Things* in the activities of Eliot's son Charles and his friends), or because they do not interest him. It is simply that in the context of the Cambridge novels these things are outside his concern. There is testimony that Snow was an inspiring teacher during his own time at Cambridge during the thirties, but it would probably be true to say that he had little feeling for the student radicals of that time because they did not appear to him to be serious. The activities of Charles's group (another group) impress him more because they are aimed directly at the centre of power.

This is the word to which one comes back. The whole sequence is an impressive and wholly personal statement about what Snow himself has called 'the power-relations of men in organised society'. It is this, rather than any emotional resonances relating to Lewis Eliot, that is the unique achievement of *Strangers and Brothers*, and it is necessary again to refer to Snow's life in considering his attitude. Much of this life has been spent as an administrator, first as Tutor at Christ's, and later on many committees, as a Civil Service Commissioner, and as a Minister in Harold Wilson's second Labour government. Much has also been spent in scientific research which ended, according to William Cooper, when 'a piece of research went wrong through oversight.' But although his active research ended in the early or mid-thirties, Snow's varied scientific interests have been maintained. No other writer in this century has been both a serious scientist and a professional administrator, and Snow's way of looking at people and at art naturally reflects the principles that have guided his own life. Many of the characters in his books are scientists, civil servants, administrators of one sort or another. These people run the world, and it is right that they should do so. For the scientists in particular Snow shows a strong vein of hero-worship.

Against these men, most of them liberal and humane, are posed other figures unable to accept the structure of power and the limits it places on behaviour. The most important of them are George Passant and Roy Calvert, but they can be found in other books—in *Last Things* Calvert's daughter Muriel shows a good deal of his cold recklessness in supporting student revolution. On this other side also are people like Eliot's brother Martin who refuses the chief administrative appointment at 'Barford', the research station for atomic work; Charles March who chooses obscurity rather than success; and a gallery of people defeated by the world, like Eliot's own father, or Sheila, or Margaret's father Austin Davidson, who take refuge in clowning or neurosis. In *Last Things* Davidson becomes totally absorbed in the progress of the stock market, and is delighted when Eliot manages to persuade him that he has made money by following the dying old man's advice.

These are the winners and the losers, and Snow's finest portraits, affectionate, humorous and discerning, are mostly those of the winners; the icy Hector Rose who is discovered in this last book occupying a Pimlico flat with the new wife to whom he is surprisingly affectionate, the burstingly energetic scientist Walter Luke, the Minister Bevill, 'the man to be kept informed of what was going on, the supreme post-office'. It would be beside the point to say that nobody else had handled similar characters so well, for no other modern novelist has treated them seriously at all. Snow sees their weaknesses, but they make up for him a sort of corporate hero of our time, the man who knows what things should be done and how the doing of them can be organized.

The losers are treated compassionately, although they sometimes prompt Snow to write with the yearning romanticism that is his greatest weakness, as in the recollection of Roy Calvert as a sort of Rupert Brooke, 'a young man, mischievous and mocking, the sleeves of his sweater tied round his neck, as when we walked away from cricket in the evening light'. The eccentrics among the losers are all done very well, but outstanding among them is undoubtedly George Passant, the talkative solicitor's clerk whose refusal to accept the limits of freedom takes him to prison. The picture of Passant has a richness and fullness unusual in Snow's work, although it is made clear that he is on the wrong side. What all his fine ideas come to, it seems in *The Sleep of Reason*, is the participation of his niece and her lesbian friend, who were 'on the fringe of our crowd', in the murder of a child. Denying any responsibility for their act, Passant says that he advised them only to act 'according to their nature', but were they not doing just that? Under cross-examination Kitty Pateman admits that she admires the books of Camus because 'they go to the limit, don't they, I like them when they go to the limit.' For Snow, as for Eliot, going to the limit must always be wrong, and it is also something that he cannot emotionally understand. He knows a great deal about personal loneliness and misery, but the elements in the human psyche that led to the development of the concentration camps are as alien to his comprehension as those that prompted the Sharon Tate murders.

To say this is only to say that Snow's work is not of the deepest imaginative order. His kingdom extends no further than the world he has known personally, and within it his writing does not flare with the furious energy of Zola, nor does it have the savagery in much of Trollope's later work. Yet to mark out the limits of what he has done is not to deny its validity. The whole sequence is finer and deeper than any single work within it, and it offers a view of professional British life in the twentieth century magnificent in its scope and remarkable for the faithfulness with which it is maintained. This should not be taken as half-hearted praise. Few other novelists in our time have attempted as much, few have spoken with such generosity and lack of malice, none has shown insights into his chosen material that are more delicate and true.

(1970)

The Figure in the Amis Carpet

The Riverside Villas Murder by Kingsley Amis

It has been suggested that, so far from there being any figure in the Kingsley Amis carpet, there is not even actually any carpet, but only a collection of discordantly coloured rugs loosely stitched together. So roughly stitched (the metaphor goes on, pushed a bit far) that any critic unwisely trusting himself to one of these rugs finds it slipping from under his feet so that he ends in a pratfall, watched by the amiable Amis while sipping one of the wines or liqueurs he recommends monthly in *Penthouse*, to sharpen or assuage emotions aroused by other features of that magazine.

The Riverside Villas Murder offers no comfort to those who look for consistency in Kingsley Amis's work. There have been rumours for some time that he was writing a detective story, and not just a detective story but a classical puzzle, of thirties style though seventies vintage. 'Perhaps no detective story can attain the pitch of literary excellence. Perhaps it can only offer ingenuity raised to the point of genius,' he suggested in an essay on great detectives from Dupin to John Dickson Carr's Dr Fell, who seems upon the whole to be his favourite detective. (He regards H.M., the creation of Carr's alter ego Carter Dickson, as an old bore, which seems a curious view when H.M. and Dr Fell are very similar huffing and puffing rhetoricians and mystifiers.) But Amis recognizes, although with regret, that the great detective has had his day. 'The light in Gideon Fell's study is burning low . . . His heyday came to an end somewhere about 1950, and there died with it the classical detective story . . . of which Fell's creator has been the greatest exponent.'

This new book is an attempt to revive the tradition. It has been given a period dust-jacket, it is set in the thirties, and it uses a trick of the time in offering particular pages for study by those who 'may wish to pit their wits against the author's and solve the mystery for themselves'. (They will be very lucky if they get any help from the pages named.) The victim, who in the traditional manner has done a very fair job of insulting or threatening several of the other characters

73

at a local dance, staggers in through the french windows of fourteen-year-old Peter Furneaux's home wet from immersion in the nearby river, says some audible but at the time meaningless words, and dies, apparently from a blow on the head with an improvised spiked club. The detective is Colonel Manton, Acting Chief Constable, helped by a stooge or two plus Peter. There are red herrings, a reconstruction of the way in which the victim might have got to the particular spot in the river from which he reached shore, and a last chapter called 'How Can They Prove It?'. In fact they can't, and like many another fictional detective of the period, Colonel Manton offers the criminal the only honourable way out.

But *The Riverside Villas Murder* is something more and less than a period detective story. Mr Amis is not one to take any convention too seriously, and on one plane he is simply having fun. The story is a good deal concerned with Peter's search for sexual experience, which he gets from Mrs Trevelyan next door, after having no luck with dumb Daphne, who is a year older than himself. This is enjoyable to read, although it has no direct connection with the crime. The period detail is done with beautiful unobtrusiveness, and seems just right in books and dance bands named, and in the language used by these particular people in their outer London suburb. One small scholarly demurrer: the word 'masturbate' was not in general use among the young then, and Peter would not have said 'I masturbate' to Mrs Trevelyan, but 'I toss myself off'—that is, if he said anything at all. But Peter is a good naturalistic portrait, his loving but wary relationship with his father is believable; Colonel Manton is in more than one way an unusual policeman. The trouble comes with the plot, which is shaky at best, and often outrages our willingness to suspend disbelief. Without giving away any secrets, it can be said that the reason for the reconstruction of the victim's trip down river is preposterous, and that the behaviour of both victim and murderer approaches the incredible. The plot is clumsily made, and the result is in parts lively Amis, but an indifferent detective story. Whatever its other qualities, the best work of the period, like that of Carr and Ellery Queen, ends with a surprise startling as thunder. This shock of surprise is something we just don't get from *The Riverside Villas Murder*.

The turns in Kingsley Amis's work can be understood most easily in relation to the changes in his attitude to life and society. The author of

The Figure in the Amis Carpet

his recent work is still a bit of a joker, like the author of *Lucky Jim*, and even a bit of a private joker. On an early page of *Lucky Jim* there is mentioned a certain L. S. Caton, who is 'starting up a new review with a historical bias, or something'. Caton, although his initials were not L.S., was the owner of the Fortune Press, at whose hands Kingsley Amis, like Philip Larkin and other young poets, first suffered book publication. Naming him was a way of paying off an old score. He was disposed of thirteen years later in *The Anti-Death League*, when he comes on a visit to the Blue Howards to 'address the unit on the public image of the armed forces', and is later killed during a gun battle, when a stray shot goes through his car window. In *Girl, 20*, the 'eminent Sovietologist coming down the steps of the Voyagers' Club', who is jocularly labelled by Sir Roy Vandervane as 'another bloody Fascist', is evidently Amis's friend and occasional collaborator Robert Conquest, who once wrote a spoof anti-academic article called 'Christian Symbolism in *Lucky Jim*'.

But although both the author of *Lucky Jim* and of the recent *Girl, 20* see the behaviour of people as comic, there is a great difference in tone and attitude between the two books. The basic difference is that the thirty-year-old poet and lecturer at Swansea who wrote *Lucky Jim* and its successor, *That Uncertain Feeling*, enjoyed nothing more than cocking a snook at authority in general, and bumbling provincial bureaucracy in particular. Twenty years later, Amis is not exactly in favour of authoritarianism, but is looking for a philosophy of life 'pitched between ancestral verities and the next Conservative Party policy statement'. The progress is charted clearly in 'Socialism and the Intellectuals', a talk to a Fabian Society summer school given in 1956 and later printed as a Fabian Tract, and 'Why Lucky Jim Turned Right', which first appeared as a Conservative Party pamphlet. (Is it a record to have pamphlets published by both main political parties in little more than a decade?)

Both Fabian Amis and Conservative Amis are attractively open and naive in attitude, and both conspicuously avoid theory. 'I am not a politician, nor am I specially well-informed about politics,' Fabian Amis says. He calls himself 'an elderly young intellectual with left-wing sympathies', adding that the intelligentsia now is if anything right-wing. George Orwell is rapped sharply for having become 'a right-wing propagandist by negation' and a 'supremely powerful—though unconscious—advocate of political quietism'. However, there was little enough that the intellectual could do for the Labour

Poets, Novelists, Critics

Party except vote for it, which Fabian Amis had done and would do until the end of his days 'unless something very unexpected happens', and if some intellectuals had moved to the right 'this is not necessarily unmixed loss to the left.' Conservative Amis asks himself why he has crossed the floor, attacks Labour policy on education (passed over by Fabian Amis), mentions—in 1967—the rise in the cost of living, mentions the threat of Communism, and comes on very strong against the Lefty who is not only soft on Communism, but 'buys unexamined the abortion–divorce–homosexuality–censorship–racialism–marijuana package', a Lefty who often looks remarkably like Fabian Amis. A postscript written in 1970 stresses that Lefties hate England and those who have done England credit, like Drake, Queen Victoria and Winston Churchill. 'I wish somebody would undertake an analysis of the Lefty psyche, with special attention to its horror of father- or family-figures.' But of course left-wing attitudes have been examined long ago from very much this point of view by that 'right-wing propagandist by negation', George Orwell. And it was long ago too that those who adored the Soviet system and its leader from a distance were said to do so because they really longed to have Stalin up their arses.

All this is elementary stuff, like Amis's suggestion in answering a 1967 questionnaire on the Vietnam War that 'the communists simply have to be convinced that they cannot win. They will collapse then.' Both Fabian and Conservative Amis offer emotional reactions rather than reasoned arguments. What is remarkable is that such attitudes have produced some of the best and most subtle comic writing since the war. The central character of *Girl, 20* is Sir Roy Vandervane, a TV celebrity who sums himself up as 'a failed composer and mediocre fiddler ending up as a hack conductor.' He has bought the Lefty package in pursuit of a cult of youth, and is ready to break up his family life for a destructive girl in her teens named Sylvia. He embodies everything that Amis most detests, yet the portrait of him never descends to caricature, not even when he mentions casually turning down a commission to write the music for a film about Richard II because 'some right-wing shag had written the screamplay. Glorifying the monarchy and so on.' Roy is pathetic, comic, and in the end rather engaging. Accused by his friend, the highbrow musical journalist Douglas Yandell, of 'trying to arse-creep youth', he laughs uproariously and admits it, saying that they not only give him sex but uncritical admiration, which gets rarer as you grow older.

The Figure in the Amis Carpet

Amis seems to have learned, like Shaw, that it may pay artistically to allow the devil a lot of the best lines. Even the appalling Sylvia and Roy's daughter Penny, who has an affair with Douglas, are allowed to state their case. When Sylvia, whose behaviour throughout is at best indifferent to other human beings and at worst totally vicious, is attacked by the cautious and bourgeois Douglas, her retort has its power. 'What makes you such a howling bitch?' he asks, and she replies:

I expect it's the same thing as makes you a top-heavy red-haired four-eyes who's never had anything to come up to being tossed off by the Captain of Boats and impotent and likes bloody symphonies and fugues and the first variation comes before the statement of the theme and give me a decent glass of British beer and dash it all Carruthers I don't know what young people are coming to these days and a scrounger and an old woman and a failure and a hanger-on and a prig and terrified and a shower and a brisk rub-down every morning and you can't throw yourself away on a little trollop like that Roy you must think of your wife Roy old boy old boy and I'll come along but I don't say I approve and bloody dead. Please delete the items in the above that do not apply. If any.

Amis's eye for the pretentious and the phoney is equal to his ear for the way people talk. There is a marvellous description here of one of those tarted-up pubs which help to blight modern London. This one has war posters or reproductions everywhere, together with plastic curtains made up to look like sacking. There are signs saying Wipers Bar, Blighty Bar, Cookhouse and Dug-Out, replicas of rifles, gas-masks and grenades hang on the walls. The characters move around a London of bars and flats, searching for sex which to the girls at least is automatic and clinical. They watch wrestling matches which they know to be fakes, go to frightful concerts, bicker endlessly and meaninglessly, trapped in a world which they do not enjoy but hardly wish to escape. At the end Roy is undeterred by a beating-up he has received from young men at a concert where he was playing Elevations 9, his 'chamber concerto for violin, with parts for sitar, bass guitar and bongoes' with the Pigs Out group. He leaves his family and goes to live with Sylvia. Douglas is pleased when he finds the usually miserable Penny self-contained and happy, until she explains that she has gone on to heroin. When he tells her that she will only last two years she answers: 'That's one of the things that's so nice about it. Nothing's going to last. None of that awful business of getting married and having children and being responsible.'

'What about Beethoven?'

'He won't last me. I'll never be good enough.'

She turns down Douglas, saying that she wants nobody to take her on, and that the whole thing has worked out well for everybody. 'We're all free now.'

Girl, 20 was praised on its publication in 1971, but still not praised enough. It is a masterly novel, one in which Amis co-ordinates for the first time his tastes, his theme and his talents. The episodic form is perfect for what he wants to convey; the picture of a self-ordered hell in which people move around endlessly in the same routine has a consistent power absent from most of his writing. In general he has no great gift for narrative, and some of his books falter and fade because of his inability to devise an adequate plot. In *I Like It Here* the quest for the Jamesianly named novelist Wulfstan Strether promises a good deal, but the book slips away into jokes about the inability of the narrator's digestive tract to cope with Portuguese food. *One Fat Englishman* is similarly slight, an insular joke about the awfulness of being abroad, and especially abroad in America. *The Green Man* offers a ruthless examination of a character losing his grip on reality in a mist of drink and sex, but it offers also a ghost story which only those with a taste for the supernatural are likely to find particularly interesting. As a writer Amis has been too often reluctant to take seriously what he is doing. He evades the punch of reality by taking refuge in jokes, in James Bond or science fiction or classical detective stories, or (as a poet) in neatly turned sweet-sour sentiment. 'A Chromatic Passing-Note' is typical of the feeling in his later poems:

> 'That slimy tune' I said, and got a laugh,
> In the middle of old Franck's D minor thing:
> The dotted-rhythm clarinet motif.
>
> Not always slimy. I thought, at fifteen,
> It went to show that real love was found
> At the far end of the right country lane.
>
> I thought that, like Keats and the rest of them,
> Old Franck was giving me a preview of
> The world, action in art, a paradigm.

The Figure in the Amis Carpet

Yes, I know better now, or different.
Not image: buffer only, syrup, crutch.
'Slimy' was a snarl of disappointment.

The last verse of the last poem in the same book, one of the pieces about Dai Evans, Welsh hypocrite, drinker and lecher, makes the same point in a different way:

Nice bit of haddock with poached egg, Dundee cake,
Buckets of tea, then a light ale or two,
And 'Gun Smoke', 'Danger Man', the Late Night Movie—
Who's doing better, then? What about you?

What seems to have been lost or stifled is the good humour, and actual enjoyment of what he was doing, shown in Amis's first two brilliantly farcical novels, and most of the genuine tenderness in those books and in the early poems. Such feeling is rare in his recent work, although it can be found, for instance in a delicate little article about his father. Fabian Amis and Conservative Amis are perhaps both simpler, less sophisticated, more sensitive and easily hurt characters than either has been willing to let on.

There is one other novel which shows Amis's talents often at full stretch, the underestimated *The Anti-Death League* (1966). The springs of this book are in Amis's liking for sensational spy stories, and it may also owe something to an admiration for Chesterton, and in particular to *The Man Who Was Thursday*, a comic metaphysical thriller full of spies named after the days of the week, all of whom turn out to be policemen. In Amis's novel Captain Leonard, a spy-catcher or phylactologist, in charge of Army security on a hush-hush assignment called Operation Apollo, becomes convinced that Dr Best, the psychiatrist in charge of a nearby mental hospital, is an enemy agent. Best, on his side, is convinced—or apparently convinced—that Leonard is suffering from delusions and would benefit from hospital treatment. The nature of Operation Apollo is kept from us until almost the end of the book, but its awfulness weighs upon more than one of the officers who make up the cast of characters. A mysterious typescript appears on the recreational notice-board, describing the details of three deaths from accident or natural causes reported in the papers, and announcing the formation of the Anti-Death League in opposition to 'what happened on these occasions'. Contained within this loose framework is a send-up of spy stories and of psychiatry, or its outer trappings, a mystery thriller, and an enquiry as to the justification for assuming the existence of God.

All this may sound like a possible masterpiece, but in fact *The Anti-Death League* is a wildly funny but sadly disjointed book—rather, again, like *The Man Who Was Thursday*, in which the comedy is much more effective and intelligible than the metaphysics. There are few better comic scenes in modern novels than that in which Leonard, accompanied by Captain Hunter (a whole-hearted open homosexual, who has been told by Best that his drinking problem is caused by repressed homosexuality), goes to arrest the psychiatrist, who produces an order committing Leonard to a mental home. A nurse with a hypodermic confronts Leonard, who is armed with a pistol. After a struggle Best confesses, in terms appropriate to Walter Mitty playing James Bond, and the nurse comments: 'They're all barmy here, you know.' This is only one among many comic scenes which are successful principally because they are done with deadpan seriousness. The parody of the spy story is also well done, never drifting over to the point where the comic might look merely silly. The overtly serious side of the book, however, is pretty much of a disaster. It turns out that the League has been prompted by two personal catastrophes rather than by 'the Apollo caper', and there are some distressingly sentimental scenes between one of the officers and his girlfriend, when it is discovered that she has cancer. Anthony Powell's remark that 'there is always an element of unreality, perhaps even of slight absurdity, about someone you love' is to the point, and Powell's understanding that the conversations of lovers are conducted in clichés, so that we shouldn't be given too much of them, is lacking in Amis, here and elsewhere.

What would one wish, or hope for, from Kingsley Amis in the future? Mostly negative things, undoubtedly. It would be nice if he felt no further need to convince us of his Plain Manliness:

> I'm not at breaking wind behind a hand
> Too good. I'm not when hot the man that fanned
> His cheek with a mouchoir. I'm not that kind.
> I'm not a sot, but water leaves me blind,
> I'm not too careful with a drop of Scotch,
> I'm not particular about a blotch.
> I'm not alert to spy out a blackhead,
> I'm not the man that minds a dirty bed.

The Figure in the Amis Carpet

I'm not the man to ban a friend because
He breasts the brine in lousy bathing-drawers.

The lines are those of an earlier satirist, the attitude is admirable, but
Amis sometimes pushes it to the very edge of philistinism. In a
positive way, it is hardly possible to say much more than that a
novelist should learn what his talents are, and then work within them.
And perhaps a writer in his fifties shouldn't make too many jokes,
Catonic or otherwise. To the extent that *The Riverside Villas Murder*
is a joke or an evasion, it can only be regretted, but there is no recipe
for the production of a novel like *Girl, 20*. Kingsley Amis's gifts are
unique in his generation of British novelists. What sort of books are
produced through them depends in the end on his own ability to order
his talent.

(1973)

Deadly Rustic:
The Two Geoffrey Grigsons

Ingestion of Ice-Cream and other Poems by Geoffrey Grigson
A Choice of William Morris's Verse ed. Geoffrey Grigson

The British Museum catalogue, which is not notable for being up to date, lists more than seventy titles associated with Geoffrey Edward Harvey Grigson: books written, anthologies made, selections chosen, encyclopedias edited, artists or collections introduced. Archaeology, botany, geology, literary essays, poetry, travel, English drawing and British Museum art treasures, Cornwall and Wiltshire, the Englishman's flora and the *Shell Country Book*; he has interested himself in or been interested by all these. It seems strange that this Geoffrey Grigson should live in the same skin with the writer of sharp reviews and often sharper letters to periodicals, the author of lines like these from a poem in his new collection, *Ingestion of Ice Cream*:

> Stevas smirking from strength to strength.
> Brophy still leading by half a length.
>
> Auberon floating from sneer to sneer
> And Brophy la Belle going over the weir.
>
> And old B. Nichols and old G. Winn
> And Allsop stuck where the drains come in.
>
> For all these bleeders
> It's sink or swim.

'Life is a most disorderly river,' as he wrote in the introduction to a fine anthology called *The Romantics*, and Geoffrey Grigson is disorderly too, or at least often illogical, a man whose character is complex although his attitudes are often curiously simple. The most immediate guide to complexities and simplicities is his autobiography, *The Crest on the Silver*. The book appeared in 1950 and received a fair amount of attention but not much praise. The *TLS* reviewer granted the author considerable sensibility but deprecated the 'uneasy, bad-tempered, self-pitying, emphatic egotist, whom he

82

Deadly Rustic: The Two Geoffrey Grigsons

uses a great deal of the time as a convention to illustrate his everyday behaviour', and in the *Spectator* it was called 'a shapeless book, deliberately jazzy and unsettled alike in sequence, style and substance'. Nearly two decades later the self-pity and jazziness are not apparent. *The Crest on the Silver* is a desperate and honest book, at times it seems the work of a man at the end of his emotional tether, as interesting in the kind of thing it omits as in any revelations it contains. The self-portrait firmly drawn is that of a Cornish countryman, a boy keenly observant from childhood of what lay around him as he wandered about the garden of the 'large, awkward, ill-arranged house, facing warmly to the south over a small valley' in the parish of Pelynt, near Looe. The naturalist's eye with which the garden is seen no doubt owes something to hindsight, yet nobody could question the genuineness of the emotion that comes through:

> Of all things in this rich wild garden which I now love to remember, of all the oaks, the redwoods, and copper beeches planted by the ingenious Colonel Cox, of all the pines, and the sycamores planted by a pluralist vicar in the eighteenth century, none count so much as the laurels. Their stems were long, clean, thick and black, in their strongest black after rain. Their leaves shone on spring mornings, as one leant from the bedroom windows. Their flowers, standing up precise and white from the glistening leaves, were one of the first natural excellences of which I was conscious.

Such writing about childhood must always be near an edge of sentimentality. In Grigson's case it stays on the right side because the descriptions are enlarged by knowledge, illuminated always by curiosity. The seventh son of a clergyman three times married who was in his sixtieth year when this last child was born, he is fascinated by the family history and its East Anglian background, the clergymen and landowners, 'the arms of Grigson, with all their quarterings, in an oak frame' which hung in the drawing-room above the bureau in which his mother kept his father's love letters. Family history, local history, a taste even in childhood for antiquities, these are the things that the forty-odd-year-old Grigson records. 'I was still pretty young when I began to collect Cornish books, catalogue parish papers, examine tithe apportionments for field names, search out burrows which were ploughed almost flat, and look for chipped flints and arrow heads.'

These explorations and discoveries had their emotional content, and so had his association with the villagers—like the illiterate Bessie, 'small, neat, rufus-cheeked with darker veins among the red'. The uneasy relationship between the boy's complaisant forgiving father and his 'moderately Tartarish' mother is delicately shown. But the kind of openness with which all this is put down does not extend to other emotions, pleasures, discoveries and sorrows in his adolescence and manhood. These are no more than hinted at, presumably because they contain memories too painful for explicit description. School is mentioned as hateful ('if only I had never entered the desert of a public school'), but beside such a detailed account as George Orwell's his picture of it is impressionistic, slight. Life at Oxford is done in similar flashes, girls are mentioned, frustration indicated. The honeymoon prelude to an unhappy marriage is written about like this: 'They were not in some ways the happiest of weeks, far from it. I had known from that masculine childhood in Cornwall too little about women, and my wife was an American and I knew even less about Americans. Still the sun came out at times.'

There is a career on the *Yorkshire Post* and the *Morning Post*, the account of a journey to Salzburg at the time of Munich to bring back an Austrian girl who became his second wife. These it might be supposed are important events, but when he tries to confront them the writer withdraws as he never withdraws in writing about Cornish villages, his father, his brothers. The nightmare journey across Europe is admirably done, but the object of the journey, the girl brought back and married, remains a blank. This is said not to criticize Geoffrey Grigson (to each his reticences and revelations) but to characterize him. The man portrayed in *The Crest on the Silver* is immensely observant of the visible world, a bit churchy, a bit quirky, in some ways surprisingly naive; a man longing for close emotional relationships with other human beings but not wholly at ease with them—although this is a deduction from what the autobiography does not contain rather than from what it says.

These are recognizably the features of the man who abandoned London for Wiltshire and who has written about art and botany. Only occasionally, in comments expressing independence of what were then current literary fashions, does the editor of *New Verse* become visible. Throughout the book there is an insistence on subjecting books and pictures to the test of individual vision, a rejection of what he would call flashiness or affectation, a countryman's preference for what is solid and immediately seen over what is abstract or theoretically ingenious. Here he is commenting on Sickert:

> Sickert does not give much; for a time dingy interiors, music halls, small landscapes—those were good and within his means; but how exaggerated and coarse many of the big paintings are, as if he had stretched and pulled the little condensed pictures. His men and women are disgustingly and cruelly non-existent. In them and in much architectural drawing of his there is a scribbling shorthand which comes before apprehension, and is not apprehension seized and summarised and abstracted. . . . Better Crabbe's poems than Sickert's pictures.

Yes, the editor of *New Verse* shows through, but he does not show very clearly, and this is by deliberate intention. A decade after the magazine's demise Grigson regarded the hatching of this 'malignant egg' with some embarrassment:

> If I can bear to look into old notebooks, it is rather more than I can bear to look now in old numbers of *New Verse*. . . . The fun and the slaughter now make me, if I recall them, rather sick. They covered up too little in me of a positive affection, too little of a viable desire. The tactic was too uncharitable.

There is even a turning of the cheek towards Edith Sitwell, who had been called 'the old Jane' in *New Verse*. 'My old enemy, Miss Sitwell, is now enthroned. I was not at the coronation, I am not among her subjects. But I have no inclination left to be a reginacide or even a jeering republican. She will accept, I hope, my regret for old asperities.'

These words were written when post-war literary romanticism was at its height, when the ornate, the gilded, the rhetorical were widely admired and Grigsonics were out of fashion. Commenting on the suggestion that *New Verse* took its picric flavour from the fact that he was unhappily married, Grigson suggests that it had more to do with being unhappily born. 'I could no longer, now, billhook my victim and sit on his corpse and enjoy a glass full of his blood.' But times have changed, gold leaf has faded, and Geoffrey Grigson has drunk a glass or two of blood in the past twenty years. Young critics feel that he was much more often right than wrong, and that it is a great thing in any period to have a critic who will deal incisively with what seems to him meretricious, imitative or shabby writing.

Poets, Novelists, Critics

> His critics, in their thin and early twenties,
> Pronounced him, fat and forty, a wonderchild

as one poet excoriated by him wrote (not about Mr Grigson). Admiration of *New Verse*'s achievement ranges far beyond the young, from Cyril Connolly to moderate Leavisites in their red-brick hutches. It is an admiration that slightly surprises Geoffrey Grigson himself, who thinks that he has done much more interesting things since the 1930s. Yet what he has actually done seems less valuable, in the context of art in Britain now, than the native nonconformism he represents. What he stands for and against cannot be assessed in terms of doctrine or theory. Perhaps it can be seen most clearly in the artists he admires and the things and people he dislikes. The artists he admires, Moore and Nicholson, Saint Wystan and Philip Larkin, Dryden and Crabbe, Blake and Palmer, Chirico and Wyndham Lewis, are joined by something exact and literal in their objective view of the world (that seems almost his first requirement in an artist), linked in some cases although not in all by an inner vision of great intensity.

'He would not paint a swan or a rose. I would not write them', he says in 'A Painter of Our Day', the fine poem to Nicholson in his new book, and one remembers that Lewis also was called the enemy of the rose. What is wrong with swans and roses? A reference is probably intended to the easy symbolism used by a poet like Edith Sitwell for whom a rose was not so much an object as a nice word, but swans and roses are for Grigson, as they were for Lewis, a mark of what is slick or academic in British art and letters. Journalistic slickness and burrowing academicism are represented for him not only by the obvious denizens of Grub Street but by television commentators and pundits, art administrators and historians, biographical excavators, almost any kind of literary theoretician and almost every variety of British or American literary don. He opposes to them, in his admired artists and as he hopes in himself, qualities of individual thought and vision that are sometimes eccentric but never merely dotty, a refusal to conform to fashionable ways of thinking and feeling which still never rejects the existence of a world in which it is proper to be contemptuous of political 'realism' and angry about military murder or starvation. He is dogmatic without being doctrinaire, a socialist who may respect Marx but gives emotional adherence to Morris and Ruskin.

86

Deadly Rustic: The Two Geoffrey Grigsons

About all this there is much to be admired but something to be regretted. Gratitude that there is a Geoffrey Grigson around to puncture balloons of academic pomposity and to recognize the shoddy under tinsel trappings must be joined with a recognition that he sometimes takes for granted what needs to be proved, and is often at the mercy of his own taste for oddity. The introduction to his selection from Morris's poems begins with the decision made by the youthful Morris and Burne-Jones to become artists instead of clergymen, and refers to Morris as one of the 'seminal idealists' of the nineteenth century and to Burne-Jones as 'the now more or less disregarded, if not forgotten painter'. The comment about Burne-Jones might have been true in the 1930s but is certainly not right today when all sorts of unexpected (and non-existent?) merits are being discovered not only in the Pre-Raphaelites but also in the practitioners of Art Nouveau. And in his admiration for Morris's generosity of mind and desire to 'share the happiness of his own childhood with all of the deprived' he grants to the early poems a genuineness which they surely do not possess, as though because Morris was an excellent human being he must also at some time have been a good artist. The language that Morris used, consciously archaic and picturesque, and the thumping rhythms that mark all his verse, destroy him as a poet. It is a mark of eccentricity not to recognize that Morris as a poet was very much the equivalent of Burne-Jones as a painter, a similar mark to find room in his anthology *The Victorians* for Lord de Tabley and Jean Ingelow but not for Ernest Dowson or Lionel Johnson. Such oddities of judgement are not in themselves very important, but they are the complement of a failure ever to produce the considerable critical works on painting and literature that seemed likely twenty years ago.

Grigson has been compared with F. R. Leavis, and it is true that they are both critics who avoid doctrine and theory and consider the touchstones of their own taste and sensibility as the only means of judging works of art. The comparison shouldn't be pushed far (it is not easy to know which of the two subjects would find it more uncongenial), but it is evident that Geoffrey Grigson's abilities as a critic of books and paintings have been much greater than his performance. Most of his best essays are in *The Harp of Aeolus* (1947) yet, although no other writer could have produced all of these 'essays on Art, Literature and Nature', they are remarkable singly, a collection of brilliant bits that never make explicit the full coherent

87

attitude towards art, literature and nature that his admirers would have liked to see, and at one time expected him to produce.

Towards such a coherence he does not aspire, preferring the disorderliness of life's river to any moral or aesthetic pattern imposed on it. In doing so he has opted for minor merits and sometimes ignored major problems. His own prose is edgy, disorderly, full of images that are often enlightening, sometimes cryptic. He would agree with John Dennis (the quotation comes from one of his own anthologies, *Before the Romantics*): 'A Poet hath two ways of exciting Passion. The one by Figurativeness, and the other by the Harmony of his Expression; but the Figures contribute more to the exciting of Passion than Harmony.' In Geoffrey Grigson's prose there is always a rough edge, not much harmony. A good deal of passion is conveyed in vivid pictures. The effect, in the prose and in most of his poems, is of a writer basically uncertain about the ends towards which his means are taking him. What is it he wants to show us?

> As this wall adds up, flint
> to flint fitted,
> red shapes
> fall to the hot flints
> in the hot sun.
>
> Let us precisely state
> they are petals of
> coquelicot,
> poppy in our
> cross-channel tongue.

Let us precisely state it by all means, but we are not stating much. The style of the poem is typical of many he has written. It offers exact observation, colour—colours are important to him—and the poem has a kind of shape, but that is about all. Nobody need look for any further meaning, no chances have been taken, wall and poppies do not relate to anything outside themselves. Sometimes he reaches farther than this, as in his remarkable poem about Chirico, but not often.

Geoffrey Grigson is now in his middle sixties. There is no sign that his apprehension of the shapes and sounds of the visible world has dulled, and a generation of poets is in debt to his insistence on the importance of keeping an eye on the object and taking it as starting

Deadly Rustic: The Two Geoffrey Grigsons

point—he was a New Liner long before *New Lines*. They should be grateful also for the long campaigns against the once-triumphant 'romance' which believed 'that anything, any first impression can be crammed into formless verse without the self-discipline and self-criticism which are the sources of form; the sources of that composition in which, Henry James declared, exists the "principle of health and safety".'

Under the often considerable pressures of earning a living he has never given way to the temptations of middlebrow literary good fellowship. In spite of those pacific words in *The Crest on the Silver*, the billhook has often been in use in recent years, and it can only be by chance that Pop poets and Pop painters, Black Mountaineers and their feeble imitators here, have remained so long unscathed.

(1969)

Wilson's Way

The Bit Between My Teeth: A Literary Chronicle of 1950–1965 by Edmund Wilson

In the 'modest self-tribute' set as a prefix to this collection, Edmund Wilson says that his chief critical function has been as a sort of universal communicator ranging as widely as possible over the world's literature, and getting away from 'the academic canons that always tend to keep literature provincial'. Reviewers have dutifully taken up this theme, but there is another phrase in the self-tribute which is the true key to Wilson's finest criticism and to his critical method. 'I have also an interest in the biographies of writers which soon took the bit between its teeth.' The typical Wilson approach—think of the essays on Dickens, Kipling, Flaubert, or those on Swinburne and de Sade in this book—lays essential aspects of a writer's life before us, and interlinks them with his work. The method is now unfashionable, and it can be journalistic in the worst sense, but in Wilson's hands it has produced the most original and revealing criticism of this century. The single work about Dickens that tells us most about his art is not Edgar Johnson's patient, admirable biography, nor Orwell's creation of a Dickens made in his own image, but Wilson's psychological analysis in *The Wound and the Bow*. It is an extraordinary piece of what one would call Leavisite snobbery if it were not paralleled so closely by American academics, to assume that a serious critic must be concerned only with texts and never with the life behind them.

This is the Wilson method, but it is not an invariable rule-of-thumb which he uses on all books and writers. *The Shores of Light* and *Classics and Commercials*, his two earlier literary chronicles, contain a lot of week-to-week journalism about (for example) Greenwich Village in the twenties or Houdini and spiritualism, and the literary journalist appears in this volume too, calling attention to the almost unknown talent of the artist Edward Gorey, recounting with a touch of self-ridicule a visit to Max Beerbohm, recalling days with Hemingway and Scott Fitzgerald in Paris long ago. These pieces are

90

always perceptive and interesting, but as Wilson's critics have said they do not quite operate on the level of criticism. It is true also, to give his enemies a final hostage, that Wilson's interest in recent English and American literature is slight, and that he writes about it as though he were ninety rather than seventy years old. Sympathy and understanding seem to have deserted him when he dismisses Anthony Powell with the remark that he is 'just entertaining enough to read in bed late at night in summer'. In general, the passionate curiosity that marked the earlier volumes is absent, and when we ask what Wilson thinks about the Beat poets or Norman Mailer, the answer seems to be that he doesn't think of them at all. This Edmund Wilson is conscientiously out-of-date, inclined to be proud of his blind spots and to imply that there is some virtue in never having got around to *Middlemarch*. It is high time that he did get around to it.

Yet about the things that interest him Wilson is still our most valuable critic, and about these things he still shows his remarkable capacity for discovering documents that throw new light on his subject. The most striking instance here is the long essay on 'Myra Buttle' and T. S. Eliot. Who else, when discussing *The Sweeniad* by 'Myra Buttle' (Victor Purcell), would have gone to the trouble of digging up Purcell's earlier, seriously-intended and 'hilariously awful' book of verse, *Cadmus: The Poet and the World*, to show that what was awful in *Cadmus* contains the germ of what was lively and amusing in *The Sweeniad*? Who else has discovered or would think of discussing the lecture which Eliot delivered at a Conservative luncheon, and which was later published with a foreword by Anthony Eden? The puffed-up platitudes of the lecture are just as much part of Eliot as *The Waste Land*, and they lead on to a serio-comic analysis of Eliot's several masks, American and English. These are the Anglican clergyman (English) as heard intoning his poetry on records, the formidable professor (American), Dr Johnson, the genteel Bostonian (distinctly anti-Semitic, regarding 'any large number of free-thinking Jews' as 'undesirable' in a good society), the Christian, and the oracle. These last two Eliots are perhaps jointly responsible for such remarks as that 'tolerance is greatly over-estimated' and that 'to be educated above one's station leads to unhappiness and social instability.'

This essay was written in 1958, and it makes refreshing reading to anybody who has pulled through some of the pompous nonsense, or the even bigger mass of sensible dull textual analysis, written about Eliot. Few critics have accepted that the most illuminating approach to Eliot is that which first distinguishes between his often bigoted, sometimes ridiculous, opinions about life and society, and the revolution in poetic speech which he played so large a part in bringing about, and then shows the relationship between the opinions and the verse. One may accept *The Waste Land* as a supremely original poem and yet deplore the notes attached to it, admire 'Burbank with a Baedeker' but dislike the snobbery and anti-Semitism implicit in the poem. These truisms are voiced only to make the point that Wilson is not using a hatchet on Eliot, but on the dead critical wood surrounding him. Forget 'the idiocy of the hungry sheep who look up and do not know that they are not being fed' and you are left with the essential Eliot, who has transmuted his borrowings into essentially dramatic poetry that is masterly, original and strange, who is not thought to write 'memorable lines' but fills as much space as any modern writer in dictionaries of quotations, and to whom the aphorism from Cocteau used by Wilson is perfectly appropriate: 'The artist is a kind of prison from which the works of art escape.'

Nothing else in *The Bit Between My Teeth* is as good as the Eliot essay, but there are long articles on Sade, Swinburne, James Branch Cabell and *Dr Zhivago*, of which only the last is well known here. I have never got around to *Dr Zhivago*, but the other articles are compulsively readable, and valuable as reconsiderations of their subjects. Wilson has a voracious capacity for absorbing the raw material of literary criticism in the form of letters and diaries, and it is impressive to find him reading through the six volumes of Swinburne's letters 'with an interest and an enjoyment hardly ever fatigued'. He goes on to consider Swinburne in the light of his being unique among nineteenth-century English writers as belonging to the 'top nobility' and 'out-ranking Byron, Shelley and Landor'. There seems to be something not quite right about this point of view, but the conclusion that the picture of Victorian country-house life in *Lesbia Brandon* is unique because Swinburne knew what he was writing about is really made extremely plausible. The two essays on Sade (there is also a short piece about Mario Praz's *The Romantic Agony*) outline with great skill the facts of his life as put down in Gilbert Lely's biography and relate them closely to the work, but these essays suffer a little from Wilson's temperamental inability to admit the power of Sade's nihilistic egoism. How can a hard-headed humanist New Englander reconcile himself to the idea that such self-destructive Wagnerian romanticism may approximate to a truth about the way in which people behave, or wish to behave? 'The James Branch Cabell Case Reopened', with its pendant rather moving short epitaph written after Cabell's death in 1958, sets the author of *Jurgen*, who is now completely and unjustly forgotten in Britain, in his context as a product of the American South who exemplified its history in the bitterness of his allegorical fantasies. It is a mark of Wilson as a critic that he does not try to compel our assent to the ideas he puts forward. He appears as counsel, occasionally for the prosecution but more often for the defence, never as judge. So in the case of Cabell we do not have to agree with him that the tale of the relentless man of action Manuel the Redeemer, *Figures of Earth*, is 'on a plane, perhaps, with Flaubert and Swift', to see the strength of the case he makes out for re-reading Cabell in the terms of what he is saying, forgetting or forgiving his over-decorated prose.

Altogether, *The Bit Between My Teeth* confirms Wilson's position as one of the very few literary critics who have special insights, exceeding those of common sense, into the art of literature. As he wrote himself long ago of Bernard Shaw: 'Of his influence it is unnecessary to speak. After all, the very methods we use to check him have partly been learned in his school.'

(1966)

Little Magazines

Scrutinizing *Scrutiny*

I LEAVIS, A MAN TALKING

Some of the mistakes made about Dr Leavis can be cleared away if it is understood that often when he puts down words in print he does so really as a man talking, or more exactly as a teacher lecturing to his students. The lecture is carried on, as several of them have recalled, with the utmost informality. Sometimes wearing a raincoat (curiously identified in one recollection as a dressing-gown), in fine weather open-necked, and on other occasions no doubt accoutred in suit and tie, he enters, reads a sonnet and says that *that* is by no means a work of genius, it is by Lord Alfred Douglas; and a discussion, for which the tone has been set, begins. Or he is eloquent about a passage from Lawrence or Conrad and proposes to examine it closely. But often the close examination is not carried out, he is lured from it by a question or by something else that has occurred to him, and rambles away on a diversion that may touch on the iniquitous tricks and tedious trivialities of reviewers in the Big City or the hostility he has encountered in the home of civilization, Cambridge. At the end of the session the student may have learned something about *Nostromo* or *Heart of Darkness*, he may be convinced that a close reading and examination of texts is vital to a deep understanding of literature, but he will certainly carry away the impression of a man talking, not always coherently but with the mixture of didacticism and passion that convinces the young, about the values of literature.

To extend this informality from speech to writing, to imagine that he was talking to students when he was in fact addressing a much less sympathetic audience—that is what Dr Leavis has often done, and he has done it again in the 'Retrospect' which, with a most intelligently devised index, makes up Volume 20 in the complete reissue of *Scrutiny*. These twenty-odd pages of self-justification, praise of former Scrutineers now in seats of power, attacks on the non-standards prevailing in the sink of London letters, are written with a shoddiness and ugliness that is shameful in a serious critic, and they show also a distressing failure to organize ideas coherently.

Little Magazines

Sometimes it is a matter simply of extreme informality jarring on the reader. When, for instance, Leavis mentions 'the research students and undergraduates who used, in the early thirties, to meet at my house, which was very much a centre' and then corrects himself a couple of sentences later ('I should have said "*our* house" in the sentence before last'), one cannot help asking why he did not make this small correction before going into print, and the answer seems to be again that this is Leavis talking, making a mistake and correcting it as one does in casual speech. It is charitable to suppose that the 'Retrospect' was not revised in proof for otherwise, surely, such a phrase as 'the tough sophistication that enables young poets to offer their immaturity as a mature aplomb' must have been changed, and so must this almost unintelligible sentence about T. S. Eliot:

> It was in *Scrutiny*, too, that Eliot, invested and confirmed as we were entering on our long battle in his now time-worn institutional status, received the limiting and qualifying criticism that tells, or at any rate is justified in the sense of him and of his oddly disappointing distinction so generally expressed today.

What was it that the 'limiting and qualifying criticism' told? What difference does Leavis mean to imply between writers who were 'Marxist' and those who were 'Marxising', and why does he not state the difference directly and clearly? I am afraid the answer is that in dealing with general matters, as distinct from specific problems of writing, he does not wish to be direct and is not capable of organized argument. (Witness the rambling formlessness of his Richmond Lecture on the Two Cultures.) He prefers to talk to the students, mentioning things as they happen to occur to him. There was that 'great Establishment potentate at Cambridge' who once said that *Scrutiny* was very alarming. There was the 'advanced Cambridge intellectual' who said ' "I am not a moral hero",' there was the time thirty years ago when Mr Eliot turned down a pamphlet written for the 'Criterion Miscellany', there was the sin of Mr Alan Pryce-Jones when he was editor of *The Times Literary Supplement*: none of these things has been forgotten, all are referred to in the 'Retrospect', some with a nod to the student which says: 'I'm not going to tell you who that "great Establishment potentate" *is*, but I daresay you won't find it too hard to guess.'

If anything could destroy in advance a belief in the merits of *Scrutiny* it would be the fact that Dr Leavis is such a clumsy and graceless writer. But really *Scrutiny* was founded and run by a teacher. (There were other editors, I know, but they were teachers too.) That is a fact to remember.

The idea of *Scrutiny* sprang from the best magazine published in England between the wars, *The Calendar of Modern Letters*. Edited by Edgell Rickword, with the help of Douglas Garman and Bertram Higgins, the *Calendar*'s vigorous but uncertain life, first as monthly then as quarterly, ran from 1925 to 1927. Three issues, and these not exceptional ones, included contributions by E. M. Forster, William Gerhardi, Robert Graves, D. H. Lawrence, Wyndham Lewis, Edwin Muir, Peter Quennell, Bertrand Russell and Siegfried Sassoon. The magazine printed the work of American writers hardly known in this country, like Hart Crane and John Crowe Ransom—and this, remember, was in the middle twenties, in the heyday of the *London Mercury*. Dr Leavis has paid tribute to the *Calendar* more than once, and he does so again in the 'Retrospect'. It did, he says, 'most unquestionably represent a real offer to establish a strong and lively contemporary criticism'. Even the name of the new magazine deliberately echoed, 'as a salute and a gesture of acknowledgement', the title of a collection of essays from the *Calendar* which attacked the current valuation of such Edwardian literary figures as Barrie, Bennett and Galsworthy.

In spite of this praise, there is something astigmatic about Dr Leavis's view of the *Calendar*. It was not primarily a critical paper. The magazine's strength lay in its demonstration of what was alive in modern literature, side by side with the examination of what was no longer interesting. It was not merely a cemetery for Edwardians, but (as the stories and poems in each issue showed) a gymnasium for the exercise of living talent. It is remarkable that Dr Leavis did not notice or comment on this difference between the two magazines. In the earliest days of *Scrutiny* it was the editors' intention to print original creative work, and the first issues contained a few unimportant poems, a fragment of an important novel. Thereafter came a page or two of verse, but after its third year *Scrutiny* found no room for poems or stories. If you are going to comment contemptuously on the accepted writers of your time, each piece of creative work that you print offers a target to your enemies. It is the part of caution, though not of courage, to print nothing at all.

Little Magazines

II SCRUTINY, A NARROWING CIRCLE

The purpose of every other important English literary magazine of this century was primarily to print creative work, that of *Scrutiny* was wholly critical. It was inevitable that those who felt themselves to be writing for a 'a key community of the élite' (Leavis's phrase) should develop a hardness and coarseness of judgement, particularly in dealing with modern literature. The process can be seen steadily at work in the writings of many contributors, with some admirable exceptions like Professor L. C. Knights, and it is strikingly noticeable if one compares a pre-war with a post-war volume. One may feel, for instance, that Leavis's assessment of John dos Passos in 1932 as 'an unusually serious artist' was over generous, and that Mr D. W. Harding's review of *Tender is the Night* in 1934 was too kind, but these pieces were important in calling attention to talents not fully recognized. (Who else was offering serious criticism of Scott Fitzgerald in 1934, when the first bright gloss had gone?) In the last ten years of *Scrutiny* there are few attempts to understand the intentions of living artists, to balance strengths against weaknesses, to view with sympathy the effort of creation. George Orwell seems at first glance an exception to this rule, but on a second view this isn't really so, for he is praised as a 'plain man' critic and pamphleteer, and neither *Animal Farm* nor *1984* was thought worth reviewing. Certain *Scrutiny* touchstones have been established for modern literature— Lawrence in the novel, early Eliot and early Pound in poetry, and other writers are condemned to the degree that they diverge from them. In writing of the past, *Scrutiny* critics make an effort to understand the mind and motives of an artist, but living writers are judged from outside, by the touchstones.

It is the tendency of any magazine that relies on a tight group of contributors sharing many of the same ideas, to become monolithic, and this happened to *Scrutiny*. Such groups or sects have many merits, but there is an obligation upon the leader of the sect to make sure always that the judgements arrived at are truly sectarian, and not imposed by his own personality. It cannot be said that Dr Leavis ever attempted such detachment, and it is notable that *Scrutiny* critics have been most successful in dealing with subjects and writers where his interests were not directly involved. It is instructive to compare Mr W. H. Mellers's articles on music, for the generosity of which other Scrutineers rebuked him, with his often brutally insensitive reviews of new poetry.

Scrutinizing *Scrutiny*

Scrutiny derived its character from its university origin. Dr Leavis himself says that the magazine was the product of the real and essential Cambridge, but the phrase implies limitations as well as merits. Since Cambridge was the home of *Scrutiny*, since *Scrutiny* was 'the essential Cambridge' and was also the expression of 'a common civilization and a positive culture', it followed that everything outside was more or less removed from the true heart of culture. There are times when Leavis speaks rather as if Cambridge were a metropolis and London a troublesome unconquered province several hundred miles away. Such illusions are dangerous.

In another and more obvious way the magazine was shaped by its Cambridge background. It was founded to vindicate 'the Idea of a University' in conjunction with 'vindicating the Idea of Criticism', and what this vague phrase appears to have meant in practice is the training and education of generations of students in Leavisite ways of thought and habits of assessment. During the first years the contributors included many who were outside the circle that met round the Leavis hearth. Of Edmund Blunden and Geoffrey Grigson, Herbert Read and Norman Shrapnel, it may be said, as of Frank Harris in another connection, that they were all admitted to *Scrutiny*—once—and that once in the early days. Later, as Scrutineers sprang from the University armed for battle, things were very different. There was still a large number of contributors, but the range of their ideas had narrowed, and their responses were predictable. There is something comic in Dr Leavis's statement in the 'Retrospect', when he is discussing the sad shallowness of Auden, that 'critic after critic in *Scrutiny* (we took care to give him a number of different and clearly independent reviewers), dealing with his books as they came out, did the appropriate variant of the diagnosis, which became depressingly familiar.' Supposing that one of those 'independent' reviewers had produced a different diagnosis, what then? But that could never have happened.

Like other sects, the Scrutineers suffered for their ideas. From the beginning, from the article on 'What's Wrong With Criticism' in the second number, the magazine opposed itself to the literary Establishment of its time, in particular to the *New Statesman*, *The Times Literary Supplement*, and the log-rolling belletrism of the Sunday papers. Such attacks, which were not made elsewhere, naturally caused indignation among those sitting comfortably in editorial seats. No doubt the Scrutineers expected indignation. 'It would be unreasonable to expect that one criticize an orthodoxy, and have that orthodoxy make things easy for one,' as Wyndham Lewis wrote of his own activities in the thirties. The attacks made in *Scrutiny* were rarely answered. The magazine suffered the worse martyrdom of being ignored, and a deliberate attempt was made to pretend that it did not exist. Of several such cases one, discussed in detail in the 'Retrospect', may be mentioned. A comprehensive account of British literary periodicals, in a special issue of *The Times Literary Supplement* published in 1950 for readers overseas, omitted *Scrutiny* altogether, and a letter of protest by Leavis was not printed. The Scrutineers were right in their belief that as one Establishment reviewer succeeded another in weeklies and Sunday papers, they formed a solid front, whatever might be their other associations and inclinations, against the cads from Cambridge. Mrs Q. D. Leavis put the *Scrutiny* case against the 'world of letters' in a pungent review of *Enemies of Promise* in 1939: 'The odious spoilt little boys of Mr Connolly's and so many other writers' schooldays move in a body up to the universities to become pretentious young men, and, still essentially unchanged, from there move into the literary quarters vacated by the last batch of their kind.'

True? Well, there was enough truth in it then, there is enough now, to make those accused uncomfortable, and to make them feel that the easiest way to deal with *Scrutiny* was to sweep it under the mat, where nobody was likely to do more than trip over it occasionally.

This ostracism is a thing of the past. For at least five years references to *Scrutiny* criticism and critics have been friendly or, to use a word Dr Leavis might prefer, respectful. A sociological examination of what has happened would be interesting. *Scrutiny* ended in 1953, and I should be inclined to think that a post-*Scrutiny* generation of students has stormed or infiltrated many of the enemy positions. Whatever the reasons, *Scrutiny* has triumphed, as this reissue potently shows, but the triumph came too late to check the bad effects persecution has upon all who suffer it. Several of the Scrutineers had come to regard themselves as the only truly virtuous people, encouraged in this by their leader's tendencies towards megalomania. The *Pelican History of English Literature*, that compendium of badly-balanced and dogmatic opinions lightened by a few genuine critical articles, shows the disastrous result.

Such a jejune compilation was the worst of *Scrutiny*. What was the best, what prompted all those long articles making a cowardly amends recently in the papers that represent 'the modish literary world'? What sort of thing was *Scrutiny* criticism?

III LEAVIS, A CRITIC

It is not from disrespect to the other critics who wrote for and at times helped to edit *Scrutiny*—Professor Knights, Mr Mellers, Mr Harding, Mr H. B. Parkes and others—that one finds Leavis, and those who were directly influenced by him, at the heart of *Scrutiny* criticism. And if it is difficult to approach Leavis's criticism, it is because he has himself raised barriers that have to be climbed:

> 'Twere well, might critics still this freedom take;
> But Appius reddens at each word you speak,
> And stares tremendous, with a threatening eye,
> Like some fierce tyrant in old tapestry.

Appius in *The Essay of Criticism* was John Dennis, and the image of Dennis in his flannel nightcap and red stockings is one easily conjured up in the presence of Leavis. As Dennis cried that although they would not let his play run they stole his thunder, so Leavis finds *Scrutiny* ideas adopted without acknowledgement on every side. Is there a 'new "sociological" approach to literature, entertainment and culture'? It was 'demonstrated and established' by *Scrutiny*. Shakespeare criticism? *Scrutiny* has 'effected a reorientation' in it. The novel? It is *Scrutiny* that 'established Conrad in his now recognized place among the great', that first considered Dickens as 'one of the greatest of novelists', that 'established D. H. Lawrence as a great novelist and critic', that 'started . . . the modern cult of Henry James'. Some of these statements are well founded, others are ridiculous—to suggest that an article in *Scrutiny* rather than Mr Edmund Wilson's essay in *The Wound and the Bow* was the starting point of modern Dickens criticism is too absurd for detailed refutation to be necessary. Beyond this, however, Dr Leavis makes claims which amount in effect to saying that *Scrutiny* was always up to the minute ('first in the field with reports on Sartre and Camus . . . took prompt note of Kafka'), and so one has to say that as far as *Scrutiny* was concerned the cinema did not exist, theatre was hardly discussed, modern art was treated with wretched triviality and many important

103

writers remained unmentioned in its pages. (Brecht and Nathanael West are two in a long list.)

It would not be necessary to say these things if Dr Leavis's claims were less exaggerated. But just as, when one turns away from Dennis's invective against Pope to look at the body of his work he can be seen as the most important critic between Dryden and Johnson, so once past the barrier of silliness raised by Leavis himself it is possible to see him as a critic often profound, generous and humane. He is such a critic when his imagination is truly engaged by a work of art, as in the essays contained in *Revaluation* and *The Great Tradition*, most of which appeared originally in *Scrutiny*. To see the virtues of critic Leavis it is useful to examine one of these essays. I have chosen that on George Eliot, but half a dozen others would have done as well.

The first thing that distinguishes his criticism is the deliberate statement of a moral attitude. A characteristic of greatness, he says, is 'a kind of reverent openness before life, and marked moral intensity'. In a footnote he says that he shares with George Eliot the Puritan standards of right and wrong (although this is not his own phrase), that they seem to him 'favourable to the production of great literature' and that 'the enlightenment or aestheticism or sophistication that feels an amused superiority to them leads, in my view, to triviality and boredom, and out of triviality comes evil.' It is often said that *Scrutiny* had no philosophy, and this is an accusation to which Leavis seems sensitive, but underlying most of the important contributions to the magazine was a moral attitude like the one expressed here.

The next thing one notices is that close attention to the text which Dr Leavis impressed upon his students. Most good critics in the first half of this century worked from the general to the particular. Leavis does the reverse of this. It is true that he looks for reverent openness and moral intensity, but that is not the same thing. As he examines *The Mill on the Floss*, for instance, he makes us understand that the weakness of the book, in spite of its magnificent qualities, is George Eliot's identification with her heroine, Maggie Tulliver. The identification is generally accepted. What is unique in the analysis of it here is that, with the utmost delicacy, Leavis shows that Maggie's personality is given to us too purely from the 'inside'. Her immaturity is presented with sympathy, but it is shared by her creator. This point is made again and again, most forcibly in relation to the book's climax, when Maggie drowns. This, Leavis says, is more than 'a "dramatic" close of a kind congenial to a Victorian novel-reader':

> It has for the critic more significance than this suggests: George Eliot is, emotionally, fully engaged in it. The qualifying 'emotionally' is necessary because of the criticism that has to be urged: something so like a kind of day-dream indulgence we are all familiar with could not have imposed itself on the novelist as the right ending if her mature intelligence had been fully engaged, giving her full self-knowledge. The flooded river has no symbolic or metaphorical value. It is only the dreamed-of perfect accident that gives us the opportunity for the dreamed-of heroic act—the act that shall vindicate us against a harshly misjudging world, bring emotional fulfilment and (in others) changes of heart, and provide a gloriously tragic curtain. Not that the sentimental in it is embarrassingly gross, but the finality is not that of great art.

It is impossible to read this account of *The Mill on the Floss* without being affected in one's view of the book, and much the same thing is true of the rest of the essay. The extrication of the 'good', that is the psychologically subtle, things in George Eliot from the part that belongs to the Victorian novel and now lacks interest, is carried out in a way that is totally new. Nobody has written better about *Middlemarch*, particularly in relation to Dorothea, nobody has clearly pointed out the superiority over the rest of *Felix Holt* of everything that concerns the relationship of Mrs Transome with her family, above all nobody else has defined and established the greatness of that part of *Daniel Deronda* which Dr Leavis calls 'Gwendolen Harleth'. The things Dr Leavis claims wrongly about Dickens and other writers are absolutely true in relation to George Eliot. Everybody who writes about her now must be in debt to this essay.

Dr Leavis's approach brings such rewards when he is dealing with writers who measure up to his own standard of greatness, a standard which doesn't by any means exclude wit or emotion but insists that they must be used to illuminate significantly a moral problem. It is right, however, to look at the limits and qualifications involved in it. There is for him no question of using psychoanalysis to help interpret a work of art. Most psychoanalysts take a determinist view of human relationships and activities which he finds entirely unacceptable, and the 'marked moral intensity' that he requires of a great work of art would seem to them merely symptomatic. Nor does he regard as desirable the approach made by Edmund Wilson in his most fertile period, which attempted to use a writer's life to illuminate his work. In 1942 Dr Leavis qualified slightly patronizing praise of *The Wound and the Bow* by saying that Wilson was 'preoccupied with explaining his authors' literary development in terms of their private psychological tensions considered genetically and of the social tensions of their age'. And what is wrong with that? Just that, for Leavis, criticism should be a *moral* encounter between a reader and a work of art, and psychological and social tensions are extraneous to such an encounter. To those who would say, as I should, that literature must always be judged in part by these extraneous elements, he has made his own eloquent reply in writing about 'Literature and Society' (1943), when he says how his way of thinking differs from that of a Marxist: 'It stresses not material and economic determinants, but intellectual and spiritual. . . . It assumes that . . . human intelligence, choice and will do really and effectively operate, expressing an inherent human nature.'

You do not have to agree with this to appreciate the integrity of the viewpoint. With Leavis as with Dr Johnson the 'rightness' of his judgement is much less important than the impact of his narrow, but deeply perceptive and forceful, mind upon literature.

IV SCRUTINY, AN ACHIEVEMENT

One writes, it is inevitable that one should, about the crabbiness and occasional crankiness of Dr Leavis himself and its too faithful aping by some of his followers, about the lack of any creative measure to which critical standards could be compared (it is this that makes *Scrutiny* so much less rewarding reading than *Partisan Review*), about the ingrowing virtue that makes many Scrutineers look like missionaries stuffing culture down unwilling throats: yet all this should not be allowed to obscure the achievement. It has been worth a great deal to have these ironside incorruptibles—not corrupted, even, by payment for their work—savaging pretence, smelling out sham and nepotism, refusing to admit the politenesses by which 'literary life' is carried on. It would not be true to say that the literary life they attacked has been extinguished, but at least its typical figures are no longer in the seats of power, and Mrs Leavis should not now feel it necessary to comment as she did a quarter of a century ago on 'the advantages Americans enjoy in having no Public School system, no ancient universities and no tradition of a closed literary group run on Civil Service lines'. Weekly journalism today is infinitely less school and class ridden, more honest, more serious and more able than it was when *Scrutiny* began.

It does not seem to me probable that *Scrutiny* articles will for long be treated as sacred texts, as the recent shamefaced salaams of some reviewers have suggested, and it is even likely that as the personal influence of Dr Leavis fades and the elementary instructions he gave to each small literary grub are forgotten ('Keep your nose to the text, son, watch out for false morality or a Snow job, when you spot an aesthete don't argue, shoot') there will be a reaction—it can be seen already in young critics—against his insistent moralizing tone. But after *Scrutiny*, as after the post-war Labour government, nothing can ever be quite the same again, and any future reaction will come from those who have been influenced by *Scrutiny* even in reacting against it. The magazine's achievement, although more limited than has been claimed, is real and remarkable. Awkwardly and boorishly sometimes, sharply and intelligently always, these unpaid incorruptibles have by their teaching and writing changed the whole critical climate of Britain in relation to literature.

(1964)

A Word on Late Leavis

Anna Karenina and Other Essays by F. R. Leavis

This is a dismaying book for admirers of Dr Leavis: for admirers, that is, of his critical stance and example who yet stop short of regarding all his basic opinions as unquestionable. The collection, which ranges back in time to the early thirties but includes a considerable proportion of work produced during the last decade, might have been chosen by an enemy to show Leavis's limitations. With the exceptions of the admirable piece on *Anna Karenina* and the essay on Johnson's criticism, the general level is far below his best, and several articles show his narrow dogmatism, his lack of charity and his failures of imagination and sympathy.

Let me set about justifying these hard words. *Narrow dogmatism*: most of the articles begin not with their ostensible subject but with an attack upon some writer who has seen this subject wrongly. Almost half of a lecture on *The Shadow Line* is given to disputing what was said in *London Magazine* articles about Conrad, a piece on D. H. Lawrence's letters is concerned chiefly with the inadequacy of Professor Harry Moore's work as an editor, a long essay on Eliot begins with a sustained attack on 'Tradition and the Individual Talent'. It is characteristic of Leavis that he should approach truth through error, the error of others. Their failings are demonstrated by reference to a standard of excellence which Leavis feels no need to justify. It's all there in his previous writings, the important questions have been settled, the geiger counter need only be applied and the response is guaranteed accurate.

In the case of modern writers their attitude to D. H. Lawrence is often crucial. Thus it is a mark of Eliot's critical weakness that he had a 'profoundly personal prepossession against D. H. Lawrence', and one of Pound's sins is that he, 'like Eliot, dislikes Lawrence and is drawn to Wyndham Lewis—who also disliked Lawrence'. The chain of iniquity is a long one, for references to Lawrence are dragged into almost every essay. Why does Leavis fail to understand that the reaction of Eliot, Pound and Lewis to Lawrence is implicit in the whole nature of their thought and writing? Why instead of attempt-

A Word on Late Leavis

ing a rational discussion of their ideas does he merely abuse them,
why when discussing Lawrence's politeness towards fashionable
literary figures does he attribute this to the fact that for him Edward
Marsh 'was another human being and another centre of life' (and
isn't that the most cliché-ridden form of excuse?), whereas Eliot's
friendship with assorted Bloomsburies expressed only his 'loyalty or
docility' to them? Why, having associated Eliot with Bloomsbury,
does Leavis not give him credit for courage in advocating the merits
of the anti-Bloomsbury Wyndham Lewis? The answer is simple.
Where Leavis once argued persuasively and with perception he now
dictates received truths from on high.

Lack of charity: this recurs throughout the volume but is most
marked in the essay on Eliot where the word 'distinguished' runs
through a piece that is full of what can only be called hatred. The
book under review is 'distinguished'—but also unimportant. Eliot is
'a distinguished critic'—yet in the next phrase also a critic lacking
penetration, sureness of judgement and coherent thought. He has 'a
distinguished mind'—and at the same time a feebly conventional and
orthodox one. Those who may have thought that 'Tradition and the
Individual Talent' was notable for the clarity of its approach to
poetry will be surprised to learn that 'the essay is notable for its
ambiguities, its logical inconsequences, its pseudo-precisions, its
fallaciousness, and the aplomb of its equivocations and its specious
cogency'. Sometimes Leavis does not scruple to invent in order to
make his prepared point. Attacking the inadequate conception of art
offered in Eliot's essay he shakes his head about the idea that there
will be an essential separateness in the perfect artist between 'the man
who suffers and the mind which creates'. Is the phrase true of Tolstoy,
Shakespeare—Lawrence? Certainly not. 'But when we recognize that
the artist implicitly proposed is Flaubert, then the proposition
becomes intelligible.' What authority is there for this *implicit*
proposition? None whatever. Flaubert is not mentioned in the essay,
and its argument bears no relation to his aesthetic. It might as well be
said that Eliot was 'implicitly' proposing Oscar Wilde. Having
invented the connection, however, Leavis is then able to write of
Eliot's own 'Flaubertian kind of self-contradiction'.

Failures of imagination and sympathy: most conspicuous here on a
serious critical level is the Leavis version of Henry James's attitude in
The Turn of the Screw and *What Maisie Knew*. His essay was written
in reply to one by the American critic Marius Bewley, and there is no

space to recapitulate the arguments here, but re-reading the two pieces and Bewley's subsequent 'Rejoinder' the deep imperceptiveness shown by Leavis, particularly in relation to *What Maisie Knew*, is bound to shake one's faith in the values of this (to beg a word from him) distinguished critic.

And there are other failures too, little splutters of spleen about writers of genius or talent which are distressing because of the quarrelsome insensitiveness they reveal. 'The absurdity of our being offered Landor as a great poet . . . when one reads of Spenser's *The Faerie Queene* as a "long poem in the first rank" . . . The conventional acceptance of *The Way of the World* as a summit of civilization and literary refinement goes with an inability to see . . .' To see what, in this last case? It is hardly credible, but the sentence ends '. . . a consummateness of wit and humour and a delicate living mastery of tone, manifestations of a supreme vitality of intelligence in D. H. Lawrence.' What is the *point* of such a comparison between writers working in different conventions, in different periods, with different aims? Surely it cannot be made seriously? But alas, it is. What it seems that Leavis wants to say is that Congreve has no code of moral values and therefore cannot be a writer of any interest, but he cannot quite bring himself to so crude a statement. Hence the comparison, inappropriate though it is, with Lawrence.

It is not necessary to go on. It is easy to understand these excesses, possible (except for Dr Leavis) to forgive. Leavis's achievement as a critic was the replacement of the bland supercilious assumptions of Bloomsbury by the assertion of permanent standards. But acceptance of his view that George Eliot was supreme among Victorian novelists should not carry with it, as it does for him, the implication that her contemporaries with the exception of Dickens were negligible. (Neither Thackeray nor Trollope was thought worth discussion in the twenty-one years of *Scrutiny*.) Whatever may have been necessary in the thirties and forties in the way of overstatement to defeat the hordes of Bloomsbury, those battles are long since won. What was once passion has turned into prejudice. What was once a fresh and eager view of past and present literature has become, certainly with reference to the present (see his comments on the 'strongly distasteful' sexual details in *Lady Chatterley* and then think how ill-qualified such a commentator is to assess modern fiction), simply out of date.

(1968)

The Little Magazine and *The Review*

I HIGHBROW REVIEWERS, MIDDLEBROW AUDIENCE

What is a little magazine? The American authors of *The Little Magazine* (published in 1946, and although inevitably in some respects out of date still the best view of its subject) define it as 'a magazine designed to print artistic work which for reasons of commercial expediency is not acceptable to the money-minded periodicals or presses'. Reviewing this book at the time of publication in the little magazine *Now*, I suggested that the little magazine, as it had existed since 1910 in the USA and since 1914 in England, had always been 'the expression of a minority culture working in a literary society in process of disintegration', and that with the advance of a majority culture prepared to soak up and transform minority art, 'the little magazine will be less and less able to attract talent.' The original dates are of some interest. In America, 1910 saw the publication of Vachel Lindsay's *Village Magazine*, succeeded in the following year by *The Masses*, and a year later *Poetry* (Chicago). In 1914 *The Little Review* ('making no compromise with the public taste') first appeared. In England *Rhythm*, edited by Middleton Murry and Katherine Mansfield was published in 1911, to be succeeded in 1913 by Murry's *Blue Review*, which did not pay contributors but optimistically contemplated sharing profits at the end of nine months, and in 1914 by *Blast* and *The Egoist*.

It is necessary only to mention the names of such magazines, and to look through some of their contents in a library, to see the weakness and timidity of what we have now. What magazine today could contemplate anything comparable to *The Little Review*'s publication over a period of three years of *Ulysses*, with the consequent confiscation and burning of various instalments? And if it is said that there is no book which would similarly outrage contemporary taste, would not *Lolita* have been a candidate for serialization a few years ago, and might not Terry Southern's *Candy* be eligible now? What magazine today would dare to put out an issue almost entirely blank, because no interesting work had been received — *The Little Review* again? Or would attempt anything as typographically unconventional as *Blast*? What little magazine now can even call regularly upon the best-known poets of a particular generation, as could *New Verse* in the thirties? The questions are rhetorical: but still, the answers are interesting. Look at that original definition of the little magazine. What work is there today which 'for reasons of commercial expediency is not acceptable to the money-minded periodicals or presses'? When Eliot was writing the poems contained in *Prufrock*, there was no place except the little magazines in which his work would have been printed; even in the thirties it would have been unlikely, if not unthinkable, that a new poem by Auden, Spender or Day Lewis would have been printed in a Sunday paper; but today, if Thom Gunn or Philip Larkin writes a poem, there are half a dozen papers in which it may be printed, papers all of which have enormous circulations by the standard of little magazines. A parallel situation exists in other arts. Abstract, automatic and pop painting is dealt with in colour supplements where once it was ridiculed or ignored; experimental plays receive the columns of considered opinion that was once given to middlebrow drama; young men come down from universities and slip smoothly, and as it seems quite naturally, into reviewing or editorial positions that would once have been the prerogative of long-service hacks. An unrecognized revolution has taken place in British art and letters since the war, a revolution based partly upon the economic well-being that has carried with it an immense horizontal spread of cultural interest throughout society, partly upon the insistence on newness and youth that is at the heart of a culture which has planned its own obsolescence in advance, so that new 'movements' must replace old ones at ever-shortening intervals.

At first glance it seems obviously right to say hurrah for this revolution. The standards of weekly book reviewing are immensely higher than they were in the days when Ralph Straus and Gerald Gould regularly dipped every new middlebrow novel in the treacle of praise, when all except mock-Georgian new verse was likely to be patronized or jeered at, when art criticism was less provincial than parochial. It would be wrong, though, not to recognize the limitations that go along with the enlightenment. It is a horizontal and not a vertical revolution. People read *Lolita* and *The Group*, laugh at the stylistic repetitions in a Pinter play, look at the new poems printed in large circulation newspapers, but as an audience they are not very different from that which took Straus and Gould as guides for the library list. They pay a respectful visit to the Gulbenkian 54–64 exhibition at the Tate, they know that it is not proper to laugh at the three panels shown there which appear at first sight to be plain black but can be seen after close examination to be black patterned on black, but the eyes with which they look at pop or abstract art have the same vision or lack of it as the eyes that used to look at 'Dignity and Impudence'. Highbrow reviewers now occupy the seats once warmed by middlebrows, but the revolution that has taken place is one imposed from above, imposed with the blessing of Arts or local Councils, and with the enthusiastic co-operation of up-to-date magazine and newspaper executives, art editors, industrial designers. It is really all these distributors of patronage who have been converted to 'highbrow', unpopular art. The conversion is very welcome, but it should not be confused with the much more radical change in taste, springing from the roots of a society, that can come after a war or a revolution.

II REVIEWING *THE REVIEW*

The effect of this revolution upon the little magazine primarily concerned with literature has been dual and ironic: its financial position has been eased at the same time that its vital organs have been removed. Several little magazines today receive subventions from the Arts Council, and these small sums of money help to ensure their continued existence. But why should they exist, what minority art do they print? Well, there is some work that would still be excluded from mass-circulation papers. But the impression of thinness and feebleness that one gets in reading little magazines nowadays springs from the basic fact that their editors have little talent to call upon. If they are verse magazines they are not likely to get the best poems, if they print other kinds of creative work they are not likely to get the best, not only because they cannot pay much money but because almost all writers prefer to reach the largest possible audience. Who can doubt that Eliot and Pound would have been delighted to see their early poems appear in *The Times*— poetically a still-unbreached citadel? It should be said parenthetically that *Encounter* and *The London Magazine* should largely be exempted from these remarks, *Encounter* because it is concerned so much with sociology and day-to-day politics. *The London Magazine* among other reasons because it is the only English magazine that consistently prints short stories, for which there is in this country no commercial market. Some new category is needed to differentiate a large, flourishing monthly like *Encounter*, which is published for and was supported by the Congress for Cultural Freedom, from little magazines dealing wholly with art and literature. Among these 'traditional' little magazines *The Review* is outstanding, and its progress offers interesting sidelights on the fate and function of the little magazine today.

The first issue of *The Review* appeared in 1962, and the most recent, Number 11–12, is a double number on the thirties. During these two years the size of the magazine has increased from forty pages (the early numbers) to sixty-four larger-sized pages and now to ninety-six pages for this double number. The price has increased from half a crown, to three shillings for ordinary numbers and five shillings for the thirties issue. The magazine has a single editor, Ian Hamilton—who should not be confused with the former editor of *The Spectator*—and is conducted single-handed. The increase in size and number of pages after Number 3 was based chiefly on assistance given by the Arts Council.

The Review is sub-titled 'a magazine of poetry and criticism', but the criticism is more in evidence than the poetry. Number 9 is exceptional, in the sense that more than half of it is taken up by poems, including the remarkable last poems of Sylvia Plath, but much more typical are Number 3 and Number 8 (four and seven pages of poems respectively). This shortage of poems is no doubt caused partly by the difficulties already mentioned, which confront all little magazine editors, but partly also by Mr Hamilton's determination not to abate the sharpness of his own approach to poetry, so that poems with celebrated names at the bottom of them have been returned. That is absolutely as it should be, and as it rarely is nowadays, but it does mean that *The Review* must be judged primarily as a critical magazine. As such, it is a considerable achievement. Although its home is Oxford it has remained triumphantly unacademic. Some of its contributors are well known— F. W. Bateson, Donald Davie, A. Alvarez—but several are not often to be encountered outside the pages of *The Review*. It is tempting to believe that they are all pseudonyms for Mr Hamilton, but I believe that is not the case. Their names are less important than the fact that some of the best recent criticism is to be found in the long articles, among which those on Roy Fuller (Number 3) and Yvor Winters (Number 8), should be mentioned, and in some of the special numbers. One can imagine Mr Hamilton saying to himself, when he received the promise of support from the Arts Council: 'How can this money best be used, given the present conditions for the existence of little magazines?' His answer is contained in the special numbers on T. S. Eliot (Number 4), William Empson (6/7), Black Mountain Poetry (10) and the thirties, numbers which are all permanently valuable for consideration of their subjects.

It is this sort of intelligent strategy, involving the conception and execution of projects on a shoe-string budget, that makes *The Review* so interesting. Mr Hamilton is aware of present-day possibilities, as well as limitations, and he has sensibly made a good deal of use of tape recordings. The first issue contained the transcript of an interesting, though unnecessarily rambling recorded discussion between Alvarez and Davie, the Empson number included a conversation' with its subject, and in the thirties number there are more conversations, in which questions are put by an unnamed interviewer—presumably the editor—to Edgell Rickword, Claud Cockburn, Edward Upward and James Reeves. In a way such interviews are a substitute for criticism, but they have their value, in lightening a tone that threatens sometimes to become merely scholastic, and in giving the chance of asking questions that might otherwise be missed.

The thirties number cannot fail to be interesting to any inhabitant of what was not only a period in time, but also a way of thinking and feeling. The cover alone, a previously unpublished picture of the Three, Auden, Spender and Isherwood, all wearing open-necked shirts and laughing like crazy, is almost worth the cost of the magazine. There is an article on *Scrutiny* in the thirties, one on the Spanish Civil War (poetically considered), a very odd piece about American poetry, critical articles on Auden (two), MacNeice, Bernard Spencer. Altogether an interesting, although uneven, number, notable for its compelled or voluntary omissions. No justification, condemnation or comment on the past from the Three, nor from Day Lewis (weren't they asked or didn't they want to say anything?), nothing from Geoffrey Grigson about *New Verse* in spite of editorial approaches. I missed any understanding among the younger contributors that the thirties was a self-contained movement involving a very particular use of language. It was much more 'aesthetic' than appeared at the time, and the only parallels to it in English literature are the Nineties and, more indirectly, the pre-Raphaelite movement. There should also have been something about homosexuality, which is mentioned only in passing, by Claud Cockburn. (One can't help wondering, though, whether the Arts Council would have been pleased by a piece on 'The Homosexual Syndrome in Thirties Literature'.) On the other hand the best article, Francis Hope's 'Then and Now', is by a contributor born in the thirties. This assessment of the period from a sixties vantage point gets right to the core of thirties feeling, and assesses it generously. 'The worst of their poems may only be read for the light they throw on their decade; but the study of their decade will continue to throw some light on even the best of their poems.'

Nobody who buys *The Review* should expect to like everything in it. When a large part of one number was handed over to Mr Charles Tomlinson to make an anthology of the 'Black Mountain Poets', who stem from William Carlos Williams, a denizen of the thirties could only look at the result with horrified incomprehension. (Is it Williams and the Objectivist Press, yet? And when are they disinterring Amy Lowell and Maxwell Bodenheim?) But still, I suppose the irritation is of the kind a little magazine should engender. An ambitious future programme, announced in the thirties number, includes occasional verse pamphlets to be distributed as part of the magazine, and special issues on the Imagists and World War II poets. *The Review* is worth buying: better still, worth a subscription.

(1964)

POSTSCRIPT, 1980

As every reader of little magazines will know, *The Review* was succeeded by *The New Review*, and now that too is a thing of the past. It had the same editor, Ian Hamilton, and in relation to poetry the same firm standards; it printed some interesting articles, and short stories that would have been unlikely to appear elsewhere; but it was never anything like so good a magazine. Some of the reasons for this rested in the editor's inability to print his personality on a large

116

The Little Magazine and *The Review*

magazine with a wide range of material, as he had on a small one concerned exclusively with poetry and criticism, combined with an inability to keep within a generous subsidy provided by the Arts Council. But the end of *The New Review* prompts less personal, more general reflections.

The process noted in my article sixteen years ago is now much further advanced. *Advanced* is indeed the word: the appetite for anything that can be called artistically new—an arrangement of bricks, a Warhol soup tin, a concrete poem, 'performance' art—is insatiable. Such activities are immediately taken up by the colour supplements, most often in an adulterated form, rather on the lines that a concrete poem shaped like a pear might be used as a whimsically ornamental way of presenting 'a partridge in a pear tree' in a Christmas issue. The message such movements carry to the middlebrow audience is that art is easy, art is fun, art is quite the reverse of a discipline. Eric Gill's belief that every man is a kind of artist has been transformed into the idea that anything at all is art.

The conception of an *avant-garde*, however—that is, a group of writers or painters who use techniques or put forward views that are unacceptable to most literate people—implies the opposite of this. It suggests work that is in some way outrageous, and it is now almost impossible to outrage conventional susceptibilities. When Duchamp in 1917 submitted a lavatory bowl to an exhibition as a ready-made work of art, he caused genuine feelings of offence and shock. Today such ready-mades (cf. Warhol) would be thought immensely amusing by a great many people. When Joyce used the word 'cunt' in *Ulysses* it had an effect that such words no longer possess. The short story writer Ian McEwan, discovered by *The New Review*, was taken up within a matter of months by fashionable magazines, although the content of some of his work must have been regarded as disagreeable.

In such a world there is no place for the heavyweight *avant-garde* magazine of the past like *The Criterion*, embracing philosophy, politics and poetry. In *The London Magazine* Alan Ross has skilfully steered an eclectic course for nearly twenty years, giving space or illustration to almost every current movement, but keeping a broad base of material that shows regard for technique, and an awareness that art did not begin with Pollock and Stella, or poetry with Ginsberg and Creeley. Such eclecticism has its own value, but it is not that of the *avant-garde*; and *The New Review*, also, with its space-filling dips into political journalism and its pieces about the 'sub-

117

culture of football hooliganism' as exemplified in supporters' songs, was not an *avant-garde* magazine like its predecessor.

If there is one British periodical at present that earns what should be an honourable title, it is *Poetry Nation Review*. The title is earned no less because those offended by the magazine's attitude are likely to be 'progressives' in politics and literature, or because its approach to art and society resembles (with inevitable differences) that of *The Criterion*. The truly valuable little magazine of today and tomorrow will be small in size and sectarian in approach, confined to a small circle of writers sharing common aims, suspicious of all easy or popular art. Its editors will bear in mind Auden's question long ago, in another difficult time:

> What can truth treasure, or heart bless
> But a narrow strictness?

Those, after all, were the principles on which Ian Hamilton founded *The Review*.

The *Cri*

The most interesting literary reviews are generally those which support an idea or a group of ideas, very often embodied in an individual temperament. So *New Writing* in its early and best days was essentially a coterie publication for publicizing John Lehmann's contemporaries and those who sympathized with them, so *Horizon* and *Scrutiny* took their characters from Cyril Connolly's delicate hedonism and F. R. Leavis's bony moralizing, so everything in the early (and again the best) years of *Partisan Review* was coloured by the editors' dissident Radicalism. Everybody can name his own exceptions to such a generalization (a prime one would be the *Calendar of Modern Letters*, which in the creative work it printed was surely the best literary magazine of the last fifty years), but it is one that applies with particular force to the *Criterion*, which is today chiefly of interest as an expression of T. S. Eliot's ideas about life, art and society.

A few facts first. Born, October 1922, died January 1939. Founded, with the financial help of Viscountess Rothermere, as what she hoped might be a 'chic and brilliant' successor to *Art and Letters*, then supported by other private helpers until in 1925 it was taken over and backed by Faber and Gwyer, later Faber and Faber. At first a quarterly, price 3s 6d later advanced to 5s 0d, then in the late twenties a monthly for just over a year, price half a crown; from June 1928 a quarterly again, price 7s 6d. What, at this prohibitively high price for a review that contained two hundred pages of print but no art plates or even line drawings, was the circulation? It was said never to exceed 400 copies, although of course there were many more than that number of readers. A dishonourable practice of my youth was to maintain an out-of-date set of the magazine by asking Fabers for sample back numbers, which they supplied for the cost of postage.

In the fourth number Eliot suggested that a literary review should maintain principles 'which have their consequences also in politics and in private conduct', but it was not until 1926 that a famous editorial on 'The Idea of a Literary Review' laid down the lines on which the magazine was thereafter firmly conducted. To print merely

119

'good stuff' was a wretched policy with no end but the production of a miscellany which would be 'the feeble reflection of the character of a feeble editor'. The editor should choose his collaborators and occasional contributors carefully to embody a 'tendency' rather than a 'programme', and if he chose well 'the bound volumes of a decade should represent the development of the keenest sensibility and the clearest thought of ten years.' What was the modern tendency which the review should exemplify? About this the editor was vague, invoking dubiously the word classicism and plumping for 'a higher and clearer conception of Reason'. But he named recently published works by some writers interesting to a modern mind, including Sorel, Charles Maurras, Benda, T. E. Hulme and Maritain, and books by others who represented 'that part of the past which is already dead'— Wells, Shaw and Bertrand Russell.

This declaration in favour of authority and against liberalism (which Eliot often called a nineteenth-century idea) was repeated with many variations in the quarterly 'commentary' that was often the liveliest and most provocative part of the magazine. Eliot insisted that he was not interested in day-to-day politics, only in new political ideas, but the commentaries became more and more concerned with the condition of European society and a good deal of space was given in them, and in long articles, to sympathetic discussion of both Fascism and Communism. What 'really mattered' about Fascism, Eliot said in the pre-Hitler days of 1928, was not whether certain individuals were harshly treated but 'whether Fascism is the emergence of a new political idea, or the recrudescence of an old one'. There was never any comment on Hitler or the Nazis, but Communism received friendly treatment as a possibly inferior but still powerful religion which, again, might represent the modern 'tendency'. Yet although Eliot was prepared to consider Communism seriously he had little but contempt for British 'progressives', eager to support all good causes, who showed what he had stigmatized in writing of Wells, Shaw and Russell as the cardinal error: 'Intelligence at the mercy of emotion'. In an ironic note on a number of peace appeals he had received, including one headed 'War and Writers', he remarked coolly: 'Civilization has almost too many friends', and two years later at the height of the Spanish Civil War he condemned 'the irresponsible anti-fascists, the patrons of mass-meetings and manifestoes', whose minds were 'doctrinaire without being philosophic', and who were dangerous because they were misunderstood abroad and helped to 'distract attention from the true evils in their own society'.

These were unpopular words at the time, and they are no more popular today. It would be easy but wrong to identify them with support of Fascism, although this accusation has been repeated often, particularly since Eliot's death. What he hoped for was a movement firmly based in authority and tradition which in everyday political and economic affairs would be heterodox and even revolutionary. The task of governments was to administer society for the greatest good of the governed. The governed were deceived when they thought that independence had anything to do with the use of the ballot box, they were being tricked when their rulers persuaded them that a liberal *laissez-faire* approach could possibly solve the problems of the modern world. Some of these ideas Eliot got from Wyndham Lewis, others from Ezra Pound, and as during the thirties his own religious thought developed so that 'a right political philosophy came more and more to imply a right theology', the tone of the *Criterion* became often that of a moral censor and its editor appeared at times to be concerned less with literature than with the conduct of an ethical crusade.

How did these ideas work out in practice? The poems and prose fiction printed were little affected by Eliot's social theories and certain issues remain dazzlingly good, like Number 8 in which the principal contributors were Proust, Yeats, Virginia Woolf, Cavafy, Hugh Walpole, Osbert Sitwell, Frederic Manning and Harold Monro. 'The Waste Land' appeared in the first issue, a good many of Pound's Cantos were printed, there was a section of Hart Crane's 'The Bridge', 'Paid on Both Sides' was published when Auden was in a public sense completely unknown. In the thirties Eliot's sympathy towards the younger poets was unfailing, although their style and approach must often have been uncongenial to him. Allott, Barker, Empson, Madge, MacNeice, Spender—the list does not end there. He printed not only poems by Dylan Thomas, but two of his stories. The fiction includes Conrad Aiken's remarkable 'Mr Arcularis' and *The Woman Who Rode Away*, and surprisingly there is our own Henry Miller writing nothing sexational or scatological but discussing, yes, so many years ago, the diaries of Anais Nin. Yet the prose is a thin haul, as the poetry is a rich one. Eliot said he was 'quite incompetent to judge fiction', and the truth is that he regarded the novel as an outworked middle-class liberal art form and prose fiction generally, with a few exceptions like *Ulysses*, *Nightwood* and *The Apes of God* (which remained unreviewed although two sections appeared in the magazine), as belonging to the dead past. Certainly his remark in the final editorial, 'Last Words', that 'there were fewer writers in any country who seemed to have anything to say to the intellectual public of another' is extraordinary in a time when the talents of Sartre and Brecht were being brought to a British public by John Lehmann. And in other ways the *Criterion*'s view of literature was cramped and curious. Biography as a literary form was practically ignored, except for a damaging attack on Lytton Strachey, and such an experiment as *The Quest For Corvo* remained unreviewed. History was similarly neglected, and no consideration was ever given to the possibility that a specifically modern approach to either history or biography might exist.

It is on the purely critical side, though, that the magazine looks now most dismally old-fashioned and uninteresting. This was partly a consequence of Eliot's own academic cast of mind. A worthy determination to avoid the horrors of the familiar essay and the Squirearchy led him to print a great many articles, particularly about English literature, that might have rested for years in desk drawers before being dusted off and set up in print. Almost every issue contains some long, stiflingly dull article, on the evolution of English blank verse, the poetry of Rossetti, the scansion of Shakespeare. These looked very strange beside, say, a piece of Pound's about Antheil, and I suppose in a perverse way this combination of dullness and make-it-newness might be called one of the *Cri*'s attractions. Basically the critical failure sprang from the inadequacy of many of Eliot's collaborators, who had respect for authority and tradition but sadly lacked sensibility and sharp intelligence. The monthly dinners at a Soho restaurant where 'we naturally discussed literature more than anything else, but the atmosphere was entirely gay', did not help very much in forming the 'phalanx' of enlightened minds that Eliot envisaged. Few of these collaborators were sympathetic towards the most interesting critical developments of the period, the close examination of texts or the pressure towards a social and psychological interpretation of literature. To a certain extent Eliot acknowledged this. In one commentary he remarked: 'The relation of the forms of art to the social background is a very important part of criticism which has not been adequately explored.'

In the *Criterion* it never was explored. Such an approach had determinist implications very uncongenial to one who distrusted profoundly the idea that writers represented first of all 'the spirit of the age'. New critics were brought in as some of the old guard dropped out, and often they were lively writers, yet liveliness seemed to desert them when they came to write for Eliot. As the review became more authoritarian in feeling the criticism lost individuality and took on a *Criterion* tone which was much less interesting than the characteristic *Scrutiny* manner. The contributors did not swim against the prevailing humanist liberal current, they simply expressed contempt for it as they were carried towards the rapids of the war. The bound volumes of a decade do not represent the clearest thought of those years. They simply express shades of slightly unconventional right-wing opinion.

As an expression of Eliot's ideas the *Criterion* remains both interesting and revealing. When he wrote his 'Last Words', confessing his staleness and observing that right economics depended upon right ethics, perhaps he was acknowledging that authoritarianism had developed in a way very different from his expectations in the twenties. He was too humane a man not to have felt horror at the development of Nazi Germany, yet he had neither condemned Nazism nor even permitted books discussing it to be reviewed. In a way this is not surprising, for Nazism was a terrible caricature of his own desire for 'authority', and conveyed the real nature of the 'tendency' he had tried so hard to develop. Europe was moving towards a clash between those out-of-date liberal humanist forces he detested and an authoritarian society which he could not possibly support, although it embodied many of his ideas. It was time to put up the shutters.

(1967)

Keeping Left in the Thirties

Left Review: October 1934 to May 1938 (8 volumes)

There is a good deal of nostalgia for the thirties about at the moment. Writers too young to remember the period, dismayed by the built-in obsolescence of so much art today, look back to the time as one of enviable assurance about art's nature and objects. That wasn't the way it looked then, but such feelings may well be reinforced by reading the eight volumes of *Left Review*, just reissued. The idea that artists should not be simply individualists barricaded in their 'ivory towers' (a cliché now mercifully out of use) was very general, but in *Left Review* it was pushed much further. 'A writer's usefulness depends on his influence: that is to say, on the size and enthusiasm of his public. . . . A book, a play, a poem, could be itself a blow struck against the plans for war,' wrote 'Ajax' in the second number. No New Leftist admirer of Beckett, Pinter, Robbe-Grillet, would echo such words today. The magazine is an important and in many ways a painful document of the period.

It appeared monthly from October 1934 to May 1938, when publication ceased, officially to make way for 'a wider project, which can reach a vastly greater mass of the people', in fact because of financial troubles. The paper was well produced, with attractive covers, and of course at sixpence for 60 to 80 pages it seems now amazingly cheap. The original editors were Montagu Slater, Amabel Williams-Ellis and Tom Wintringham. In January 1936 Edgell Rickword took over the editorship, and in July 1937 he was succeeded by Randall Swingler. Most, perhaps all, of the editors belonged to the Communist Party, and it would have been difficult to find Party members more sympathetic to the values of literature. Rickword especially showed while running the *Calendar of Modern Letters* a sensibility and discernment unsurpassed by any editor of a literary magazine in our time. How did it happen that these sensitive and intelligent men so often confused literature with propaganda and printed so much that now looks derivative, dishonest and dull?

Unproved assertions? Almost any issue provides their justification. For dullness try the attempts made by these middle-class intellectuals

124

to encourage a 'proletarian' literature, the bits of working-class novels, the nine workers describing a shift in almost identically crude language, the three competition-winning 'encounters' with people, one of which begins: 'Muffled in an old overcoat bought at Paddy's rag market, Lawrence, the old negro, sat shivering in his dockside lodging in Liverpool, coughing his life away and drinking himself to death.'

Of this exercise in sentimental sinking Amabel Williams-Ellis observed with amiable condescension that 'if the style seems a little influenced by Conrad, what of it?' If indeed. For the derivative, look at the poems expressing windy rhetoric in the language of Hopkins adulterated by Day Lewis:

> Comrade, what joined severs us
> and what I love I hate,
> granite may Marxism grow in us
> wings apart fit for flight, but together elate

And dishonesty? It was inherent in the worshipful attitude to the Soviet Union and in the editorial readiness to print material relating to Russia which they would have condemned out of hand had it come from any other source. An article on 'What the Nazis Have Done for Culture' mentions the 'amazing extravagance' of poems about Hitler:

> There were the uprooted masses, surging, wild,
> A chaos of thoughts, a volcano
> Of passions—and before them stepped a Man.

Three issues later Bert Marshall (every Herbert was a Bert in those days) prints a translation of a Russian poem:

> You lay dry and arid, oh earth,
> You were fruitless and barren, oh earth,
> You were groaning from thirst, oh earth,
> But Stalin remembered you, earth!

In the same article Marshall deprecates the work of Pasternak ('far removed from Soviet actuality') and remarks on the significance of the fact that Bukharin had 'implied that the future development of Societ poetry should be along the line of Pasternak, rather than Mayakovsky'. The 'significance' of course rested in the fact that Bukharin was awaiting trial as a member of the Rightist-Trotskyite *bloc*.

Little Magazines

All this is ancient history, and although it should not be forgotten history, the reasons why such work was printed are today more important than the mere facts. *Left Review* is interesting especially because it was the only real attempt to organize the British literary and artistic Left in the thirties, an attempt that included a branch of the Writers' International and a British Artists' Congress. A determined effort was made to keep the middle-class writers in the same fold with the young proletarians, but the levels of their work were so different that at times the magazine seems almost to be split in half with Spender and Day Lewis (who were proudly announced as regular contributors in October 1936, although Spender was one for only a short time) writing about subjects like poetry and revolution, the proletarians producing their slices of reportage. The idea of a free-ranging left-wing periodical was admirable, but as time passed the area for ranging narrowed sharply. The pressure of events towards conformity of tone and subject became increasingly great, and more and more the editors bowed to them. There were sacred cows that must not be criticized, like the Soviet Union; a tone of revolutionary optimism had to be adopted in writing, for instance, about Spain, no matter what was happening there; and worst of all, it had to be accepted that 'a writer's usefulness' was also the measure of his talent. As the years went by, adherence to these tenets became very clearly a denial of reality. How could Amabel Williams-Ellis, who had said in 1934 that the speeches of Radek and Bukharin at a Soviet Writers' Conference 'will echo for a long time in Russia' accept easily their extinction as enemies of the Soviet Union? How could that criterion of a writer's usefulness be seriously maintained for long? Of course these things *were* maintained by many of the contributors, but only at the cost of ignoring reality in favour of a set of ideas which were increasingly difficult to believe.

But something, even a good deal, has to be said on the other side. The benefits of unity, of a closely knit group exchanging and developing ideas, is seen most clearly in the first two years, before the demands of propaganda became too great. The critical level at this time is high, with excellent articles by Rickword, Slater and Alick West, and outstanding pieces by Douglas Garman on Eliot and Tennyson, and by Ralph Fox on T. E. Lawrence, 'the only hero whom the English ruling classes have produced in our time'. Several of these pieces would probably have been thought too difficult or ideologically incorrect later on, including certainly Spender's questioning article about Max Eastman's *Artists in Uniform*. There are stories by Edward Upward and James Hanley that were worth resuscitation, although almost all of the proletarian stories are a dead loss, a reflection of the movement's failure to discover any interesting working-class writers. The writers appeared afterwards, when there was no literary movement. Rickword may have been right in suggesting a quarter of a century later that 'the Weskers and Sillitoes were reading their elder brothers' copy of *Left Review*'—or their fathers' copy perhaps?

There is a curious sequel to the *Left Review* story. It was succeeded by a rather dismal small verse magazine called *Poetry and the People*, and this was followed in February 1941 by *Our Time*. Ironically *Our Time*, which was a deliberately 'popular' illustrated monthly without obvious propagandist intentions, blended different kinds of writing much more successfully than *Left Review* had done, and reached a considerable working-class readership. It 'achieved a larger circulation than any Left Wing cultural magazine had ever done', to quote Rickword again, during its six or seven years of life. A reprint of it in this excellent series would be welcome.

(1968)

Criminal Matters

The Crime Collector's Cabinet of Curiosities

Who wrote the first full-length detective story? The obvious favourite is Wilkie Collins, whose *The Moonstone* was called by T. S. Eliot in a famous phrase the first, the longest and the best of detective novels in English. The book was published in 1868, and very likely Eliot made that 'English' qualification because he knew that Emile Gaboriau's first crime story, *L'Affaire Lerouge*, had appeared in serial form as early as 1863. Collins and Gaboriau, however, are not the only contenders. The first full-length book recommended in the 'two centuries of cornerstones' making up Howard Haycraft's and Ellery Queen's 'definitive library of detective-crime-mystery fiction' is *Bleak House*. Claims have been made for Godwin's *Caleb Williams*, for *Le Père Goriot* and other works by Balzac, and for Bulwer Lytton's *Pelham*. None of these, though, has a crime and its detection at the heart of the story, although they contain detectival elements.

My own candidate is *The Notting Hill Mystery*, which I read for the first time several years ago, when I was working on a history of the detective story. The book, which in some ways anticipates the style and themes of later detective stories, quite bowled me over. The year of publication was 1865, the author was said on the title page to be Charles Felix. I shall say more about the book, but my immediate concern was with the author. Who was Charles Felix, and what else had he written?

The name had an air of pseudonymity about it, and this was confirmed by the British Museum catalogue, which said: FELIX, Charles (pseud.) See HENDERSON, R., and O'T, T. But the BM catalogue, as anybody who has used it soon learns, is subtle, deceptive, and full of traps for the innocent. R. Henderson was fictional—was, indeed, the narrator in *The Notting Hill Mystery*, which is said to be 'compiled by Charles Felix from the papers of the late R. Henderson, Esq.' and T. O'T., the author of *Barefooted Birdie*, 'A Simple Tale for Christmas', proved also to be Charles Felix. There were two other books listed under Felix's own name, *Velvet Lawn* and

Criminal Matters

Ram Dass. I read these three-decker novels as well as *Barefooted Birdie* in a quest for Felix, and also in the hope that he had written something else as good as *The Notting Hill Mystery*. The pages of *Ram Dass* and *Barefooted Birdie* were uncut, and as I slit them in a surreptitious way with a nail file (against the Museum's official instructions, which I did not know at the time) I felt not only slight guilt, but also an explorer's sense of excitement.

Not for long, however. *Barefooted Birdie* proved to be the most dismally sentimental of Victorian Christmas stories, *Velvet Lawn* no more than a competent melodrama, and *Ram Dass* a variation on the standard Victorian theme of the wicked man from the East lusting after a white girl. I turned to bibliographers of detective fiction, and in particular to John Carter of Sotheby's, who nearly half a century ago produced the first serious catalogue of detective fiction. Carter's interest in the subject had long since waned, but he treated me with his customary urbanity. He knew nothing about Charles Felix or his book, but told me of several guides to minor Victorian fiction which might be useful. Alas, Felix was too minor for any of them. I found out also that *The Notting Hill Mystery* had first appeared anonymously as a serial in the journal *Once a Week* in 1862. *Once a Week* was a rival to Dickens's *Household Words*, and the book was probably written in the hope of a success comparable to that of Wilkie Collins's *The Woman in White*, which had recently appeared in Dickens's magazine. The anonymity of the original publication suggested that the author was perhaps on the staff of *Once a Week*. A history of Victorian magazines might have told me something about him, but although almost every other aspect of Victorian life has been explored in sometimes excessive detail, I found no such history. The last glimmer of hope came when I learned that the book had been reprinted as late as 1945, in *Novels of Mystery from the Victorian Age* chosen by the doyen of crime critics, my old friend Maurice Richardson. The gleam was extinguished when Maurice told me that they had reprinted from *Once a Week*. He had never heard of Charles Felix, and did not even know that the serial had appeared between book covers.

So far the mystery of Charles Felix. When this article was published in *The Times* several amateur historians set out to discover his identity—without success, although I hope the mystery may be solved one day. But something more should be said about *The Notting Hill Mystery*, both to justify my view that it is an original and interesting work, and to explain why it is not in print.* It has what was for the time an unusually factual approach. Ralph Henderson, the narrator, is an investigator for a life assurance company, and tells the story in reports to his employers. These reports include extracts from correspondence, journals and memoranda, passages from a doctor's diary, statements and depositions by people of all classes involved in Henderson's attempt to discover whether Baron R. was responsible for the death of the wife whose life he had insured with five different companies at £5,000 a time. The effect is very much like that of a modern documentary crime story. Statements made by working-class characters, in particular, have the right sort of jerkiness and brevity. Felix lets himself go in relation to such things as the spelling of semi-literates, like that 'most excellent person' Mrs Taylor, who is looking after the Honourable C.B.'s children: 'I am trewly thankfull to sai the dere children are both quit wel wich miss Kattaren made erself Hill on tuesday and pore miss gerterud were verry bade in consekens for 3 dais but his now quit wel agen.'

The book also includes a map of the Baron R.'s basement, a facsimile marriage certificate and another facsimile of a torn letter fragment written in French (Henderson evidently knows the language, and provides a translation). This was something absolutely new at the time. I have not traced the next use of visual clues, but they were still regarded as unusual when Conan Doyle used similar devices thirty years later, like the letter fragment in 'The Reigate Squires' or the code figures in 'The Dancing Men'.

With all these merits, and with a strikingly modern ending in which Henderson asks his employers whether a crime has been committed at all, and if it has 'are crimes thus committed . . . of a kind for which the criminal can be brought to punishment', the novel is based upon such outrageous premises that one can't take it seriously. Baron R. is 'the most powerful mesmerist in Europe', and his plans are based on the sympathetic feeling between Catherine and Gertrude. It is suggested that poison administered to the one may have killed the other. The possibility of sympathetic transference of feelings through mesmerism much engaged the Victorians, but although the contrast between the sensational plot and the factual manner of its telling is remarkable, in the end it has to be said that Charles Felix was not

---

* The book has now been reissued in an American collection of early crime stories.

Criminal Matters

Wilkie Collins, and that *The Notting Hill Mystery* is not a master-piece in the *genre*, but one of its most engaging curiosities. Its quality as such has been recognized recently. John Carter sent me a Christie's catalogue in which a copy of it was included in a lot of otherwise unremarkable volumes. I went along prepared to pay £20 for it, but the lot fetched more than £50.

This was the most interesting discovery in the BM research which occupied me for a year, during which I read or looked through an average of some eight books a day, reminding myself of many works which I had read in youth but had since forgotten, often mercifully as it proved. Who now remembers Sir Clinton Driffield, Chief Constable of Blankshire, or Sergeant Bobby Owen, or Superintendent Wilson who varied so strangely in height? Well, those who still read J. J. Connington, E. R. Punshon and G.D.H. and Margaret Cole, is the answer. Crime fiction is an interesting field for the collector, because there is no accepted value to most of the first editions. There are now several specialist booksellers in the field, but until a couple of years ago it was comparatively easy to pick up a first edition of Christie or Carr, let alone Connington, for a few pence on secondhand bookstalls. Even now, an energetic collector who placed a limit of a fiver on any single volume could quickly amass a considerable library of first editions.

The question is, where do you stop? Anybody setting out to collect the several hundred odd works of John Creasey would have little room in his library for other prolific authors. I remember once urging Creasey to cut down his output. 'I try,' he replied soberly and sincerely, 'I do try to keep myself down to twelve books a year, but I can't do it, I find myself writing fourteen.' Creasey, the whole literary bulk of him, might I suppose count as a curiosity, and so certainly would the pseudonymous works of my friend the poet Ruthven Todd. In 1945 Todd wrote with more than Creaseyan speed ten detective stories in six months under the name of R. T. Campbell, to pay off his debts. But was it really ten, did he write ten books or twelve, were ten published or eight? *Death Is Not Particular*, *Death Is Our Physician*, *No Man Lives Forever* and *The Hungry Worms are Waiting* were announced, but did they appear, were they even written? The publisher, John Westhouse, is long since defunct, and the BM catalogue is unhelpful. When I asked Ruthven about this he said that the four books were 'probably written, but not published'. I like that 'probably' very much. The note of uncertainty is very much in the crime story's tradition. Anybody who has one of these books certainly possesses a rarity.

The London Library is a splendid place for the browser into ephemeral fiction published before World War II. After that date lack of space, of money, or of both has greatly limited their buying of novels, and particularly (as it seems to me) of crime stories. Picking books more or less idly off the shelves in my usual way, looking into them for five minutes and putting them back, I came across an extraordinary work called *Sudden Death: Or, My Lady the Wolf*, written by B. C. Skottowe and published in 1886. One of Carter's recommended guides told me that Britiffe Constable Skottowe was a historian of sorts, and also wrote a couple of textbooks. I discovered later that he was the fourth Baron Skottowe in the French peerage, the barony having been created by Louis XVIII.

Sudden Death, apparently his only work of fiction, is the first crime story with a transvestite theme. Its murderous hero/heroine is the dashing Gordon Leigh, who has beautiful eyes, small white hands, a slender figure, and altogether 'something irresistibly attractive, almost fascinating' about him. The narrator, like most men, feels 'strangely drawn to him from the very first'. In his feminine incarnation Gordon is the wicked Astarte, 'or Miladi Louve as they call her in Paris'. Her double identity is plain to the reader (perhaps I should say to the modern reader) long before it is revealed in the last chapter to the narrator. Gordon/Astarte confesses to three murders, and says that she dressed generally as a man 'because I liked it better and it seemed to come more natural to me.' As an unconscious case history—for there is no overt sexual ambiguity—the book is fascinating.

Curiosities abound in the field of detection. I am sure the London Library alone has more to offer than the things I have casually discovered, and if the amateur collector is not attracted by the thought of being surrounded by Creasey under his twenty-four different names, there are plenty of other possibilities. He might try collecting the books in the Haycraft-Queen 'definitive library' already mentioned, or those in my own selection of the Hundred Best Crime Stories. A more limited field might be the murder dossiers composed by Dennis Wheatley with the help of J. G. Links, in the thirties. These artefacts with their photographs of characters and scenes, and their real clues of hair, matches and pills enclosed in transparent envelopes, are undoubtedly curiosities. There are four

Criminal Matters

Wheatley/Links dossiers, and the fourth, *Herewith The Clues*, is a rarity because it was an almost complete flop. In America they were paid the compliment of imitation, again without repeating the success of the first dossier, *Murder Off Miami*, in Britain.

It would be possible to collect crime comic strips. A correspondent wrote to me recently, excited by the discovery of a 1934 strip called 'Secret Agent X-9', drawn by 'the then top comic strip artist Alex Raymond', and written by Dashiell Hammett. Making a collection of crime short stories published in book form might be a financially rewarding, as well as pleasurable, enterprise. According to Ellery Queen no more than 1,500 volumes of short stories had been published up to 1950, although this number has perhaps doubled in the last quarter century. They included such rarities as R. Austin Freeman's first book, *The Adventures of Romney Pringle* (written in collaboration with a medical friend and published under the name of Clifford Ashdown), of which only six copies are known to exist in the first edition, George R. Sims's *Dorcas Dene, Detective* (1897), and books that few people on this side of the Atlantic have seen, like Percival Pollard's *Lingo Dan* (1903), of which the author wrote that although he did not expect the success of Sherlock Holmes or Raffles, his book was 'at least one thing the others are not: American'. Few modern short story collections are rare, and most can be picked up cheaply.

My own fancy, which I have indulged only casually, would be for collecting parodies. There are not many good parodies of crime stories, perhaps because the form is so easily mocked. The best parodies, like Beerbohm's, have an edge of seriousness to them. 'Scruts' and 'Perkins and Mankind' are nearly Bennett and Wells on off days, Cyril Connolly's 'Told in Gath' gets close to Aldous Huxley; but in the crime story what is called parody is usually just pastiche. Ellery Queen says that 'The Stolen Cigar Case', a story written in 1902, is 'probably the best parody of Sherlock Holmes ever written'. Perhaps, but it is more likely to have been a pastiche, like the Queen collection of thirty-three pastiches and burlesques, *The Misadventures of Sherlock Holmes*, which was suppressed by the Doyle estate.

There have been attempted parodies of almost every great amateur detective, Poirot and Thorndyke, Father Brown, Nero Wolfe and Peter Wimsey, as well as of James M. Cain and Raymond Chandler, but Dwight Macdonald did not think any of them good enough for inclusion in his anthology of parodies. Even Connolly's much-

136

The Crime Collector's Cabinet of Curiosities

praised 'Bond Strikes Camp' seems to me too camp itself, too knowing, for total success. The best crime parody I know, a distinct achievement in the sense that it is carried on through a whole book, is *The John Riddell Murder Case*, by John Riddell.

Who was John Riddell? That question I *can* answer. He was an American humorist named Corey Ford, and the author parodied was S. S. Van Dine, whose languid, elegant, intolerably erudite aristocratic detective Philo Vance was then at the height of his fame. The pomposity of the Van Dine style is perfectly caught:

> The series of uncanny and apparently unrelated events which constitute this palimpsest of horror began on a mild, luxurious morning in early April, when I was breakfasting with Vance in the little roof-garden atop his apartment on East Thirty-eighth Street. Vance was a young social aristocrat who had acted several times in the past as a sort of *amicus curiae* for his friend John F.-X. Markham, the District Attorney; and for the past five years I had deserted the cause of literature to devote my pen exclusively to his sanguinary experience . . . On the fatal morning of which I write, Vance had come to breakfast rather late, having been occupied most of the previous night preparing a brief monograph on early Hittite stamp-collecting for *The Philatelist Quarterly*—a task which the bizarre events of that morning rudely interrupted.

And so is Vance's style of conversation, as he translates a comment in Walter Winchell's column which reads:

> 'John Riddell, local tome solon, will fold up in his verb-and-adjective garage at 9 this (Monday) yawning.'
> 'I beg of you, old dear', Vance protested with a quizzical smile. 'Middle-Broadway Winchell is a most difficult language. Coptic and Assyrian and Sanskrit are Abecedarian beside it. However, let me give you the literal translation of a few phrases.' He opened the dictionary and adjusted his monocle. ' "*Tome solon*, n: fiction referee; novel-and-poetry arbiter; current Mencken. *Verb-and-adjective garage*, n: book mausoleum; reading asylum. *Fold up*, v: to close down; bump off; go pfffft". . . Put into English, it reads: "John Riddell . . . book reviewer . . . will meet his death . . . in his library . . . at nine o'clock this morning." '

The tone is just right, an exaggeration that never becomes preposterous. The book's form is highly ingenious. Riddell's body is surrounded by the season's best sellers, which include works by Theodore Dreiser, Sherwood Anderson, Erich Maria Remarque and Beverley Nichols. Lively caricatural illustrations of them, as well as of Van Dine himself, are provided by Miguel Covarrubias. Each chapter carries on the story (more or less), and each is written as a parody of the best-selling writer, in the manner of Beverley Nichols, Anderson or Dreiser. The result is a devastating criticism of Philo Vance, and naturally of Van Dine.

One must avoid grandiose claims. Few people now read Van Dine, and fewer still recall some of the best sellers parodied, like Peggy Hopkins Joyce (who had a great success with her daring autobiography *Men, Marriage and Me*), the traveller Richard Halliburton, or the poet Joseph Moncure March, whose *The Wild Party* was causing a stir. *The John Riddell Murder Case* is amusing, adroit and occasionally witty, but it is also out-of-date. It does deserve, though, a place of honour, beside Charles Felix and Baron Skottowe, in the crime collector's cabinet of curiosities.

(1976)

Agatha and *Agatha*

Agatha by Kathleen Tynan
Ten Little Indians   by Agatha Christie
Destination Unknown by Agatha Christie
The Mousetrap and Other Plays by Agatha Christie

I

First, the life.

Agatha Mary Clarissa Miller was born in 1890, the third child of an idle well-to-do American father, and a mother who was markedly sensitive and aesthetically perceptive. Her upbringing was unusual only in the fact that she never went to school, but instead was taught at home by her mother and a succession of governesses. Not, of course, by Mr Miller, who lived like a super-typical leisured gentleman of the time. He left their house in the seaside resort of Torquay every morning, went to his club, was brought back in a cab for lunch, returned to the club for whist in the afternoon, and was home again to dress for dinner.

Such a way of things seemed natural to Agatha, who said afterwards that her parents' was one of the four completely successful marriages she had known. She was eleven years old when Fred Miller died after a series of heart attacks. Most of his money had vanished in ways that he never fully understood, but he survived to the end without having to do a stroke of work. Agatha considered him a totally agreeable man, and he provided a model for the many similar figures in her books. Another model must have been her much-loved brother Monty 'Puffing Billy' Miller, who said to his sister once that he owed lots of money to people all over the world and had led 'rather a wicked life . . . but, my word, kid, I've enjoyed myself.'

But Agatha's mother Clara was the formative influence on the girl who never had any formal lessons. She must have been, by her daughter's account, a remarkable woman: almost clairvoyant at times, fascinated by things mysterious and strange, a woman who saw life and people in colours 'always slightly at variance with reality', as Agatha put in her autobiography. These qualities were

139

passed on to the child, who evolved elaborate games which she played alone, observed the adults who were her chief companions, and accepted a code of manners and morals that stayed with her for life. Servants worked incredibly hard, but then of course they really liked it. They were professionals, and were to be treated always with the utmost courtesy. It was natural to be a true blue Conservative, a believer in the supremacy and benevolence of the British Empire, because although people with other opinions were known to exist, one never met them.

Certainly they were not to be found at the dances where Agatha always had a female companion, because 'you did not go to a dance alone with a young man.' The girl who in 1914 married dashing Archie Christie was exceptionally innocent and naive, and remained so all her life. She adored Archie, who became one of the first pilots in the Royal Flying Corps when World War I began, but it is doubtful if she ever understood him. Trains and houses were, as she mentions casually in her autobiography, always more real to her than people, and she was horrified and astonished when in 1932 an otherwise amiable German said that all his country's Jews must be exterminated. Could such things be? Apparently they could, but she never cared to write about them.

Her marriage to Archie Christie was effectively ended when, after twelve years, he told her that he was in love with another woman. There followed the single public event in the life of this notably private woman. She left home, abandoned her car, and disappeared. The police treated the case as one in which her violent death could not be ruled out, but after nine days she was found living in a hotel in the spa resort of Harrogate, using the name of her husband's mistress. There were immediate suggestions that the disappearance was a publicity stunt, and that her explanation of amnesia was inadequate. The facts point the other way. She was under immense stress at the time (her mother had just died, and Archie had told her that he wanted to marry his mistress), and she had no need of the publicity—in fact, her sales declined after the affair. The idea of a publicity stunt must also seem preposterous to anybody who knew her.

'Life in England was unbearable,' she said afterwards, and she left the country, travelled a good deal, divorced Archie after holding out for a year in the hope that he would change his mind and return to her, married the archaeologist Max Mallowan, and became more and more successful as the years passed. 'From that time, I suppose, dates my revulsion against the Press, my dislike of journalists and of crowds.' She became morbidly sensitive to any mention of the disappearance, and her natural shyness was accentuated to a point at which she refused to make any public appearance which would involve speaking even a few words. When she died in January 1976 she was certainly the most famous detective story writer in the world.

Kathleen Tynan's *Agatha* is a 'novel of mystery' about the disappearance. It is a complementary work to the film made with Vanessa Redgrave as Agatha, and reads very much like the book of the film script. The book is a contemptible production, ill-written, utterly vulgar in conception and execution, and a work that must cause extreme distress to Agatha Christie's family, who have unsuccessfully opposed both book and film.

According to her publishers, Kathleen Tynan 'became fascinated by the story several years ago' and now 'poses an ingenious imaginary solution to an authentic mystery'. Her solution suggests that Agatha knew what she was doing all the time, and that it was her intention to commit suicide. She goes to Harrogate because her husband's mistress Nancy Neele is there, and conceives a plan for her own electrocution at Nancy's hands, by inducing Nancy to turn on the current of a treatment called the Galvanic Bath. Nancy obligingly, and innocently, turns the switch, but Agatha is saved at the last moment by an admiring journalist who is half in love with her. 'Suicide's one thing, but to pin a murder on your husband's mistress . . .' he says reprovingly. Agatha denies this, but it is not easy to see just what her intention was, except that she says she wanted to get Nancy in her sights. 'I used to do that with the leopards when we went on safari.' In fact she never went on safari with Archie Christie.

The characterization is on the same plane as the rest of the book. Agatha uses phrases like 'I think we'll give it a miss', and 'Have you noticed that a woman, if she's naked, walks on tiptoe?', which are both out of period and out of character. The other figures are mere shades, from Archie, 'a handsome man of 37' who won 'countless medals in the War' (in fact three), to the extraordinarily dull journalists. It takes some exceptional quality to make journalists dull, but Kathleen Tynan has it. The story is a piece of total nonsense, but it may be taken seriously by readers and cinema-goers who will feel that the author can hardly have made it all up. Altogether, this is the kind of book of which we can hardly have too few. One is more than enough.

Criminal Matters

II

And then the books.

In World War I Agatha Christie worked in a hospital, and eventually found herself an assistant in the dispensary. There she conceived the idea of writing a detective story. Since she was surrounded by poisons, what more natural than that this should be a poisoning case? What kind of plot? 'The whole point of a *good* detective story was that it must be somebody obvious but at the same time, for some reason, you would then find that it was *not* obvious, that he could not possibly have done it.' That is just what happens in *The Mysterious Affair at Styles*. And the detective? She was devoted to Sherlock Holmes, but recognized that she must produce a character outside the Holmes pattern. She rejected the kind of detectives flourishing at the time—like the super-scientific Doctor Thorndyke and the blind Max Carrados, whose sense of smell was so strongly developed that he could discern the spirit gum in a false moustache across a room—feeling rightly that these were not her kind of people. Her man was meticulous, neat and orderly, faintly absurd. He was small, so she named him Hercules. His nationality was derived from a colony of Belgian refugees near her home. Somewhere the name Poirot appeared, the 's' vanished from Hercules, and—although he had to wait five years before he got into print—a Great Detective was born.

The people in Agatha Christie's books look back, more than those of any other modern writer, to the world of her childhood and adolescence, that time when social life was settled and people knew their places in it. Her love for Ashfield, the sizeable villa in Torquay where she grew up, is responsible for the many country houses in her books. She reflected late in her life that one of the things she would miss most, if she were a modern child, would be the absence of servants, and there are dozens of servants in her stories; butlers and housekeepers, housemaids and under-housemaids, gardeners and odd-job men. There were servants in all moderately comfortable households in England up to 1939 and World War II, but not on the Christie scale. She was looking back always to a style of behaviour that had ended in 1914. Her characters adjust to the clothes, and more or less to the speech of the period in which the books are set, but not to the occupations and behaviour. Old buffers retired from the Indian Army or Civil Service linger on after their time, and there is a sharp

142

division between gentlemen occupied in the professions and trades-men, with doctors and dentists somewhere in between. There must be very few cases of tradesmen proving to be guilty parties in Christie novels (I cannot think of one), although of course the case would have been different if they were gentlemen in disguise. Servants almost vanish, naturally enough, in books set in the 1950s and 1960s but still no Christie male ever has to light a fire or do the washing-up. Women may be employed as secretaries or typists, but they are rarely seen working.

All this is not said in denigration, but to emphasize how totally the novels are set in a fairy tale world, the world that a critic has wittily named Mayhem Parva. It is one that perfectly fits the artificiality of her wonderful plots. The plots also can be traced to her childhood, to the endless stories that the happy but lonely child told herself about imaginary kittens who were also human beings, and her invention of three railway systems in the garden, with the stations marked out on a sheet of cardboard. Behind the middle-class English lady, remote and shy, whose perfectly appropriate occupation seemed to be the pouring of tea from a silver jug into thin china cups on a green lawn, was somebody else, somebody perhaps not so nice but more interesting.

This other Agatha Christie knew a lot about poisons (the use of poison in one of her later books was copied in real life), was fascinated by murder and its methods, and held opinions about the need for capital punishment that are all the more startling because of the naivety with which they are expressed. She was capable of thinking out criminal plots of outlandish improbability but dazzling cleverness. Who can believe that the ten people in *Ten Little Indians,* all nursing some guilty secret, would have accepted that mysterious invitation to visit a small island? But such things happen in the world of Mayhem Parva, and once we have taken the leap and accepted them, we can applaud the masterly skill with which the plots are handled. As death after death occurs in *Ten Little Indians,* we understand that soon only two people will be left, so that one must be the murderer. But there is still a trick to be turned. The book's last sentences run: 'When the sea goes down, there will come from the mainland boats and men. And they will find ten dead bodies and an unsolved problem on Indian island.'

For a long while this extraordinary ingenuity in plotting worked against success in the cinema, which has never found it easy to give full value to such visual clues as the dropped cigarette end or the bloodstained thumbprint, let alone such arcane tricks as those Christie played with verbal misinterpretations or reverse images in mirrors. I have never seen René Clair's version of *Ten Little Indians* (1945), but if this justifies the high praise it has received it remains a lonely example among a mass of dismal B films. Even the best of these, *The Alphabet Murders*, bears such a distant relationship to the original book, *The ABC Murders*, that it shows how nearly impossible film directors found it to adapt Christie plots. Billy Wilder's *Witness For the Prosecution* (1957) was a successful film, but its stage origins were evident.

In 1974, however, *Murder on the Orient Express*, and in 1978 *Murder on the Nile*, showed that Christie plots could be transferred to the screen without alteration and with commercial success. And what plots they are. Raymond Chandler said of *Murder on the Orient Express* that its outrageousness would knock the keenest mind for a loop, and that 'only a halfwit would guess it.' The central element of the first death in *Murder on the Nile*, similarly, is so unlikely that only a lunatic would try to carry it out. Nevertheless there is a fascination in seeing it done, and in one of the film's flashbacks we *do* see murder done.

We accept and enjoy on the level of a fairy tale, something that Chandler didn't realize. Nothing could be more unlikely than the ritual gathering of suspects in both films, but we are concerned with fictions as strictly conventional as Restoration comedy, not with literal reality. It is entirely right that the paddle-steamer going up the Nile should be as luxurious as a pre-war Atlantic liner, that Jack Cardiff's photography should present an Egypt good enough to eat, without a hint of dirt and with only a few token swishings to indicate the presence of flies, that the characters should be stereotypes or caricatures.

Here Angela Lansbury is triumphant as an ageing hard-drinking nymphomaniac romantic novelist, and one can take no exception to the crooked lawyer (Arthur Kennedy) presenting papers for the heiress (Lois Chiles) to sign in a crowded lounge with people around, and Poirot listening at a corner table. That's the way people behave in Agatha Christie films. It follows that Albert Finney, the Poirot of *Orient Express*, is more successful than Peter Ustinov in *Nile*. Finney looks remarkably like the Poirot of the books, egg head cocked to one side, boot black hair, patent leather shoes. He looks, as his creator said he should, like a hairdresser. The performance is artificial, and succeeds because Poirot is a totally artificial creation. Ustinov looks simply like Ustinov plus neatly-curled moustaches. He goes through what one may call the Ustinov act in a relaxed manner, without making any particular concessions to Poirot. It is a naturalistic performance, out of place in such a film.

For all that, *Murder on the Nile* is a success. Dame Agatha said that *Murder on the Orient Express* was the first film made from her work that she had liked, but she would have enjoyed this one too. None of the films in which Miss Marple appeared gave her similar pleasure, and she is known to have been particularly indignant about the filmic transformation of St Mary Mead's implacable knitter that found her, in the person of Margaret Rutherford, doing the twist, fencing, and turning down a proposal of marriage from Robert Morley. The Miss Marple of the four Rutherford films was, certainly, a travesty of Agatha Christie's demure spinster detective. She felt no similar indignation about the Finney Poirot, because she was able to agree that Poirot was an artificial creation. She could not, however, accept the evident truth that a country spinster of seventy-odd who solved crimes while living in an English village of a kind that was out-of-date before World War II was equally artificial. It would have been difficult for any actress to have produced a Miss Marple satisfactory to her creator.

Nor would she have accepted the fact that the Miss Marple stories, though some are ingeniously turned, will always seem to most addicts inferior to the best Poirot tales. Good though *The 4.50 From Paddington*, *A Caribbean Mystery* and one or two other puzzles are, they are not quite of the same order as *The Murder of Roger Ackroyd* and *The ABC Murders*. And Miss Marple, as Agatha Christie reluctantly recognized, was never more than a second string to Poirot. We are assured that she was not intended as an idealized picture of her creator, but she was viewed with a distinctly sentimental eye. Poirot is saved from absurdity by the fact that Agatha Christie regarded him as a comic character from the start.

III

And last, the puzzle.

Agatha Christie's success has not been checked by death. It is not

Criminal Matters

merely that *The Mousetrap* has been running in London for a record twenty-six years, nor that she has been outsold only by the Bible and Shakespeare. Her books have lasted in a literal sense. No more than a handful of other crime stories published in 1920 or earlier are in print today, but *The Mysterious Affair at Styles* still sells edition after edition. What is it that has made the books last?

Certainly not the quality of the writing, which is at best no more than lively, and at worst as bad as that in the opening sentences of *Destination Unknown*, a work of the fifties:

> The man behind the desk moved a heavy glass paper-weight four inches to the right. His face was not so much thoughtful or abstracted as expressionless. He had the pale complexion that comes from living most of the day in artificial light. This man, you felt, was an indoor man. A man of desks and files.

The tautology of this, and its general ineptness, does not need demonstrating.

Yet if Agatha Christie was an indifferent writer, she was a most intelligent craftsman, who had considerable sensibility about the form in which she worked. Ira Levin, in an introduction to eight of her plays, points out that she adapted three plays from novels that included Poirot, but eliminated him for stage purposes. This was partly because she felt a distaste for Poirot as she grew older, but partly also because she rightly regarded him as a drag on the dramatic action. In one play she changed the murderer, and in *Ten Little Indians* altered the ending to let two characters survive. *Witness for the Prosecution*, which she adapted from a short story, has at its heart an old but brilliantly used stage trick. To see any of the plays is to realize both that dialogue and settings are period in the fairy tale sense already mentioned, and also that the mystery in them is devised and concealed with great skill.

This is true also of the best books, most of them written in the 1930s and '40s. The construction of the puzzle in them is done with unexampled skill. A Christie initiation might begin with *The Murder of Roger Ackroyd* (1926), and then go on to *The ABC Murders* (1935), *Peril at End House* (1932), and of course *Ten Little Indians*. Thrillers, like *Destination Unknown*, should be avoided. Agatha Christie was a mistress only of puzzles pure and complex.

Other bad writers have been skilful craftsmen without lasting like Agatha Christie. Perhaps the nearest one can get to explaining the puzzle of her enduring popularity is to suggest that although the detective story is ephemeral, the riddle's attraction is lasting. There are those who find the detective story's origins in the Apocrypha, the story of Oedipus or Voltaire's *Zadig*, but these are scholastic arguments. What is certainly true is that human beings have a passion equally for concealment and revelation. Agatha Christie's stories appeal strongly to very many people because they fulfil this passion in the world of the fairy tale, a world only nominally linked to reality.

(1978)

A View of Simenon

The Family Lie, The Girl with the Squint, Maigret's Pipe, Maigret and the Hotel Majestic and *The Iron Staircase* by Georges Simenon

His life is obsessional, far beyond that of most people or most writers. Everything is arranged in advance and happens on time. He is bothered by a pencil out of place in his study, looks for the known reflection of light in a particular place on a piece of furniture, and is disturbed if it has moved. And he withdraws from the outside world into his house and his family, just as within the house he withdraws into his study. His wife D, the three children living at home, what more does one want? The nurse, maids, secretaries in the house are necessary, but they are also an irritant if they intrude at the wrong times. The children are loved, but still he is disturbed 'if they burst in when I'm alone with my wife . . . for instance when we're having coffee after lunch'. Food is taken at exact hours, give or take five minutes. D, his wife, has her occupations too, or perhaps they should be called her duties. 'The least slip-up, the least whim, spoils everybody's schedule.'

This obsessive need for organization extends to the work. The 'Do Not Disturb' signs, the four dozen newly-sharpened pencils, pad of yellowish paper, envelope giving the names, ages and addresses of characters, these are all necessary preliminaries to beginning a book. Another disagreeable necessity is physical sickness, expressive of his deep anxiety about the work to be undertaken. Then eight or ten days of total absorption in the book until it is done. Or perhaps no luck. 'A little shame, I admit, at D, the children, the staff, seeing me come out of my office before time.'

With the book finished, celebration. An urgent, and again obviously obsessional, need for sex. After completing one book he goes to a night club with D, and there takes the telephone numbers of four performers. The need for them is not emotional, but 'a necessary hygienic measure' purging those 'dreams and vague urges . . . which I believe poison most marriages'. Emotion is reserved for D, this routine sex is 'a kind of inoculation'. It is indeed only a faint echo of the sexual activity of his youth when he was at times 'like a dog in rut'.

148

A View of Simenon

This need is, he thinks, perhaps not for the mere act of sex, it is part of a desire to 'penetrate humanity' . . .

This account of Georges Simenon's activities when he was still writing novels (he has now given up fiction, but dictates book after book of journals) comes from *When I Was Old*, the notebooks he kept between 1960 and 1962. He was nearing sixty, and suffering traumatic fears and doubts which left him after this period. The novel *Pedigree*, written twenty years earlier, is generally taken to reflect the reality of Simenon's early life, although he has said himself that it may be much too literary, and also that it is not really accurate. *Pedigree* is an essay in concealment rather than in revelation and is, perhaps for that reason, a dullish book.

When I Was Old, on the other hand, is disturbingly honest. Nobody reading these journals could doubt Simenon's love for his wife and children, but who could be really happy living in that thirty-six-room château outside Lausanne, with every word and action fitted to Simenon's needs? It is not surprising that for much of this time D is suffering from some mysterious mental illness. Simenon tries to help her, and notes with regret that what he does often has an opposite effect. 'What did I say to provoke a painful crisis? I don't know at all . . . There she is, depressed, beaten, and anything I say hurts or wounds her.' He plays with his children, is fascinated by their development as individuals and has no desire to own them, yet it is inevitable that his activities should shape their lives.

Shape and, one must add, damage. Nearly a decade after keeping these journals, Simenon was living in relative isolation with his twelve-year-old son—plus, it is true, a staff of twelve including two private secretaries. D, and their eighteen-year-old daughter, were at this time both in a psychiatric hospital, and for almost a year Simenon was not allowed to see his daughter. During a remarkable television interview in 1971 with a psychiatrist and a forensic pathologist, Simenon talked about these things and expressed his sorrow for what had happened without feeling any responsibility for it. He discussed himself impartially, playing the roles of both doctor and patient. At the end of the interview he took up a question by the pathologist about whether he liked Van Gogh, and answered it with his customary candour:

I see maybe they make a kind of comparison with him because van Gogh was completely unconscious of what he was doing and it is

149

the same with me, we are about the same. Maybe I am not completely crazy, but I am a psychopath, and they know it I am sure.

One cannot understand Simenon's work without considering his personality. In one sense it is true to say that what we are is what we do, but in another sense what we are is what we desire, and often Simenon's desires seem the opposite of what he has done. His life is full of self-imposed restrictions but what he wants, as he told the television interviewers, is the total liberty of a man without possessions, typically a tramp sleeping under a bridge in Paris. Such a tramp would be a truly superior man. 'It's superiority not to need all those gadgets, a house, a woman, anything—you just sleep on the stones, eat some old bread with a piece of sausage and a bottle of wine. I consider that is superiority.' It is easy enough to point out that Simenon's life in practical terms shows a passion for acquisition—of boats, houses, women—but his unique quality as a writer springs from the intensity with which he is able to imagine quite different existences.

He has said more than once that for the time during which he is working on a novel (which may be less than a week, and is rarely more than a month) he becomes the central character, so that it is not through his intelligence that this character goes down on the page, but by his instinctive understanding of what such a person would say and do. His hard novels—that is, those that do not concern Maigret—fall into two main groups. In the first a few characters are pressed into close contact with each other like people in a crowded train. The claustrophobic contact breeds conflict, and the conflict ends in violence. In the second group of stories there is a central figure who tries to fulfil that desire of Simenon's to start out all over again, something expressed in his own life only by gestures like getting rid of all his furniture every time he moves. 'To start one's life over each time from scratch!'—that illusion of the tramp's freedom is used in these fictions to generate stories of remarkable power.

A perfect example of this kind of story is *The Man Who Watched The Trains Go By* (*L'homme qui regardait passer les trains* of 1938) in which Kees Popinga, managing clerk to the leading ship's chandler in Groningen, discovers suddenly that he is ruined. He realizes that the whole pattern of his life is a fraud, including the devotion he has given to the loving family by whom he is in fact bored. Inspired by the defalcating boss of his firm, who is about to stage a fake suicide and disappear, Popinga decides to start again from scratch, and in the course of doing so becomes a multiple murderer. He ends in a lunatic asylum, visited occasionally by his wife, who consults him just as in the old days about family matters. He starts to write an article headed 'The Truth About the Kees Popinga Case', but gets no further than that heading. As he says to the doctor, 'Really, there isn't any truth about it, is there?' Popinga has no responsibility for the things that have happened, he is the victim-villain of his destiny. This theme is elaborated in many books—for instance in *Monsieur Monde Vanishes* (*La Fuite de Monsieur Monde* of 1946) and *Act of Passion* (*Lettre à mon juge* of 1947) in which a murderer writes a book-long letter to his judge before committing suicide, maintaining that 'we are almost identical men.'

Three recently published books emphasize the other theme, of emotional claustrophobia. *The Iron Staircase* (*L'escalier de fer* of 1953) is about a husband who believes that his wife is poisoning him so that she can marry a lover, and faces the truth he has never admitted, that she poisoned her previous husband to marry him. He sets out to kill the lover, but ends by shooting himself. *The Girl with a Squint* (*Marie qui louche*) belongs to the same period. Two girls come to Paris from the provinces. Sexy, calculating Sylvie tries to use men to make a fortune, her friend the squinting Marie remains wretchedly poor. Sylvie uses her friend to destroy a will that would prevent her getting an inheritance, but finds herself linked indissolubly to the other woman afterwards. In *The Family Lie* (*Malempin* of 1940) a doctor watching over his young son who is critically ill, meditates on his own childhood and forces himself to admit and accept the fact that his parents murdered an uncle who was said at the time to have disappeared.

For Simenon, close emotional contact almost always implies physical expression—the image of the crowded train with bodies rubbing against each other is a fitting one. The urgent sexuality of the wife in *The Iron Staircase* and of the narrator's aunt in *The Family Lie* are potent elements in the crimes, and although the relationship of Sylvie and Marie is never physical, its sexual nature is made plain.

One is inclined to call these groups of books characteristic, yet nothing in Simenon can truly be called that because his range is so wide. Many stories exploit different themes—*The Little Saint* (*Le Petit Saint* of 1965), for instance, of which the author said that it

151

expressed his basic optimism and pleasure in life, and that 'if I were allowed to keep only one of all my novels, I would choose this one,' or the universally admired *The Stain on the Snow* (*La Neige etait sale* of 1948). Yet even such books, which appear to be out of the main stream of Simenon's writing, suggest his deep interest in extremes of conduct. The little saint is a delicate freak, brought up in the violent world of working-class Paris before World War I. He accepts willingly all the insults and rebuffs showered on him, and fulfils his dream of becoming a successful painter. Frank, in *The Stain on the Snow*, becomes a pimp and murderer from disgust with his own background in prostitution and crime—nothing less than some equivalent extreme of conduct will do, and such a life is also perhaps his destiny.

Some generalizations can be made about these hundred-odd hard novels. Simenon is Belgian by birth but French in sympathies, and in its plotting his work belongs to a sensational French tradition that takes improbabilities for granted. In *The Girl with a Squint* the crucial event is Marie's destruction of the will. How did she manage to steal this will under the noses of the family; did the will exist at all? Because Simenon is interested only in the relationship between Sylvie and Marie, the question is cursorily dismissed. Another recent book, *The Hatter's Phantom* of 1949, asks us to accept the preposterous idea of a mass murderer who has killed his wife while maintaining the fiction that she is still alive, and so has to murder all the old school friends who are coming to see her on Christmas Eve.

Yet if the plots are often incredible, we always believe in the characters. Simenon writes with the same recording angel's understanding and impersonal sympathy about all sorts of professional men (especially doctors and lawyers), petty bourgeois shopkeepers, crooks and workmen, less often and less well about the upper classes in society. The range of his women characters is equally wide, but he shows them less sympathy than the men. They are often destroyers (like Louise in *The Iron Staircase* or the delinquent who wrecks the life of a successful lawyer in *In Case of Emergency*), sometimes victims (like the girl suicide in *Teddy Bear*) or earth-mother figures like Gabrielle in *The Little Saint*.

The details of these lives are marvellously convincing. One of Simenon's greatest gifts is for using the experience of his first forty years—childhood in Liège, early reporting jobs and travels on his own account and for periodicals—and transporting it to different scenes and periods. The creation of the stationer's shop in *The Iron Staircase*, with Louise down in the shop, Etienne in bed, and the iron staircase linking shop and bedroom, perfectly evokes an atmosphere in which Etienne is at the mercy of the poisoner. He seems all the more a victim because the fairground just opposite the bedroom window offers the promise of gaiety and freedom. The opening chapter of *The Girl with a Squint* conveys superbly the petty restrictions and sly sensualities of the provincial boarding-house where Sylvie and Marie share a room and a bed. Simenon gives us the appearance and atmosphere of places better than any other living novelist. It is, very often, first of all through the places that we know his people.

To say this is not to endorse his admirers' view that Simenon is a great novelist, let alone one with the amplitude of Balzac. His stories look inward, not outward. Where Balzac and Zola stretch out to comprehend their society, Simenon compresses society into the shapes of his obsessions. His stories gain something through the speed and intensity of their production, but there are losses too. The central character seems often not to be fully visualized, but to be a figure invented for the expression of problems occupying his creator. One remembers Simenon's description of himself as a psychopath. When asked whether he cured himself through writing, he agreed that this was so.

His almost total lack of interest in history and politics limits the subject matter of the stories, and there are other limitations. 'Suppress all the literature and it will work,' Colette told the young Simenon, and he took the advice very literally, trying 'to simplify, to suppress, to make my style as neutral as possible'. Purple passages have been eliminated, but the result is not a prose that has the Orwellian clarity of a window pane. Simenon's neutrality gives us a prose that has no vices, but few virtues. At times he offers us information with the blankness of a computer. The writer of the hard novels is the most extraordinary literary phenomenon of the century, but that is not the same thing as being a great novelist.

And so to Maigret. Not before time, it may be thought, but this relegation of the Maigret stories to a secondary position among his works would meet the author's approval. Maigret is a kind of Old Man of the Sea that Simenon cannot shake off, as Conan Doyle was unable to get rid of Sherlock Holmes. The success of the Maigret stories compared with the hard novels can be summed up in the fact that almost all of the outstandingly successful Penguin Omnibus volumes contain two Maigrets and one hard novel. This does not please Simenon, and *When I Was Old* contains several slighting references to the detective. He is 'an accident to whom I attached little importance'. The books are 'semi-potboilers', and they compare with his 'difficult books' as 'light sex' compares to physical love with a beloved person. 'There is no morality or immorality in Maigret', he said to his television interrogators with a trace of irritation. 'He is a functionnaire who does what he has to do.' Yet Simenon himself has emphasized the similarity between the two kinds of book by introducing some characters—Lucas and Lognon are two—into both Maigret and hard novels.

The Maigrets recently published are certainly not very good. Simenon does not shine as a short story writer, and *Maigret's Pipe* is a distinctly inferior collection. The length at which the books are written is perfect for his gift of compressing into a novella material that most writers would put into a work of double the length. His short stories read rather like film outlines awaiting expansion. *Maigret and the Hotel Majestic* (*Les Caves du Majestic* of 1942) is a good deal better, particularly where it deals with the workings of the hotel, but if the Maigrets are minor Simenon, this is minor Maigret.

These books, however, are not typical of the Maigret canon. The Maigret tales have changed a good deal more than the hard novels over the years. Simenon is not in the ordinary sense of the words a detective story writer at all. He has no interest in the apparatus of clues, deductions, scientific examination of tyre marks or blood-stained hammers. Maigret, as he often says, has no method but operates by instinct. In the half dozen Maigrets that launched the Chief Inspector, as he then was, on the world in 1931, Simenon accepted the need to make some concessions to convention. An example is *The Madman of Bergerac* (*Le Fou de Bergerac*) of the following year, when Maigret knows that a murderer must have visited his hotel room because he has dropped a vital railway ticket in the passage outside the door. Several of the early Maigrets have sensational plots in the tradition of Gaboriau, du Boisgobey and Gaston Leroux, and Maigret himself sometimes plays an active role for which he is really not suited.

After this flood of early books, Maigret was put into cold storage for several years. He emerged again in 1942 in more relaxed and coherent works, as the pipe-smoking philosopher interpreted by Jean Gabin and—of all unlikely figures—Charles Laughton in the cinema, and by Rupert Davies in the remarkably successful and sympathetic television series. Maigret reached his peak during the late forties and early fifties. The later stories tend to find him drinking in bars, considering Madame Maigret's cassoulet, or philosophizing at the expense of the story.

If we say that the Maigret tales are second-class Simenon compared to the best of the hard novels, a qualification must be made: Maigret himself is the most fully realized character in the whole *oeuvre*. He has developed greatly, from the casually conceived figure equipped with appropriate detectival properties like his pipes and heavy overcoat, to a man fully and lovingly known. He is based on Simenon's beloved father, as the many overbearing power-hungry women in the stories derive from his mother.

We know about Maigret in a factual way through *Maigret's Memoirs* of 1950, which introduce an unusual element of humour in the young man's courtship of Louise Léonard, but we also know his mind. Maigret is in many ways the ideal French bourgeois, although his father was bailiff at a château in the Auvergne, and even though he is called in one story a proletarian through and through. His love of food, drink and comfort, the cushioned life provided for him at home by Madame Maigret, his lack of interest in politics, his commonsensible reactions to sex, poverty, crime — in all of these things Maigret is the average sensual man, gifted with an intuitive understanding of criminals' feelings and attitudes that makes him an uncommon detective. It is an irony he would appreciate that a writer so little interested in detective stories should have created the archetypal fictional detective of the twentieth century.

(1977)

Raymond Chandler:
An Aesthete Discovers the Pulps

Fairyland is Everyman's dream of perfection, and changes, dream-like, with the mood of the dreamer. For one it is a scene of virgin, summery Nature undefiled by even the necessary works of man . . . For another it is a champaign, dotted with fine castles, in which live sweet ladies clad in silk, spinning, and singing as they spin, and noble knights who do courteous battle with each other in forest glades; or a region of uncanny magic, haunting music, elves and charmed airs and waters.

That is Raymond Chandler writing in 1912 for *The Academy*.

The man in the powder-blue suit—which wasn't powder-blue under the lights of the Club Bolivar—was tall, with wide-set grey eyes, a thin nose, a jaw of stone. He had a rather sensitive mouth. His hair was crisp and black, ever so faintly touched with grey, as by an almost diffident hand. His clothes fitted him as though they had a soul of their own, not just a doubtful past. His name happened to be Mallory.

That is the opening paragraph of Raymond Chandler's first story for the pulps, 'Blackmailers Don't Shoot', which appeared in *Black Mask*, December 1933.

Between the two pieces lay twenty-one years in time and the Atlantic in distance, but they had a common emotional basis. The Chandler who wrote for the pulps was still a man who dreamed of fairyland. As I have said elsewhere it is emblematically right that in this first story the detective should be named Mallory, echoing the *Morte d'Arthur*. His carapace of iron (only iron could survive those frequent assaults with cosh and blackjack) conceals a quivering core, and whether his name is Mallory, Carmady, Dalmas or Philip Marlowe, he is truly a knight errant. Chandler's stories about criminals and a detective carried over into an alien field the literary aestheticism of his youth.

Raymond Chandler became a writer for the pulp magazines

Raymond Chandler: An Aesthete Discovers the Pulps

because he was broke, not because he wanted to write for the pulps. 'Realism and Fairyland' was one of the last pieces he published in England before he gave up the hope of making a literary living there, and he printed nothing in America until 1933. In between he had a variety of jobs, lived with his mother, married a woman eighteen years older than himself as soon as his mother died (his wife Cissy knocked ten years off her age for the marriage register), became vice-president of a group of oil companies, drank hard, had affairs, was eventually sacked. At the age of 44 he had no money and no prospects. At this point he listed himself as a writer in the Los Angeles directory, and began to study the pulp magazines. It struck him, as he said, that he might get paid while he was learning.

He was not likely, as he must have known, to get paid very much. The pulp magazines, so called because they were printed on wood pulp, began in the nineteenth century with the publication of the Nick Carter stories. The *Nick Carter Weekly* first appeared in 1891 and, like Sexton Blake in England, was the product of multiple authors. The chief of them, the bearded Frederic Dey (that is, Frederick Marmaduke Van Rensselaer Day) produced a 25,000 word story every week for years, and did not get rich. In 1929 he shot himself in a cheap New York hotel. Nick Carter's fame endured, and indeed endures, so that when *Detective Story Magazine* began publication in 1915 its editor was named as Nicholas Carter. *Black Mask*, in which most of Chandler's early stories appeared, was founded in 1920 by H. L. Mencken and George Jean Nathan, but did not take on its true character until Captain Joseph Shaw became editor in 1926. During the decade of Shaw's reign the magazine published stories that moved sharply away from the conventional detective story aspect of earlier pulp fiction (Edgar Wallace was one of the stars of *Detective Story Magazine*) to reflect the violence of American society and the vivid colloquialisms of American speech.

Chandler's approach, his background and his age made him a very unusual figure among the pulp writers. Most of them were hacks, although they would have called themselves professionals. They were hard-working, sometimes hard-drinking men who wrote fast and wrote for the money. To make a fair living they had to write a great deal, for the basic rate of one cent a word meant that you had to write a million words to make $10,000 a year. Many of them, like Erle Stanley Gardner, used several names, and some wrote romances and Westerns as well as crime stories. Such a literary netherworld exists in

Criminal Matters

England now, although because there are no magazines its inhabitants write books, turning out ten or a dozen a year to make a reasonable living. In America during the Depression years similar writers worked mostly for the pulp magazines. Few of them had the specialized knowledge of Dashiell Hammett, who had been a Pinkerton agent, but most had familiarized themselves with some aspects of the law and crime, and knew a good deal about firearms. Many of them appeared to write with an ink-dipped cosh rather than a pen.

Chandler resembled them very little. He had read only three or four detective stories when he set out to make a living in the field, and he learned the technique of the crime story in the spirit of a young artist copying masters in the Louvre. He read everything he could find, in particular Hammett, but also Gardner and other pulp writers. He made a detailed synopsis of a Gardner story, rewrote it, compared the result with the original, rewrote it again, and then apparently threw it away. He took what he was doing seriously, because if he had not done so he could not have justified doing it. He was writing for *Black Mask* and *Dime Detective Magazine*, and he knew that what he did was hack work, but he gave to this hack work the care he had devoted to the literary pieces produced for English magazines long ago.

He knew little about the technical aspects of crime, and never bothered to learn, relying instead on textbooks. From the beginning he sensed that for a writer like himself such things were not important, and that any success he won would come through sharpness of language and observation rather than through expert knowledge. In a battling introduction to a collection of his short stories published in 1950, when he had become famous, he defended the pulp crime story by saying that 'even at its most mannered and artificial [it] made most of the fiction of the time taste like a cup of lukewarm consommé at a spinsterish tea-room.' He said also that he wished the stories being republished were better, but that the distinction of the imprint meant that he need not be sickeningly humble, even though 'I have never been able to take myself with that enormous earnestness which is one of the trying characteristics of the craft.' In fact he took himself very seriously indeed, and strongly resented adverse criticism from others, although he was prepared to make it himself. He also made claims for the form in which he was working that must seem over-stated. 'The aim is not essentially different from the aim of Greek tragedy, but we are dealing with a

Raymond Chandler: An Aesthete Discovers the Pulps

public that is semi-literate and we have to make an art of language they can understand.' The aim may be similar but the results, as he should have seen, are so different that the comparison is absurd.

Chandler remained by temperament a romantic aesthete. His feebly literary early essays and poems are full of either/ors like sciences and poetry, romance and realism. Are we to be saved 'by the science or by the poetry of life'? That, he said, 'is the typical question of the age', and he came down on the side of poetry as opposed to science and of romance against realism. Or rather, of realism seen romantically, so that 'any man who has walked down a commonplace city street at twilight, just as the lamps are lit' would see that a true view of it must be idealistic, for it would 'exalt the sordid to a vision of magic, and create pure beauty out of plaster and vile dust'. The phrases echo Chesterton, and also look forward to the famous peroration of 'The Simple Art of Murder' which runs: 'Down these mean streets a man must go . . .' It was Chandler's strength, and his weakness, that he brought this basically sentimental aestheticism to the crime stories, so that they had increasingly to be about a romantic hero whose activities gave the novels at least 'a quality of redemption' so that he could think of them as art. That was the weakness. The strength lay in the fact that by treating seriously everything he did Chandler achieved even in his early stories for the pulps more than his fellow practitioners.

To talk about Chandler as a romantic aesthete may make him sound like an intellectual, but in fact he disliked intellectuals and the magazines for which they wrote. In the few meetings I had with him near the end of his life, it was possible to sense his distrust. Was this another of those damned critics trying to get at him? He was fond of using big words like art and redemption, but shied away from such things when they moved from the general to the particular. He could be deeply imperceptive and philistine. 'I read these profound discussions, say in the *Partisan Review*, about art, what is it, literature, what is it, and the good life and liberalism and what is the definitive position of Rilke or Kafka, and the scrap about Ezra Pound getting the Bollingen award, and it all seems to meaningless to me. Who cares?' he wrote to his English publisher Hamish Hamilton. He got on well with fellow pulp writers, partly because they regarded him, as one of them put it, as 'a professorial type, more of an intellectual than most of the other pulp writers I knew'. He was the oldest of them, a year older than Gardner and six years older than

159

Hammett. They respected him, and so made him comparatively at ease. In general he avoided places and people through which he might be involved in literary discussion, preferring to talk to garage men and postal clerks. Other writers, and his opinions of them, he preferred to put on paper.

Second only to romantic aestheticism in giving his work its colour and character was his loneliness. He seems to have been from youth a shy person who found it hard to make friends, and this shyness was accentuated by his marriage to a woman so much older than himself. In these years also they were poor. For a decade Chandler scraped a living, writing for the pulps and publishing crime novels that received critical praise but were far from being best sellers. They moved from place to place, had few friends, went out little. Out of this loneliness, now and later, Chandler created his best work. When he began to write for films and became involved in the social life of the studios he wrote little, and that little was usually not very good. Shut up in an apartment, with Cissy in the next room and with 'life' making no demands, he sparkled on paper.

The third important element in Chandler's writing was its Anglo-American character. He had been brought up in England, he longed to return (and on the whole was not disappointed when he came), and the delighted disgust with which he saw California came partly from the contrast between its brash newness and English good taste. When he read Max Beerbohm he felt that he too belonged to an age of grace and taste from which he had been exiled. 'So I wrote for *Black Mask*. What a wry joke.' No doubt he would have felt hopelessly out of place in an age of grace (if such an age ever existed) and would have written ironically about it, but that is not the point. The flavour of his stories is individual partly because, even though, as he said, all the pulp writers used the same idiom, his is filtered through an English lens.

The very intelligent notes on English and American style which he put down in his notebook end with a striking observation of differences in verbal tone:

The tone quality of English speech is usually overlooked. This tone quality is infinitely variable and contributes infinite meaning. The American voice is flat, toneless and tiresome. The English tone quality makes a thinner vocabulary and a more formalized use of language capable of infinite meanings. Its tones are of course read into written speech by association. This, of course, makes good

Raymond Chandler: An Aesthete Discovers the Pulps

English a class language, and that is its fatal defect. The English writer is a gentleman (or not a gentleman) first and a writer second.

Most of these distinctions seem to me very good ones, but in any case they were important to Chandler. Once he began to write, he became absorbed in the verbal problems involved, in particular the problem of giving an English variability to the 'flat, toneless and tiresome' pattern of American speech. The best of his work is witness to his triumphant success.

Chandler was not a prolific writer. He wrote in all twenty stories for the pulps, at the rate of two, three or four a year. It is true that almost all of them were much longer than the usual story, and that they might almost be called short novels, but even so the output was small. It has been said already that he was poor in the decade after he started to write crime stories. His average yearly earnings during the late 1930s and early 1940s were between one and two thousand dollars. In truth, there was no way of making a reasonable living by writing for the pulps unless you published ten or twelve stories a year. It is a mark of Chandler's integrity as a writer that he refused to do this, or was incapable of doing it, as later he refused to do what he was told in Hollywood when he was employed there at a salary gloriously or ludicrously large compared with his earnings at the time from stories and novels.

About the pulp stories considered as stories there is little to say except that they are not very good. 'Everybody imitates in the beginning,' as Chandler said himself, and the writer he imitated most was Hammett. The young blond gunman in 'Blackmailers Don't Shoot' is obviously derived from Wilmer in *The Maltese Falcon*, the sadistic thug in 'Pick-Up on Noon Street' is based on Jeff in *The Glass Key*, and there are other echoes. Standard scenes and characters appear in most of the stories. There will be at least one night-club scene, a variety of villains will appear in every story, and some of them will be gangsters or gamblers who own the night clubs. The hard men who hit the detective over the head will be exceptionally stupid, and the gangsters will be only just a little smarter beneath their veneer of sophistication. The police will be tough, cynical, and occasionally corrupt. There will be a lot of shooting, with an Elizabethan litter of corpses piled up by the end. At the heart of the trouble there will be a girl, and she is almost never to be trusted, although she may have 'the sort of skin an old rake dreams of' (Rhonda Farr in 'Blackmailers

161

Criminal Matters

Don't Shoot') or hair that is 'like a bush fire at night' (Beulah in 'Try the Girl') or even hair that 'seemed to gather all the light there was and make a soft halo around her coldly beautiful face' (Belle Marr in 'Spanish Blood'). The women in the short stories are not as deadly as they become in the novels, but they are dangerous enough.

These standard properties are used in a standard way. The detective himself is not much more than a man whose head is harder and whose gun is faster than his rivals'. This is true of Marlowe, who appeared first in 1934, as much as of Mallory or Carmady. But the basic defect of the stories is that the length to which they were written did not fit Chandler's talent. The weakness of his plotting is more apparent in the stories than in the novels. The demand of the pulps, he said later, was for constant action, and if you stopped to think you were lost. 'When in doubt, have a man come through a door with a gun in his hand.' The novels gave more space for the development of situations and the creation of an environment. One of Chandler's great merits was his capacity to fix a scene memorably. He sometimes did this in a phrase, but he could do it even better in a paragraph or a page. The stories did not give him time to create anything of this kind. Everything that did not carry forward the action was excised by editors.

If we read these stories today it is for occasional flashes of observation that got by the blue pencil, and for the use of language. Chandler's ear for the rhythms of speech was good from the beginning, but it developed with astonishing speed. The stories written in the later 1930s, like 'Killer in the Rain', 'The Curtain', 'Try the Girl' and 'Mandarin's Jade' are often as well written as the novels, where the early tales are full of clichés. 'Smart-Aleck Kill' (1934) has eyes that get small and tight, eyes with hot lights in them, eyes that show sharp lights of pain. There are cold smiles playing around the corners of mouths, and mirthless laughter. But within a very few years these have almost all disappeared, and we recognize the sharp cleverness of the novels when we are told that the garage of a modernistic new house is 'as easy to drive into as an olive bottle' or that a smart car in a dingy neighbourhood 'sticks out like spats at an Iowa picnic'.

It was these later and better stories that Chandler cannibalized, to use his own word, to make three of the novels. This was an extraordinary process. Other writers have incorporated early material in a later work, but nobody else has done it in quite this way.

162

Raymond Chandler: An Aesthete Discovers the Pulps

Most writers who adapt their earlier work take from it a particular theme or character and jettison the rest. Chandler, however, carved out great chunks of the stories, expanded them, and fitted them into an enlarged plot. Where gaps existed, like spaces in a jigsaw, he made pieces to fit them. It meant, as Philip Durham has said, adapting, fusing and adding characters, blending themes from different stories, combining plots. Much of his first novel, *The Big Sleep*, was taken from two stories, 'Killer in the Rain' and 'The Curtain', plus fragments from two other stories. About a quarter of the book was new material, but the passages from the two principal stories used were much enlarged. There could be no better proof of the limitation Chandler felt in being forced to work within the pulp magazine formula.

Almost all of the enlargements were improvement. They added details of description, vital touches of characterization, or they were simply more elegantly or wittily phrased. They also helped to make the stories more coherent. In 'The Curtain' the detective does not call on General Winslow in his orchid house until chapter three. In the novel Chandler, realizing that this was a splendid starting point, begins with it. (He economically kept chapter one for use years later in *The Long Goodbye*.) The difference in the effectiveness of the two scenes is startling. What was no more than adequate in the story has become memorable in the novel, with the old half-dead General emerging as a genuinely pathetic figure. One would need a variorum text to show exactly how Chandler did it, but here are one or two significant changes. The General is telling Marlowe to take off his coat in the steaming hot orchid house. In 'The Curtain' he says:

'Take your coat off, sir. Dud always did. Orchids require heat, Mr Carmady—like rich old men.'

In *The Big Sleep* this becomes:

'You may take your coat off, sir. It's too hot in here for a man with blood in his veins.'

It is the last sentence that gives real flavour to the bit of dialogue, telling us more about the General than would haf a dozen descriptive phrases. And, freed from the blue pencil, Chandler let his love of simile and metaphor run free. The smell of the orchids is not just like boiling alcohol as it was in the story, but like boiling alcohol under a blanket. In the story the General just watches the detective drink, but now 'The old man licked his lips watching me, over and over again, like an undertaker dry-washing his hands.' These are samples from thirty similes or metaphors brought into the scene. Is some of it a little too much? That is obviously partly a matter of taste, but the exuberance of it, the sense of a man using his own talent in his own way for the first time, cannot be anything but enjoyable. This 50-year-old colt is kicking up his heels in sheer pleasure. And Chandler now is on the look-out for clichés. In 'The Curtain' the General has 'basilisk eyes'. Now they just have a coal-black directness.

The famous, and at the time rather daring, pornographic books passage in *The Big Sleep* appeared first in 'Killer in the Rain'. This too has been transformed. In the story the detective knows in advance of the pornographic book racket, while in the novel suspense is created by our learning with Marlowe the meaning of 'Rare Books'. In the book store he meets a girl with silvered fingernails. A comparison of texts shows the value of Chandler's enlargements.

> She got up and came towards me, swinging lean thighs in a tight dress of some black material that didn't reflect any light. She was an ash blonde, with greenish eyes under heavily mascaraed lashes. There were large jet buttons in the lobes of her ears; her hair waved back smoothly from behind them. Her fingernails were silvered.
>
> She gave me what she thought was a smile of welcome, but what I thought was a grimace of strain.
>
> ('Killer in the Rain')

> She got up slowly and swayed towards me in a tight black dress that didn't reflect any light. She had long thighs and she walked with a certain something I hadn't often seen in bookstores. She was an ash blonde with greenish eyes, beaded lashes, hair waved smoothly back from ears in which large jet buttons glittered. Her fingernails were silvered. In spite of her get-up she looked as if she would have a hall bedroom accent.
>
> She approached me with enough sex appeal to stampede a businessmen's lunch and tilted her head to finger a stray, but not very stray, tendril of softly glowing hair. Her smile was tentative, but it could be persuaded to be nice.
>
> (*The Big Sleep*)

The hall bedroom accent and the businessmen's lunch are the phrases that principally lift this from the commonplace to something hallmarked Chandler, and the elaboration of the scene from one page

Raymond Chandler: An Aesthete Discovers the Pulps

to three, with a client coming in to change a book, add a lot to its effectiveness.

The blonde reappears, both in story and novel, as the companion of a gangster named Marty (in the book Joe Brody). In both versions the detective gets a gun away from her, she sinks her teeth into the hand with the gun in it, and he cracks her on the head. A couple of grace notes are added in the novel. 'The blonde was strong with the madness of fear,' it says in the story. The sentence is rhetorical, and somehow inadequate. In the book it becomes: 'The blonde was strong with the madness of love or fear, or a mixture of both, or maybe she was just strong.'

The final touch is not in the story at all. After Brody has handed over some compromising photographs from which he was hoping to make money, the blonde complains of her luck. 'A half-smart guy, that's all I ever draw. Never once a guy that's smart all around the course. Never once.'

'Did I hurt your head much?' Marlowe asks.

'You and every other man I ever met.'

It is a perfect pay-off line, marvellously done.

One could go through the whole book, and through the other novels that have a basis in the stories, showing how, passage by passage, Chandler converted the mechanical effects of the stories into something unique in style and delivery. He discovered his own quality as a writer through the freedom given him by the form of the novel.

The pulp magazines had shaped him, but once he had learned the trade they were a restriction. The novels enabled him to burst the bonds and to express the essential Raymond Chandler: a romantic aesthete and a self-conscious artist, an introvert with the power of catching the form, the tone, the rhythm, of American speech supremely well on paper. In its kind Chandler's mature dialogue is perfect. One cannot see how it could be better done. The stories are not much in themselves, but without them perhaps we should never have had the novels.

(1977)

Dashiell Hammett:
A Writer and His Time

I THE LIFE

Dashiell Hammett's life and works have a legendary fame in the United States. A novel has been written about his early adult life in San Francisco, and Jason Robards recently played him on the screen in *Julia*. In Britain he is less known than his lineal follower Raymond Chandler, and in an account of him it seems worth briefly recounting his life, which was far more interesting than those of most crime writers, and also has a direct connection with his work.

Samuel Dashiell Hammett was born in Maryland in 1894. His parentage was mixed Scottish and French, and the emphasis in Dashiell should be on the second syllable (it is derived from De Chiel), a difficulty in pronunciation eliminated in Hammett's lifetime by abbreviation of the name to Dash. He left school at fourteen, and then experienced what sometimes seems a standard American practical education by doing rough jobs like those of freight clerk, stevedore and nail-machine operator, before finding work as a Pinkerton detective. He spent four years as a Pinkerton man before enlisting in the Army. There he contracted tuberculosis, and for the rest of his life had intermittent struggles with the disease.

In 1919 he went back to his Pinkerton job, and in the following year married a nurse at the hospital from which he had been discharged with his file marked: 'Maximum improvement reached'. He was involved as a detective in the Fatty Arbuckle case, which he later characterized as a frame-up. In 1922 his first short stories were published. He used for these first stories a name which suggests the self-dramatizing and secretive elements of his character: Peter Collinson. A Peter Collins was at one time American criminal slang for a nobody—so at least Hammett said, although the slang dictionaries I have consulted do not endorse him—so that Peter Collinson was nobody's son. By this time he had parted from his wife and small daughter, and was drinking hard. Later, when he had achieved a measure of success they rejoined him, and he had another
166

Dashiell Hammett: A Writer and His Time

daughter, but the marriage had ended long before his divorce in 1937.

Nobody's son was soon replaced by the name of Dashiell Hammett. It quickly became clear to editors and readers that Hammett's stories about a small fat detective called simply the Continental Op, the Continental being the name of his agency, were superior to other work of the kind in their knowledge and their style. The Op was based on a man named Wright in Pinkerton's Baltimore office, and the approach to realism in the Op's assignments and his attitude was something new. So were the direct suggestions of graft in American life in some of the stories.

For seven years Hammett made no more than a reasonable living from writing short crime stories about the Continental Op, mostly for *Black Mask*. Two novels, *Red Harvest* and *The Dain Curse*, appeared first in the magazine and then in revised form as novels, without outstanding success. Then in 1930, with the publication of *The Maltese Falcon*, Hammett became famous. The book went through more than twenty hard-cover printings in a few years. It was filmed in 1931 and again by John Huston ten years later, with Humphrey Bogart, Mary Astor and Sydney Greenstreet playing the parts originally acted—and acted more faithfully than critics have granted—by Ricardo Cortez, Bebe Daniels and Dudley Digges.

Hammett described himself in a letter of this time as 'long and lean and grey-headed and very lazy . . . no ambition, no recreations'. He might have listed drinking and gambling as recreations, but perhaps he considered them as his lifetime occupation. Now, as the money poured in, he felt no need to go on working. He wrote two more books, *The Glass Key* (1931) and *The Thin Man* (1934) plus a small handful of short stories. Apart from that he went to Hollywood and saw his books made into films, with the Thin Man providing a whole series, a couple of them from his original screenplays. The money came in, he went on drinking, he met the youthful Lillian Hellman who recalled that at their first meeting he was recovering from a five-day drunk. They lived together, and he encouraged her to write. In 1934 her first stage play, *The Children's Hour*, was a triumphant success. The beginning of her career marked the end of Hammett's. He lived for another twenty-seven years, but never completed any other work. His life as a novelist had lasted for only six years, his whole life as a writer for twelve.

Why were there no more books or stories? The screenwriter Nunnally Johnson, who knew Hammett well from the late twenties, wrote to me that only somebody who 'had no expectation of being alive much beyond Thursday' could have spent himself and his money with such recklessness. Hammett told Johnson that he saw no reason to write when he not only had all the money he needed, but was assured of things staying that way until his life ended. In this he was mistaken, but the error was excusable. In the late thirties it seemed likely that Sam Spade and Nick Charles would remain a continuous source of revenue through radio and film series and cartoons, without Hammett having to provide more than an occasional idea and a few pieces of dialogue.

During these years Hammett had become involved in Hollywood left-wing politics. It is an indication of the seriousness with which he took any moral stance that in September 1942 he joined the US Army Signal Corps. He was forty-eight, and must have been far from fit, but he was accepted, and quickly volunteered for overseas duty. He was sent to the Aleutian Islands and enjoyed life in this Siberian climate where, as he said, you had snow in the winter and mud in the summer, both up to your waist. He became known as Pop, ran a four-page daily paper for the troops, lent the boys money and paid their bar bills. He left the Army soon after the war ended, having contracted emphysema. There was little diminution in his income. The Hammett boom continued, with the reissue of the Continental Op stories in paperback. He took up drinking again in a big way, until he was rushed to hospital and warned that if he continued to drink he would be dead in a few months. He gave up drinking completely.

He had twelve more years to live, and they cannot have been happy ones. He wrote one of the speeches in a play by Lillian Hellman, a speech in which a retired general talks of the turning-point in a life, when you wipe out your past mistakes, 'do the work you've never done, think the way you'd never thought'. He deceived himself into believing that for him this time was now. He told his agent that a new book was on the way, and it was announced under the title of *December 1st*, and then as *There Was a Young Man*. But those books were never finished, perhaps were not even begun. The only work from this time ever printed, and that after his death, was an 18,000-word fragment of a novel called 'Tulip'. This Hemingwayesque piece is interesting chiefly because it shows Hammett's wish to move away from the kind of book that had made him famous. With 'Tulip' given up, he made no further attempt to write.

Before the writing of 'Tulip' he had gone to prison. He was a trustee

Dashiell Hammett: A Writer and His Time

for what was probably a Communist front organization called the Civil Rights Congress. He was sent to prison for six months because he refused to tell a Congressional committee the names of the contributors to the bail bond fund of the Congress. Lillian Hellman says that he had never been to the Congress office and did not know the name of a single contributor, but that he told her: 'If it were my life, I would give it for what I think democracy is and I don't let cops or judges tell me what I think democracy is.' Before discounting this as rhetoric, one should remember that, as Hammett's insistence on taking an active part in World War II showed, he was a man who in all important matters meant what he said. He wrote to Lillian Hellman that his prison job was cleaning bathrooms and that he cleaned them better than she had ever done. After coming out of prison he maddened her by saying that prison had not been so bad after all. But, as she reflected, she should have guessed that he 'would talk about his own time in jail the way many of us talk about college'.

Now the rich days were over. Although he was not one of the Hollywood Ten, and it is likely that his active connection with Communism was slight, Hammett was expelled from Hollywood favour. There were no more commissions to work on screenplays, his radio shows came off the air, the short story collections went out of print and remained so. Joe McCarthy moved to have Hammett's books taken out from the shelves of overseas libraries. He was sued for $140,000 in back taxes. He lived in a small ugly country cottage in Katonah, New York, moving out in the summer to Martha's Vineyard. He read a great deal, referred dismissively at times to his own books, became increasingly a recluse. In January 1961 he died, not from tuberculosis nor from alcoholism, but from an inoperable lung cancer discovered only two months before his death.

II THE STYLE

It is difficult today to imagine the effect of reading Hammett short stories in the early or mid-1920s. Their plots were like others of the time, cramming as much violence as possible into a few pages, but the harsh tautness of the writing was new, and so was the hatred of corruption implicit in several stories. It was implicit, because Hammett never explained things. In these stories, as later in his books, he described events as they happened, without any comment

169

by the author. Yet in spite of this deliberate detachment, an attitude is being conveyed in the opening sentence of the very early (1923) story 'House Dick': 'The Montgomery Hotel's regular detective had taken his last week's rake-off from the hotel bootlegger in merchandise instead of cash, had drunk it down, had fallen asleep in the lobby, and had been fired.'

The suggestion, without a word being positively said to that effect, is that if you are a detective you should be honest, you shouldn't get drunk, and if you are dishonest and drunk on the job, it is right that you should be fired. This code of honesty is extended to include all sorts of loyalties, loyalties which are always personal and not corporate. 'When a man's partner is killed he's supposed to do something about it,' Sam Spade says, and this is so even though the partner is fairly worthless. A similar code of loyalty between men is invoked in *The Glass Key*, although there all sorts of subtleties and contradictions are involved. There is also an ethic of the job. The princess in 'The Gutting of Couffignal' (1925) is certain that the Op won't shoot her if she tries to escape, and is astounded when he puts a bullet through her calf. This deliberate shooting of a woman must have outraged many readers at the time, and so must the Op's subsequent comment: 'You ought to have known I'd do it! Didn't I steal a crutch from a cripple?' Several of the early stories anticipate scenes in the novels, and the Op's treatment of the princess prefigures Spade's sending up of Brigid O'Shaughnessy.

The obvious likeness of style in early Hammett stories to those of Hemingway's first work has prompted arguments about possible influences. Hemingway could not have influenced Hammett because before 1925 he had published nothing in America, and it is not likely that early Hammett influenced Hemingway. Times of social change are often accompanied by changes in literary style, and the United States after World War I was a society in turmoil. The new world created by Prohibition, gangsterism and the loosening of sexual and social restrictions could not be adequately expressed in the prose of Edith Wharton or even by the flat realism of Sinclair Lewis. Hammett and Hemingway used a prose which seemed to them at the time the only possible way of showing the world they were writing about: in Hemingway's case a world often of warfare and almost always of action, in Hammett's a violent, brutal and corrupt section of society. It was their intention to eliminate as far as possible the author's voice, in the hope that what emerged would be genuine and not synthetic.

170

Dashiell Hammett: A Writer and His Time

Hammett put it clearly a little later, in one of his rare literary pronouncements:

> The contemporary novelist's job is to take pieces of life and arrange them on paper. And the more direct their passage from street to paper the more lifelike they should turn out. . . . The novelist must know how things happen — not how they are remembered in later years — and he must write them down that way.

One must not claim too much for the short stories. Hammett himself thought little of them, and allowed them to be reprinted only after constant pressure by publishers. Their merits are those of sharpness, hardness, bareness, but the determination to cut out unnecessary adjectives and to avoid purple passages means that the author is sometimes not much more than a photographic recorder. The style is interesting, particularly in comparison with what was being published elsewhere, but it is deliberately drained of colour, so that even scenes of action tend to be played down rather than up.

Such personal stylistic notes as Hammett permits himself in the stories come usually in the openings. 'It was a wandering daughter job . . . I was the only one who left the train at Farewell . . . Sam Spade said "My name is Ronald Ames".' The turning-point that Hammett wrote about much later in fact came for him in the middle twenties, when he became discontented with what he was doing, and realized that it would be possible for him to write a full-length book in which he could criticize the society in which he lived through the medium of a violent story about crime.

The book was *Red Harvest*, which was printed in four long sections in *Black Mask* at the end of 1927 and the beginning of 1928, and published as a book in the following year. It was revised page by page for book publication, always with a view to making it more colloquial. The result is a novel remarkable in its attitude towards violence and towards the police, and in the way it conveys through the acid prose the stench of society in Personville, which is called Poisonville. This is a town in which all of the police are crooked, not just one or two. When Noonan the police chief has one of the gangsters holed up so that he can't escape, the gangster gives money to a subordinate and tells him to buy his way out. After he has done so a uniformed copper holds the back gate open for the gangsters, muttering nervously 'Hurry it up boys, please', and a car takes them to safety. The Op, who is with the gangsters, is characteristically casual in telling us the car's origin: 'The last I saw of it was its police department licence plate vanishing around a corner.' The Op cleans up Poisonville by playing one gangster against another, so that they are wiped out. The end of the story offers little cheer to believers in good government. Personville, with all the gangsters dead (there are twenty-eight violent deaths in the book by my count, but it is not easy to be exact) is 'developing into a sweet-smelling and thornless bed of roses', but it is under martial law. Bill Quint, the red-tied union organizer introduced in the opening chapter, has given the place up as a bad job.

In *Red Harvest* Hammett also for the first time gave full play to his strong visual sense and his skill in conveying character through visual description. Here is old Elihu Willsson, 'the czar of Poisonville':

> The old man's head was small and almost perfectly round under its close-cut crop of white hair. His ears were too small and plastered too flat to the sides of his head to spoil the spherical effect. His nose also was small, carrying down the curve of his bony forehead. Mouth and chin were straight lines chopping the sphere off. Below them a short thick neck ran down into white pyjamas between square meaty shoulders. One of his arms was outside the covers, a short compact arm that ended in a thick-fingered blunt hand. His eyes were round, small and watery. They looked as if they were hiding behind the watery film and under the bushy white brows only until the time came to jump out and grab something. He wasn't the sort of man whose pocket you'd try to pick unless you had a lot of confidence in your fingers.

The portrait of Dinah Brand is created against type, in a way unique at the time in this sort of literature. The Op is told that she is tremendously attractive, a de luxe hustler, a woman greedy for money but fatally attractive to men. When he meets Dinah he finds that she has 'the face of a girl of twenty-five already showing signs of wear', with eyes that are large and blue but also bloodshot, a mouth that is big and ripe but has lines at the corners. Her coarse hair needs trimming, her lipstick is uneven, there is a run down the front of one stocking. She is very mean, and a tremendous drinker. Hammett's achievement is to convey the charm and sexual attractiveness of this untidy girl.

Red Harvest is a strongly moral book about civic corruption, and it has a brutality that reflects something in Hammett's own character.

Dashiell Hammett: A Writer and His Time

There are a good many jokes in the book, but they are all bitter. Any drink Polly de Voto sells you is good, Dinah tells the Op, except maybe the Bourbon. 'That always tastes a little bit like it had been drained off a corpse.' When the Op blackmails Elihu Willsson into acting virtuously by threatening to make public the letters written by the old man to Dinah he says that the letters are hot, and adds: 'I haven't laughed so much over anything since the hogs ate my kid brother.' The Op's own activities become so dubious and so vicious that one of the operatives sent out to work with him thinks that he has killed Dinah, and goes back to San Francisco. It is not surprising that *Roadhouse Nights*, the film said to have been based on *Red Harvest*, retained nothing of the plot and gave no screen credit to Hammett. The dialogue would sound marvellous, but even in the day of Dirty Harry the greed and violence of the characters might be too rough for the screen.

III THE ART

After *Red Harvest*, it would seem that Hammett felt there was a limit to what could be achieved by direct accounts of violence, that the same points could and should be made more subtly. His first attempt to do this was the confused and disappointing *The Dain Curse*, with a distinctly softened Op telling the story. *The Maltese Falcon* (*Black Mask* 1929–30, published as a novel in the same year) replaced the Op by Sam Spade, and also took most of the violence off-stage. We are told about people being killed, but don't see it happening.

Hammett's books can be seen from one point of view as a series of dialogues and confrontations through which the plot is revealed and tension built up. In *The Maltese Falcon* we begin with Spade and Brigid O'Shaughnessy, and move on to Spade-Dundy, Spade-O'Shaughnessy, Spade-Cairo and so on. Much the same applies to *The Glass Key*. These are stories in which conversation is made to do the work of description, and also of characterization. We are never in doubt that Gutman and Joel Cairo are villains, but what about Spade himself? 'Don't be too sure I'm as crooked as I'm supposed to be', he says to Brigid, but he never directly answers her question, when she asks whether he would have gone along with the villains if the falcon had been real. And in *The Glass Key* we are left in doubt about the relationship between Ned Beaumont and Paul Madvig. We can see that Madvig is a crooked politician in the American style, bluff and shrewd but really not too quick in the uptake. Beaumont works for him, protects him by staging a fake quarrel which Madvig believes to be real, later gets beaten up for him, but what is Beaumont's own attitude? Are we to regard him as less corrupt than Madvig, and if so why does he work in Madvig's organization? To such questions Hammett deliberately returns no answer. These ambiguities are essential to the art with which, in these two books, he approaches the complexities of guilt and innocence.

They helped him to create a new type of hero-villain, a character now common enough, but never rendered with the depth that is brought to the depiction of Spade and Beaumont. Such a hero-villain was characteristically an American of the Prohibition era and the Depression. He reflected the contradictory feelings of respectable people towards bootleggers and gangsters. The activities of bootleggers were to be deprecated, their casualness about human life was horrifying, yet because the respectable citizen patronized them they were seen as good fellows, genial and at times even heroic. The events of the Depression, together with the rise of Fascism, encouraged in the same respectable citizen the belief that the judicious use of force was the best protection against organized labour.

Like Raymond Chandler later on, Hammett used scenes and devices from the Op stories in these novels. The clue to Archer's death, the fact that he let his killer approach close enough for powder burns to show, comes directly from 'Who Killed Bob Teal?', and *The Glass Key* is in some ways a reworking of *Red Harvest*, which in turn owes a good deal to the story 'Nightmare Town'. But Hammett transformed these scenes and devices in using them again, and did so with remarkably little loss of realism. The problem that he faced was that of reconciling the 'passage from street to paper' of violent scenes from life, with the need to give these scenes the shape of art. He did so first by cutting down overt violence, and then by conveying indirectly the things he wanted to show. Hammett once said to James Thurber that *The Maltese Falcon* had been influenced by *The Wings of the Dove*, and although the comparison may seem far-fetched (the central characters in both books are concerned with a fabulous fortune) this does suggest the seriousness with which Hammett approached his work.

He was entirely serious in his masterpiece, *The Glass Key*. The

174

Dashiell Hammett: A Writer and His Time

manifold subtleties of this book range from the intricacies of motive already suggested to those of the plot, from the clever crookedness of the hat trick played by Beaumont on Bernie Despain to the deliberate destruction of the publisher Mathews. In this book Hammett also approached for the first time the question of American class relationships. Madvig is a big man in local politics but is still not really acceptable at the Senator's house because he wears silk socks with tweeds. At the same time the Senator needs him, so he gets invited to dinner. Beaumont is acceptable because (although we are never told this in so many words) he knows the social mores of the Senator, even though he may not adhere to them.

In these books Hammett pushed outwards the boundaries of the American crime story. Homosexuality was not unknown in such fiction, but it was not a common theme, and Hammett's depiction of the homosexual gunman Wilmer and his relationship with Gutman was very bold. So, of course, was the fact that Spade slept with Brigid. Within the context of the time, Hammett's treatment of sex was extremely frank. The beating-up of Beaumont by the apish Jeff in *The Glass Key*, Jeff's insistence that Beaumont likes it ('I never seen a guy that liked being hit so much or that I liked hitting so much ... He's a God-damned massacrist, that's what he is'), and the use of Jeff's instinctive sadism by Beaumont in killing Shad O'Rory, remain perhaps the most horrific scenes of their kind in any crime story. In *Red Harvest* the Op speaks of getting a rear out of violence, and this is made specific in *The Thin Man*, where Nora asks Nick, after he has tangled with Mimi Jorgensen, 'Tell me the truth: when you were wrestling with Mimi, didn't you have an erection?' The question was omitted from the magazine version of the book, and also from the English edition. Erections did not at that time exist in the English novel.

The Glass Key is a masterpiece of plotting, but one hopes and believes that Hammett ranked it in a different class from the rest of his books because in it, for the first time, his mastery of technique was truly used for artistic ends. The relationships between the characters, and not just the chief characters but those concerning such a minor figure as Opal Madvig, are conveyed with wonderful restraint. In addition the main theme of corruption, social and personal, is handled in a way beyond the reach of any other American novelist of the time. The book can bear comparison with any American novel of the thirties: it does not look out of place when put beside what

175

Criminal Matters

Hemingway, Faulkner, Fitzgerald, were writing at the time.

After *The Glass Key*—or so one sees with hindsight—Hammett could go no further with fiction in the form of the crime story. It had become hampering to him, as once it had been a liberation. If he stuck to it now, there was no way he could go but down. And down, sure enough, Hammett went in his last, and immensely popular, book *The Thin Man*.

This was begun in 1930 as a story designed to follow *The Glass Key*. Sixty-five pages were written and then, as Hammett said later, he put the book aside for nearly three years, when he 'found it easier, or at least generally more satisfactory, to keep only the basic idea of the plot'. Apart from the use of the names Guild and Wynant the unfinished typescript, he said, had 'a clear claim to virginity', although some of the incidents were used in the film *After the Thin Man*. I have not read the complete typescript, but it is clear that the characterization of both Guild and Wynant was on a different and deeper level than anything in the book Hammett eventually produced.

It was written in an interlude between drinking sessions in, Lillian Hellman tells us, a cheap and dismal hotel run by Nathanael West.

Life changed: the drinking stopped, the parties were over. The locking-in time had come and nothing was allowed to disturb it until the book was finished. I had never seen anybody work that way: the care for every word, the pride in the neatness of the typed page itself, the refusal for ten days or two weeks to go out even for a walk for fear something would be lost.

The book that came out was a sparkling comedy done in terms of a murder mystery, in many places a very funny story. For Hammett, however, it was taking an easy option. He returned to first person narration, which had been given up in the two previous books and the unfinished version of *The Thin Man*. This provided for him, as for Chandler later on, a comfortable ration of wisecracks and side-of-the-mouth comments. Everything is sacrificed to easy, flip reactions and to the relationship of Nick and Nora, which is done very well but necessarily remains superficial because, after all, this is just a comedy. No doubt Hammett deceived himself into thinking that this was an interim book, written between better ones, but if there had ever been a chance of this, the novel's tremendous success made it impossible. *The Thin Man* was the end of a career.

176

Dashiell Hammett: A Writer and His Time

In his twelve years as a writer, Dashiell Hammett did a great deal, apart from being the Onlie Begetter of the true American crime story. *The Glass Key* is a magnificent novel, *The Maltese Falcon* remains a model of the detective thriller, no other book of the time gives violence and corruption the raw reality of *Red Harvest*. Almost everything he wrote, after the earliest pieces, was stamped with a personal mark. He was an original writer in style and approach, and there are few of whom one can truly use the word. The least of his work is interesting, the best has a permanent place in literature.

(1979)

Personal meetings

Ruthven Todd:
Some Details for a Portrait

A group photograph that includes Ruthven is beside me as I write. It was taken at the 1936 London Surrealist exhibition. Between Salvador Dali and a forgotten British surrealist stands an eager innocent figure, evidently much the youngest in a group that includes Paul Eluard and Herbert Read. This was Ruthven (the name was pronounced Riven) Campbell Todd, then 22, who had some unofficial and possibly unpaid job connected with the exhibition.

Ruthven was the eldest of ten children sired by an Edinburgh architect. He went to school at Fettes, and after that embarked on the literary life, a life which sustained him, more or less, until his death this year. At certain stages on this voyage—the beginning and for a period near the end—we were close friends. Our affection was deep, and emerged untouched after long stretches of time when I hardly heard from him and did not see him at all. At the same time some aspects of Ruthven's life were little known or unknown to me, so that this piece offers no more than details for a portrait which, if it is ever completed, will be that of a brilliant and variously gifted man who never used his gifts to the full. It will also be a portrait of one of the few talented literary bohemians of our time.

In appearance Ruthven was rather above medium height, dark haired, with a long pale face that became longer and narrower as he grew older. He wore thick glasses to correct pronounced myopia, glasses with large lenses and enormously wide side arms. He smoked, drank and talked almost continuously. The cigarettes were by preference French and the drink by preference whisky, but he would smoke or drink anything if what he preferred was not available. His talk was anecdotal, and he always made the assumption that you knew the people he was talking about, so that the listener was likely to be deluged by Christian names. Some of the stories about Wystan and Norman and Louis and Geoffrey and David and Stephen—and although these happen to be poets, one could substitute for them dozens of other names of painters, or printers, or literary and artistic hangers-on—were funny, others unlikely, some obviously untrue.

Personal Meetings

Yet it was unwise to assume that any particular story was untrue. No doubt when he said at parties that Picasso, Miro and others had given him pictures he was often disbelieved, but he was telling the truth, for the pictures were given to him at or after the Surrealist exhibition. And when he said that he knew Eliot, Pound or Wyndham Lewis, it was again unwise to doubt him, for Ruthven knew everybody. It might be said that knowing people was his occupation, or one of them. When, late in his life, I asked if he had met my old friend Robert Conquest, received one of his rare negatives in reply, and took him to a party at Bob's flat, Ruthven was delighted. He liked Bob but, more than that, Bob was now established as one more link in the tremendous chain that connected Ruthven with thousands of poets, novelists, artists, librarians, curators and scholars all over the world.

It may sound as though Ruthven himself was no more than a hanger-on, but this would not be true. He was a creator, at least in his first forty years, and he was also in his particular field of art history a fine and exact scholar. It may sound also as though he was a bore, and certainly there were people who found the manic energy of his conversation tiring. Yet there was an overflowing good humour about him, and a true sweetness of character, that gave the excesses of his conversation their own fascination, and even charm. Or perhaps I am saying only that you could enjoy Ruthven's conversation particularly if, as I did, you let a good deal of it roll over you like waves. He was in some respects like an eccentric clergyman, 'a nineteenth-century Country Clergyman who has mysteriously managed to get born and to survive in this hectic age', as Auden put it. Julian Maclaren-Ross produced in his memoirs a caricature of Ruthven that still catches some essential truths. He touches perfectly on a characteristic Ruthven conversational ploy when at their first meeting, after some confusion about names (Maclaren-Ross mistook Ruthven for Reverend), both identities were established.

Ruthven cried: 'But I discovered you.'

'I thought Cyril Connolly discovered me.'

'On my recommendation,' Todd shouted, his voice still pitched to carry above a crowd, though the pub had now emptied around us. 'I happened to be in *Horizon* office when your stuff came to light, I sat down and read it through, then I went straight to Connolly and told him: 'Whatever else you do you've got to publish this bloke.'

Ruthven Todd: Some Details for a Portrait

True or invented? Maclaren-Ross obviously thought the latter, yet it may well have been true, for Ruthven worked at *Horizon* in the first months of the war.

I first met Ruthven in 1935, when he was on a visit to London, made while working in Edinburgh for a magazine called the *Scottish Bookman*. On leaving school he had tried life in his father's office and disliked it, and then spent two years working as a farm labourer on the island of Mull. There he wrote poems which he sent to Geoffrey Grigson, who did not publish them in *New Verse*, but passed them on to the *Bookman* (English) which printed two or three. Geoffrey became, and remained, a sort of literary exemplar for Ruthven. Our first meeting, which I have described in detail elsewhere along with the evening's drinking which followed it, was in a tea-shop off Fleet Street where we were both waiting for Geoffrey.

We became close friends two or three years later when he married, got a job as copywriter in an advertising agency, and took a basement flat in the Pimlico square where I lived. I spent a good many evenings with Ruthven and his wife Cicely drinking beer, talking about poetry, making plans for books. The seeds of my first crime story, *The Immaterial Murder Case*, were sown in conversation there, and in notes sent across the square. The locale, the Surrealist exhibition, was sketched, characters and plot talked about, then typed and talked about further. The book was meant to be a collaboration, but Ruthven never did any writing. I wrote it, made him the murderer, and put the typescript into a drawer for several years.

The Ruthven of that time was a less frenetic figure than he later became. He seemed content with domesticity, tolerated his job, cut down his drinking, wrote poems which were published in little magazines. When his son Christopher was born, he and Cicely rented a small house in Hampstead. There I spent part of a Christmas with them, and there Ruthven wrote in three weeks a biography of Alexander Dumas called *The Laughing Mulatto*. The book was dedicated 'To Christopher but for whom this book would never have been written', and it was a piece of hackwork, done for the £30 advance that helped to pay for Christopher's birth. He had already published a novel, *Over the Mountain*, a Kafkaesque fantasy with a political flavour, and altogether an extraordinary, original book. This too had been written with great speed, on a visit to Cicely's parents in Edinburgh. 'For ten or more hours a day, I wrote, in a small and probably rather illegible hand.' The manuscript was

183

written in eight days, typed and revised in the same number of weeks, and sent to Geoffrey Grigson, who at the time was an adviser to Harrap. Geoffrey persuaded them to publish the book. When the first royalty statement arrived, it had sold 189 copies.

Soon after Christopher was born, Ruthven and Cicely gave me a beautiful blue Persian kitten they owned, because they were afraid that it might sit on the baby's face and stifle him. The gift gave rise to one of those stories that delighted Ruthven, and went into his repertoire for frequent repetition. The kitten, christened Trotsky by me, passed in due course to my mother, who whenever possible abbreviated the uncongenial name. Ruthven would give a rendering of her calling the cat in at night: 'Trot Trot Trot' (loudly), then (voice sunk to a whisper) 'Trotsky Trotsky Trotsky.' After rendering this only mildly comic anecdote Ruthven would laugh with such furious conviction that other people, people who had never met my mother and very likely had never heard of me, tended to laugh too. Some of Ruthven's stories ran into each other, as one thing reminded him of another, some shifted into recitation. He loved nonsense, and I must have heard him recite Samuel Foote's 'The Great Panjandrum' fifty times, beginning at great speed and slowing down as he came to 'the gunpowder ran out at the heels of their boots'.

When war came the Todds removed themselves to Edinburgh, and Ruthven like me registered as a conscientious objector. He wrote to me in April 1940, partly about his objections ('Do you know that the ants are the only other creatures on earth to conduct war—and that man has not yet discovered that he is superior to them?—I have put this in my statement to the Tribunal which is perhaps scarcely tactful'), partly about his poems and his own life:

> Looking at the poems I've been writing recently I think that they are really all an Ode on I. of I. ['Intimations of Immortality'], concerned with the shades of the prison-house. The older I grow the more I realise that upon the treatment of the child depends the whole of his life as a man. It is only within the last few months that I have been able to break down the hard shell that I have erected round myself and, in consequence, to know a little about myself and what I desire.

Two years later his first collection of poems, *Until Now*, appeared. Taking the book from the shelf I see with surprise something I had forgotten, that it contains a note thanking me for help in its

Ruthven Todd: Some Details for a Portrait

preparation. Many of the poems have a standard thirties preoccupation with myths and heroes, but there are more individual ones about painters—Miro, Klee, Christopher Wood, Samuel Palmer—and some that embody impressively his feeling for Edinburgh, 'this city of grey stone and bitter wind', and awareness of the importance of his ancestry:

> My face presents my history, and its sallow skin
> Is parchment for the Edinburgh lawyer's deed:
> To have and hold in trust, as feeofee therein
> Until such date as the owner shall have need
> Thereof. My brown eyes are jewels I cannot pawn,
> And my long lip once curled beside an Irish bog,
> My son's whorled ear was once my father's, then mine;
> I am the map of a campaign, each ancestor has his flag
> Marking an advance or a retreat. I am their seed.

Ruthven had four brothers and five sisters, but so far as I know saw little of them. When he was in company with one of his sisters I was surprised to find his usual geniality turned to a snappiness and sarcasm I would have thought wholly foreign to his nature.

Whatever he desired, it became clear during the war, it was not domesticity. He parted from Cicely in 1943, worked in Civil Defence, but was rejected as unfit when he was found to have a duodenal ulcer. After that he took a job in Zwemmer's bookshop and rented a flat in Mecklenburgh Square, of which I remember little except the pints of milk lined up outside the door. Milk was rationed, but Ruthven got the pints for his ulcer. He never drank it, pouring down alcohol instead, on the ground that the ulcer had to be taught who was master. There was no doubt that he suffered pain—I have seen him bent double with cramps—but he refused to submit to it and the ulcer disappeared, or perhaps finally learned who was master. Maclaren-Ross, who also visited the flat, says that there was a complete signed set of Wyndham Lewis's works, and that Ruthven told him how Lewis had put him up in the basement of his own flat on Ruthven's first arrival in London, and had also given him the signed copies. Ruthven embroidered reality at times, but so far as I know never invented totally, and so I suppose there must have been some truth in this story, but certainly it was not literally correct. When in 1938 Lewis made some drawings of me, he was looking around for portrait

185

commissions, and Ruthven was eager to be painted. I mentioned his name to Lewis and Ruthven went to see him, but the result was not happy.

'Your friend Dodd,' Lewis said to me severely the next time I saw him, 'is agreeable enough, but he has no money. Dodd is not a man of substance. He is no use to me.'

I tried without success to correct Dodd to Todd, and agreed that Ruthven was not rich, although he would have been able at that time to pay the few pounds that my own drawings had cost. It turned out, however, that Lewis had asked Dodd for some considerable sum—perhaps £100, I can't remember—and that Ruthven had said, with unusual candour, that he could not pay anything like that. Lewis referred to Dodd once or twice afterwards, with what might be called tolerant disapproval.

In the spring of 1944 a flying-bomb damaged the flat, and Ruthven went down to live at Tilty Mill House, near Dunmow, which he had taken over from the painter John Armstrong. He managed to get everything he owned down to Essex, and the house was filled with splendid things, including pictures by many friends, and literally dozens of presentation copies of books. The journey to Tilty, however, was long and not easy, and Ruthven stayed most nights of the week in town. He spent his evenings in Fitzrovia, moving from the Wheatsheaf to the Marquis of Granby to the Fitzroy, with half a dozen other pubs in between, and ending up drinking in somebody's home. He has left a lively account of this in a long introduction to an art exhibition catalogue, done in 1973. He says there, with a faintly apologetic note, that to some of his friends 'the Sahara would have appeared less arid than Fitzrovia', and I was one of these. Even though I lived as far out as Blackheath, however, I served as a convenient occasional refuge. When the telephone rang late at night, my wife K and I would look at each other and say 'Ruthven'. I would pick up the receiver.

'Hallo.' The voice was often slightly doleful. 'This is me. Just wondered if you could possibly put me up tonight.'

'Of course, Ruthven. Where are you?'

'As a matter of fact I'm at Blackheath station.'

It was on one of these occasions that Ruthven anticipated by some years an incident in *Lucky Jim*. Like many hard drinkers he seldom became obviously drunk, and never in my presence passed out. He also rarely went to sleep without reading for half an hour. This evening he began to read in bed and to smoke, fell asleep, woke to find

186

his shirt burning, took it off and flung it aside, and burned not only the shirt but sheet and carpet. He was penitent, and of course said that he'd pay for the damage, although I don't know that he did. At this time he was almost always hard up.

Yeats once said of George Moore that he had never read a book, but picked up all his knowledge about writing and painting through endless café conversation. He might have had the same feeling about Ruthven, who seemed always to be talking and drinking, yet these must in fact have been years of intense research and study. He emerged from them as one of the world's greatest authorities on Blake. He was not especially interested in Blake as philosopher or mystic, but in his artistic achievement and his quality as a technical innovator. The four essays in *Tracks in the Snow*, published in 1946, deal with Blake, Fuseli and John Martin, but they extend far beyond the ordinary range of art criticism. Ruthven was fascinated by the relationship between eighteenth- and early nineteenth-century art and science, and the artistic possibilities that came through technical development. Here he is on the substitution of steel for copper plates in mezzotint engraving as they affected Martin's work:

> The principal trouble about copper had been its comparative softness, although it must be remembered that the copper-plate up to the nineteenth century was harder than that of today, being beaten and not rolled. As a result of this softness the 'burr' on the plate soon wore down, under the strain of printing, and the mezzotint quickly lost that velvety blackness upon which its attraction depends. The introduction of the steel-plate meant that, from being a process for the production of a necessarily limited edition, the mezzotint became a method for reproducing works intended to have a wide circulation . . . So far as I know John Martin is the only artist of any reputation or standing who has seriously adopted mezzotint as a medium of self-expression.

It is not surprising that *Tracks in the Snow* has been for years one of those source books from which other writers borrow, often without acknowledgement.

Ruthven had been interested in fine printing from his teens—in 1940 and 1944 he published two little privately printed collections of his poems—and somehow and somewhere he learned a great deal about types and settings. When, years later, he wrote a poem for a limited edition series called Poem of the Month Club, produced by my brother-in-law Jack Clark, he did not care for some of the

Personal Meetings

settings, and wrote to me: 'If you see Jack, do explain that my point about putting a "brass" space between the final letter of a word and the punctuation mark (a "copper" will do after a final "r"), and longer dashes, with a copper or a brass space at each end, are serious.' His interest in wild flowers and plants also no doubt went back to youth, but it was developed in these years, and to it was added an encyclopaedic knowledge of fungi, edible and otherwise. I remember a morning at Tilty when we went out gathering mushrooms, Ruthven eagerly talkative as ever after a night's heavy drinking, I hardly able to bend down to pick the mushrooms, and feeling his words rattling at me like machine-gun bullets.

A year or two later Tilty met a sad fate. It had been lent to the painters Colquhoun and MacBryde and a Scottish poet, and these Bothy Scots (as Ruthven called them in letters to me, by analogy with Shanty Irish) had wrecked the place, selling his pictures and books, breaking windows, smashing a sixteenth-century chair here and an African carving there. Lasting bitterness was something almost unknown to Ruthven, but he remained distressed and angry for the rest of his life at the loss of his books and pictures.

In 1944 he published *The Lost Traveller*, another part-Kafkan near-surrealist fantasy written before *Over the Mountain*, when he was only 21. On republication in America in 1968, the book became in a small way a cult work among the young. And in 1945 he started to write crime stories for a publisher named Peter Gottleib, who had recently founded twin publishing houses under the names of John Westhouse and Peter Lunn. Ruthven got £200 a book in outright payment, and as he vaguely said at the time wrote these crime stories to settle his debts. In a history of the crime story, *Bloody Murder*, I said that he had written ten in six months, but it now appears that there may have been twelve. Much later Ruthven expressed himself as uncertain about this, a nice Ruthvenian touch.

With this money, plus that for two children's books also written for Gottleib, why was Ruthven so hard up? He spent money freely, he bought pictures—like those sold by the Bothy Scots—and books when he saw anything he liked, but still this remains a mystery. Whether the tax people were after him, or for some other reason, he left England in January 1947, and never lived here again.

I heard nothing of him for a long while, apart from a yearly poem sent as a Christmas card, until in 1956 a letter from Martha's Vineyard brought me more or less up to date.

Ruthven Todd: Some Details for a Portrait

The job at Iowa folded, so I spent quite a time nearly starving—
then I worked on an encyclopaedia until I was fired and got a better
job free-lancing on another one . . . I got married again in 1951, to
a wife from Oklahoma, with a step-daughter (now nearly 9) and a
small income from oil-wells. We got a house in New York, but
when Dylan died in 1953, Jody felt she'd had enough of New York
for the time being (I was, to say the least of it, terribly involved in
the whole business), and so, when we came up here in the summer
of '54, we rented this house and have been staying here ever since.

Four years later another letter said that he was leaving for
Mallorca—where Robert Graves had lent him a cottage—together
with Alice 'who may marry me if we find it works out right'. He had
by now become an American citizen, again I suspect for tax reasons,
and was parted and divorced from Jody, although they remained
friendly. He lived in Mallorca for the rest of his life, first presumably
in the Graves cottage, then at a small village named Galilea in the
centre of the island, where he first stayed in a pension and then rented
and furnished a cottage.

These, in particular the early sixties in Mallorca, were what he
called in a later letter to me 'my lost drunk years'. I know little about
them, but he was a legendary figure in Greenwich Village. Ruthven
ran a little private press in New York for a few years, but published
nothing original except some successful books for children about a
character called Space Cat. He came to see K and me on occasional
visits to London, and our children were enchanted by him. He had let
his hair grow long and sported a piratical ear-ring, but there were
other reasons why they loved him. He treated children almost exactly
as he did adults, rattling off the same string of names and anecdotes,
interspersed with fragments of odd information, and perhaps with
renderings of Lewis Carroll poems, 'The Great Panjandrum', or
Christopher Smart on his cat Timothy. Most children hate expla-
nations, and one of Ruthven's charms for them was that he never
explained. They understood what they could, and if they did not
laugh with him he was quite happy, as he was with adults, that they
should laugh at him. On one visit he brought a sketchbook with pen,
ink and wash drawings of the 300-odd flowers he had noted in
Martha's Vineyard. He had gone to art school after leaving Fettes,
but had decided that he was facile but lacked originality. These
beautifully executed drawings of flowers and fungi were, he said, sure

189

money-makers, and in letters from Mallorca he began to weave plans about them:

> Some of them will be used in *A Check List of the Flora of Martha's Vineyard* and then I'm boxing all the originals in vellum boxes (fifty to a box), with each drawing numbered and arranged according to Asa Gray's standard flora of North East America, and provided with an index. The best way to raise cash on these seems to be to put them up for auction at Sotheby's, and Jock Carter is sounding out whether it would be wiser to sell them in London or New York.

This sounded splendid, like so many of Ruthven's ideas, but I don't think anything came of it. I remember particularly two incidents from these visits, both typical of Ruthven. One occasion was when, with money in his pocket, he took my daughter Sarah and me out to dinner. He talked his way through the meal, eating little and drinking steadily as always, and then paid the bill. We had eaten in the basement of the restaurant, and were about to leave when the waitress rushed upstairs with a bundle of five pound notes that he had dropped. Ruthven thanked her, and we left. Another waitress ran into the street after us—he had dropped more notes from another pocket. He gave her one, thanked her, and we went on. Is it any wonder that the young loved him?

The other tale is less happy. Ruthven turned up unexpectedly at a party being given by Faber in connection with their poetry prize. He had not been over for a year or two, and I was shocked to see that he was using two sticks to get about. 'Legs gone—too much Spanish brandy,' he said with a cackle. His voice was slurred, not through drunkenness but because his teeth had been taken out and a new set had not arrived. He was wearing a shabby raincoat, and looked odder than usual. Eliot sat in the middle of the room, old and obviously not very well, and I noticed a little uneasily the raincoated Ruthven hobbling over to him and bending over his chair. A few minutes later a Faber director came up to me and said: 'Would you take your friend away? I am afraid he is upsetting Mr Eliot.' I separated Ruthven from Eliot, not without difficulty, and asked what he had said. It seemed that some years ealier Ruthven had organized a fund to help the poet Theodore Roethke, who had fallen on hard times, and that Eliot had refused to subscribe. Ruthven had then sent a card to Eliot saying: 'Thank you for your Christian charity.' He had taken the chance to remind Eliot of all this. 'I thought I should, don't

190

you think so, Julian? I thought I damn well should. And do you know what Tom said?' Ruthven asked, glaring through his huge spectacles. 'He said "Yes, I was wrong, I should have subscribed." He said that, Julian.' I got him to another part of the room and left him talking to, I think, Kingsley Amis. Five minutes later I heard his loud and as it sounded drink-sodden voice raised in song. 'Oh Fundador, my Fundador, I've been destroyed by Fundador,' he sang. At that point I took him away.

Silence for a couple of years after that, and then a letter which began: 'Voice out of somewhere?', and went on to say: 'Around a year and a bit ago I decided that either I was an alcoholic or was becoming one so I took the "cure" and haven't had a drink for fifteen months.' This began a correspondence that lasted for seven years from 1966 to October 1973, with letters coming from Ruthven every couple of weeks. He wrote about the cottage, about literary plans and possibilities, and made requests that I should find all sorts of things, from special marbled paper to hooks that could be bought only in one particular store. He asked that I should bring over a small vacuum-cleaner on the visit to Mallorca that (as I much regret now) I never made. All this was mixed up with recollections of the past, chat about people I had never heard of, and schemes for raising money. Many letters described the renovation of the cottage:

> The first room to be fixed was the guest-room . . . Two elderly crones, with about three and a half teeth between them, arrived and brewed quicklime in a cauldron in the middle of the kitchen, meanwhile giving eldritch screeches in Mallorquin. They did a marvellous job in two days and presented a bill for 221.50 ptas (£1 = 168) which included the, itemized, cost of the materials. I gave them a really good paint-scraper as a present, and 300 pesetas and told them not to go and get drunk. I hope within the next few weeks to be paid by Dover for reprinting *Tracks in the Snow* and *The Lost Traveller*, and then I will have a refrigerator and possibly a better cooking stove. I heat the house with catalytic heaters which have no fumes. At the moment there is a hot shower in the bathroom, but you cannot brew tea when you're having a shower. . . .

He added: 'In spite of my having had to give up drink, I have a pretty well-stocked bar (as a rule a choice of conaça, manzanilla, Tio Pepe or La Ina, a medium sherry, gin, vodka, Pernod — 68° absinthe

191

45° the ordinary—anis, dulce y seco and a few odd bottles.'
Some letters ran to nine typed pages. My replies were less frequent
and often inadequate, but he did not much mind that. 'My trouble is
that, living by myself, I get up at any time between 6 and 7, work most
of the day, with intervals for reading and then, in the evening, use
letters in the place of conversation.' I was only one among a number
of correspondents, and I am sure that others received letters as long
and rambling as those to me. One was Geoffrey Grigson who said
that his wife Jane read him a page each morning at breakfast.
Ruthven was delighted by this. His absorption in the past, and people
he had known in the past, was now very great. When he received a
copy of Geoffrey's *Poems and Poets*, a book dedicated to him, he was
overwhelmed. 'I read my name on the dedication page again and
again. I shake, and cry.'

Living alone . . . Ruthven was the most gregarious of men, one
dependent on women for company as well as for sex. There were a
great many women in his life—at least a dozen are mentioned in
letters to me. His attitude to women was both romantic and
egoistical, and although no doubt he fell in love over and over again,
what he wanted above all was to be loved. Living alone, as he did
through much of this time, must have been hard for him. Reading the
letters through in their entirety, as I have done to write this memoir, I
understand fully what an effort he was making to try to rebuild for
himself a life and a literary reputation lost in the wastes of alcohol.
'I'm trying, pretty desperately, to get back into print as I think it's
about time I revived myself,' he wrote, exulting in the fact that the
London Magazine was 'doing one of my "scholarly" accidental pieces
on Coleridge'. He made plans for other pieces—should he give them
to Alan Ross or not? He decided that he should, in spite of the fact
that 'Alan pays so damn badly.'

At the time of his 'Voice out of somewhere?' letter in 1966 he had
begun 'a book of memoirs of life in London and New York from 1934
to 1954 called *Dead and Other/Friends and Places*'. He told me that I
appeared largely in it, and asked if I could lay hands on any old
photographs or letters. 'Owing to my peculiar habit of changing
countries, I seem to have no papers, no photographs and only a faulty
memory upon which to draw . . . and I've got to provide about a
dozen illustrations for Hart-Davis and Holt.' After 'DAO/FAP', as
it was called for short, there would be another book of memoirs called
Love Letter to Three Islands (Mull, Martha's Vineyard, Mallorca)

Ruthven Todd: Some Details for a Portrait

illustrated by line drawings and 'a dozen first-class color reproductions of my flower drawings', and after that *In The House of My
Father*, a book about growing up in Scotland.

I never saw a word of these excellently-titled books, although I
heard a great deal about 'DAO/FAP'. In June 1966 he said an
agreement was 'waiting to be drawn up with Holt' which would give
him $100 a month while writing the book. In the following January he
was 'writing, in my smallish hand, on the right hand pages of a fat,
narrow-ruled notebook, with corrections and additions on the
opposite page—I guess I've got about 50,000 words down, and have
another 75,000 to write.' When I told him the Lewis Dodd-Todd
story, he asked immediately if he could include it. In March he said
that he was hoping to bring over a draft for me to look at, so that I
could 'make notes and criticisms, harsh as possible . . . owing to my
years of booziness, my memory ain't what it used to be', but the visit
was postponed. A couple of months later the book had reached
100,000 words, with chapters interposed dealing with some friends
who then vanished from the scene, 'but characters such as Louis and
Dylan and yourself pop in and out'. More than a year after that he
said that 'the bloody book has now, cleanly, divided into three rather
long ones. The first volume, of about 160,000 words, should be
delivered to the publishers by July 1.' And that, in effect, was all.
Questions about the book's progress brought evasive or no replies,
and after another year or so it was no longer mentioned. Was the
manuscript seen and rejected by Holt? Its fate is mysterious, like that
of 'Dylan Thomas: A Personal Account', 'a book which I am not
going to publish but will cannibalise'. This was a book he had been
commissioned to write by the Dylan Thomas estate, and the
manuscript is in Texas's Humanities Research Centre. Perhaps it was
rejected by Dent, who announced it, perhaps they asked for changes
which Ruthven was unwilling or unable to make. He was not
particularly scrupulous in dealing with publishers, although in my
experience punctilious in repaying debts to friends.

From 'DAO/FAP' he moved to other projects. 'My problem is
that, while I love having written, I don't really like writing,' he said,
adding, 'what a confession to have to make at my age'. He worked
always in bursts of energy, as he had written *Over the Mountain* in a
few days long ago, and was impatient with the work of shaping and
refining and reordering that almost every book—perhaps especially a
book of memoirs—needs. About the details of scholarship, on the

193

other hand, he was endlessly patient. He turned to preparing a new edition of his Everyman Gilchrist life of Blake. Both the Clarendon Press and the University of California Press were after it, he said gleefully, but 'Blake scholarship has advanced the hell of a long way since I started on Gilchrist at the beginning of WW II, and I've somehow got to get a grasp of all that's happened.' This, however, ended in a short book done in paperback and greatly abbreviated from his original text, with which he was disappointed. His dedicatory copy calls it 'this sadly amputated little book'.

A visit to an art exhibition in Palma brought a suggestion from the gallery director that he should write his reminiscences of Miro, with whom he had worked in New York more than thirty years earlier at S. W. Hayter's celebrated Atelier 17. Work was begun with characteristic enthusiasm. 'At 2.30 in the afternoon I sat down and set to work and, by 4.30 yesterday afternoon I'd got the rough draft, some 15,000 words typed out on the legal paper (which comes folded in quires) foolscap.' The book was

> one which could have been written by nobody else, and will reproduce material (particularly in color) which is equally unobtainable in any other place: i.e. the six poems which I did on copper plates with Miro in 1947, not only in their black and white versions, but also in various color versions printed in a method which I devised for Miro at the time.

This might all, as he said, be a pipe-dream, but he began to calculate how much money he would make if it all happened—only £600 from the Spanish edition perhaps, but what about England and America? He foresaw rich pickings in both countries. 'Although I won't be able to give you a copy with the lithograph in it (Miro lithographs now cost about $1000 apiece) I'll certainly give you a copy of the ordinary edition.' But this idea, too, faded to nothing, and so did others.

The problem of money, the problem of drink, the problem of health, the problem of loneliness: during his last decade, Ruthven fought an almost constant running battle with them all. He was a great survivor ('somehow or other the old jack-in-the-box pops up again'), but at times his poverty was extreme. There were occasions when he mentioned in passing that he had been living on pulses for a month, others—though these were rare—when he asked if I could send him some money, 'either in £10 or £5 notes, enclosed in the pages

Ruthven Todd: Some Details for a Portrait

of some pocket-book (preferably one you don't think I'm likely to have read)'. He recovered mobility so that he no longer had any need for sticks, although he tended to shuffle along rather slowly, but his total abstinence did not last, although he never so far as I know went back to spirits. When he came to stay we would give him bottles of cider or wine, which he carried about with him. He got through a gallon of cider in a few hours, and consumed wine in about the same quantity. He also continued to smoke his fierce Spanish cigarettes. His morning cough was terrifying to hear, but he did not let it impede his conversation. During one visit to England in 1970 he had to be rushed to hospital, and although he recovered, each time he was a little weaker.

How, without money, did he manage to make trips abroad? One maddening thing about Ruthven was that upon occasion he had quite large amounts of money—witness that evening at dinner already mentioned. In 1967 he got a second Guggenheim Fellowship—his references included Graves and Auden. He made plans for being careful about the money 'as travel costs so bloody much', but he was determined to get back to America. In one letter he spoke of his longing for it:

> I want to have a hot pastrami on rye, I want to look at the Charles River, I want to see Scully Square in Boston and the Italian Market the other side of the tracks. I want the smell of Bleecker Street, and even the too brilliant leaves around Groton on Hudson. I want to look at Butterfly-weed, the Galopogon and the Mariposa lily. I want to taste the difference between the Atlantic and the Pacific— the latter is saltier but not as salty as the Mediterranean. I want to walk on the beach at La Jolla and meet a seal at midnight and find an abalone on a rock at low tide, to see the tall girls in their light summer dresses, to smell the old fashioned smell of the Cedar Street Bar and the places where the Abstract Expressionists met. I want to see my friends and loves. I want to see Martha's Vineyard again.

He went back, not only on the Guggenheim (which produced no book), but again in 1972 to take a course about Blake in Buffalo, at the end of which the students gave a party for him, with a large cake which had a perfect facsimile of his signature on it. He paid another visit a couple of years later, and perhaps others too. Each time he worked out in advance that he would save enough to keep him in

Personal Meetings

Mallorca comfortably for a year, always he stayed in America until the money was gone.

When I read the brief inaccurate obituary notice in *The Times* I had not heard from Ruthven in more than four years. I hope and think that there was no estrangement between us. It seemed to me likely that he had at last given up hope of resuscitating his literary reputation (at the end of our correspondence he had turned to making a bibliography of his own writings), and so had no more need to bolster his resolution with letters to friends like me. When this memoir was almost complete I heard from his son Christopher, with some details of the last months:

> He was very ill last January, and when we saw him in the spring, we soon realized that he had not much time left. His emphysema was progressing, and causing him continual pain. He did little except listen to the jazz cassettes I sent him. I am told that during the summer he went back to smoking cigars—despite his doctor—but then he had always joked about cigarettes as his 'coughing nails'. He fell ill about two days before his death on 11 October . . . Mass was held in the village church by a most understanding priest, who did not want to offend the traditionally minded by saying the eucharist for an old heathen, but who did want to celebrate the memory of his and the villagers' old friend. Burial after mass was in a most romantic setting—in a niche behind the church, on the hillside, and in the moonlight, though it did have its comic moment, which made us all giggle. As they struggled to get the coffin into the niche (they finally had to put it in backwards), someone remarked: 'Trust Ruthven not to fit.'

He would have enjoyed the joke, but the last word about him shouldn't be comic. Ruthven had a sweetness of personality and an eternal youthful optimism that transcended the minor irritations he could cause, and there was something wholly admirable about his certainty that a life spent in pursuit of art, literature and romantic love was superior to all others. His novels are original, in the sense that nobody else could have written them. The best of his poetry was written while he was young, and it was produced while dreaming of the romantic love that was so often doomed, like that of the war-struck lovers in 'Tomorrow Will Come Soon':

Ruthven Todd: Some Details for a Portrait

To-morrow will come soon, too late
For some of these, of whom there will be none to tell
How once Love made him King of the Antipodes
And her Queen of Cockayne, or Princess of the Seas.

Perhaps the truest epitaph for him was written by Auden: 'He is that contemporary oddity, a poet who actually seems to be happy.' Happiness does not exclude passages of misery, and without doubt Ruthven knew them, but of all the friends of my youth there is no other of whom I could say with such certainty that he was a happy man.

(1978)

George Woodcock: An Old Friend

Last summer my wife and I finished a long driving and flying trip through the American south west with a visit to George and Inge Woodcock in Vancouver. We drove in an enormous air-conditioned monster across the Arizona and Mojave Deserts, staying in comfortable, efficiently run, almost identical motels on the way, and finding each motel set in the same terrible strip of neon-lighted Macdonalds ('over 19 billion sold'), Burger Kings ('have it your way'), Ramada Inns, Travelodges, Best Westerns. The list is long. Americans want the certainty of comfort everywhere, and an assurance that they can get quickly the sort of unvarying food they know, the hamburger or hot dog sloshed over with mayonnaise or given taste by mustard. The result is the strip, which is anything from one to three miles long. It is a pity that the things which make travel in America easy also make part of it hideous.

Our object was to combine a look at the south west with a quick flight to the University of Texas for a sight of my manuscripts and visits to friends—Sidney and Fanita Hertzmark in Albuquerque, Sandy and Hilary Mackendrick in Los Angeles, my lone western fan in Portland, Oregon. But I had known George much longer than any of these, since the thirties. After he left England in 1949 we had met only on his rare visits here, but I had sent a good many letters to 6429 McCleery Street, Vancouver. 'Take care you don't get off the bus at the wrong end of mythical McCleery Street,' wrote Roy Fuller, whose friendship with George went back almost as far as mine.

In fact the number comes from the baffling notation used in some American and Canadian cities, and McCleery is a short tree-lined street of considerable charm. The houses are detached and of varying design, with largish gardens kept green by sprinklers, and the architecture has the anonymous pleasantness of affluent suburbia. George and Inge's house was among the smallest in the street. There were splendid things in it, wall hangings given them by the Dalai Lama as a result of their visits to the Himalayas, a fine collection of Indian masks and artefacts. Everything about the house had an air of settled and comfortable calm, an impression somehow enhanced by

198

the food put out each night for the family of raccoons which crept up to the back porch, and the cat adopted because its claws had been removed by a previous owner so that it was unable to defend itself. For a week George and Inge entertained us nobly, with luncheon and evening parties, and a visit to Vancouver Island where, a quarter of a century earlier, they had built a house. George had arranged for me to give lectures at two local universities, and we talked on the radio for half an hour about literature and politics, George Orwell and Wyndham Lewis, our own social attitudes past and present.

George's reputations in England and in Canada are very different. In England he is known principally for critical and biographical studies of Orwell, Aldous Huxley, Herbert Read. An older generation of readers is aware of his standing as a philosophical exponent of Anarchism, and of his books on Godwin and Proudhon. His travel books, and his studies of British India and of Canada, are much less known. When shrimp-browed George Woodcock was TUC General Secretary, it sometimes used to be necessary to make conversational distinctions between them.

In Canada, on the other hand, George is a national literary asset. His book on Orwell won the Governor-General's Award, *Canada and the Canadians* is naturally a good seller, he edits *Canadian Literature*, and is much in demand on radio and television as a sort of radical analyst, particularly of primitive societies. A couple of years ago he spent some months in the South Seas with a television team, and shortly after we left them he and Inge were off to make a television film about the Doukhobors, the Russian religious sect living in British Columbia who refuse to accept state authority in the running of their lives. Primitive societies evidently attract him strongly, although it is a little difficult to reconcile this attraction with the firmly respectable occupant of 6429 McCleery Street, who appeared on any slightly formal occasion wearing a suit (I thought he looked faintly disconcerted by the jacket and trousers I wore at my first lecture), and who mixed a pitcher of powerful martinis with a certain slow gravity at six o'clock every evening. The respect and affection in which he was held, not merely in his own circle, were unmistakable. After our radio session the young technician who had been taping it came up to say how much he admired the article George had written for a little radical paper about the state of affairs at CBC, the Canadian Broadcasting Corporation. And around the luncheon and supper

199

tables there was plenty of evidence of the regard felt for George's opinions, as well as for his martinis. He made no attempt to dominate conversation, sitting for the most part like Buddha, foursquare and sympathetic, sometimes gently smiling. In fields where his knowledge was particular, however—in relation to Herzen and Bakunin, for instance—he spoke decisively. About the general iniquity of state control, and the benefits that would be derived from the decentralization of almost all enterprises, also, he talked with a certainty that hardly considered the possibility of contradiction. George's links with Anarchist groups had not been close for many years, but his feeling that Anarchism would be an ideal state of affairs if it could be achieved evidently remained unchanged.

A certain tolerance is necessary when old friends meet again after a long lapse of time. One's ideas have solidified or, as one might less kindly say, ossified and opposite points of view seem evidently wrong. During the week in which K and I were with George and Inge, I had clearly brought home to me the immense difference in viewpoint between a Western materialist like me with no faith in the perfectibility of man, and a romantic idealist like George, whose whole adult life has been based on a belief in the naturalness of voluntary cooperation among individuals within a group. As I listened to George outlining his hopes of social change in Canada, and saying that the first step was a questionnaire that would be issued in a popular magazine, as Inge told me of the spellbinding revelations in Jung's autobiography which was her current reading, I began to feel a strong kinship with almost any kind of organized society. I had an inclination to sing the praises even of Macdonald and Burger King, and to praise the architecture of Howard Johnson's. But, I reflected, there was nothing new about this. George's ideas about the organization of society and the nature of human beings had always differed greatly from mine. How odd it was, when there were so few subjects that we could talk about without at least implicit disagreement, that we had become such firm friends.

I first met George Woodcock early in 1938, after he had sent in some poems to my little magazine *Twentieth Century Verse*. The figure I met was physically and in style much like my host in Vancouver. His gentleness of manner was belied by a square pugnacious face, his serious and at times solemn conversation was starred by flashes of wit and bursts of outrageous exaggerative fancy. We met first, I think, in a tea-shop—I used to ask prospective contributors to tea so that I could look them over. George was living at Marlow and working as a railway clerk, and we got on well enough to continue seeing each other. A touch of the exaggerative fancy I have mentioned comes in George's story of a meeting in a Soho patisserie, where I told him that I had eaten thirteen cream cakes, and (he says) produced the bill to prove it. I don't doubt that George believes this to be true, but it is certainly three-quarters fabricated, by which I mean that there may have been three cream cakes but certainly there were not thirteen (would I have stopped at an unlucky number?). We were born in the same year, and I think liked each other partly because we were both loners, remote from the Bloomsbury and Lehmannesque literary circles of the time, and alien also from the homosexual sodality of the period. A little later, in the months before the war, George used to come to drinking sessions with half a dozen other poets at the Duke of York pub in Victoria Street. He has written about these himself in a lively piece of reminiscence. They sometimes ended in an underground flat I lived in at the time (the large living-room had no window, only a skylight), but I can't remember whether he ever came along there. If he did, I am sure he took no part in the mild undignified horseplay indulged in occasionally by Ruthven Todd, Keidrych Rhys and others.

His poems were Audenesque in manner and approach like much youthful work of the time, but they were not just carbon copies of the master. Some, like a poem he gave me at one of our first meetings, 'Ballad of an Orphan Hand', expressed a thwarted sexuality which marked his poetry at this time. This poem had been printed for him by the Anarchist bookseller Charlie Lahr in an edition of a very few copies, and I suppose is now a rarity. Another and more interesting poetic vein exploited the treatment of some mythical incident in a realistic yet still ambiguous manner. He did this brilliantly in a poem called 'The Island', one of the finest and most typical poems of the decade. It begins:

> The oars fell from our hands. We climbed the dark
> Slopes of kelp to the stairway up the rock.
> Scott went first, grasping the fraying rope.
> The rest of us followed, dragging the iron rack.
>
> The crest was bare, but after a scanty search
> In a bird's burrow we found the hunted man.

Personal Meetings

His flesh was naked and hard as barren earth,
His arms like scythes. His eyes spoke like a gun.

And a third Woodcockian aspect was expressed (surprisingly for me, who at this time thought of him as a thwarted puritan) in a strongly sensual feeling for luxuriant nature, expressed in poems like 'Song For the South'.

I am writing about George as a poet, and this in youth is how he thought of himself. The war did not stop him writing poems, but it crystallized attitudes that had been amorphous, shaped and hardened his character. I don't know just when he became convinced that Anarchism was a good way of life, but from the time the war began he was a pacifist, determined that he would not kill other human beings. His conscientious objections were accepted, and he worked on the land during the war. He came and spoke as a witness at my own examination, but my grounds for objection were so eccentric (refusal to be involved in a capitalist war) that my rejection was inevitable. He started the small literary pacifist magazine *Now* but gave it up after three or four issues, I suppose because he lacked funds. I went into the Army and we saw little of each other until I was invalided out early in 1944, although I remember one riotous evening when K and I, in George's company, sang 'The Internationale' loudly in a tube train. According to George and K I sang in a subterranean way. Perhaps I had had less to drink.

When I emerged again into civilian clothes we met quite frequently. We were both involved in an organization called the Freedom Defence Committee—although 'organization' is perhaps too strong a word for a loose linking of individuals who included George Orwell, Fenner Brockway, Herbert Read and a clutch of Anarchists and pacifists. The Committee's object was to help victims of bureaucratic repression, and particularly to obtain the release of people still held in detention after the end of the war. Since a good many of these had Fascist inclinations, the Civil Liberties Union was not much inclined to help them. George was Secretary of the Committee, and did an enormous amount of work.

He was now living with Inge, who later became his wife, and *Now* was revived in a much enlarged and improved form. Looking back on the issues that appeared between 1944 and 1947, it seems to me much the best periodical of a radical kind in England during those years. The general editorial attitude combined radicalism with the utmost

202

George Woodcock: An Old Friend

freedom for contributors. Everybody wrote for love (or perhaps I should say more cautiously that I was not paid for my contributions) in an air rich with the scent of almost any possibility. This is not to say that the magazine gave print to any masterpieces—although Orwell's 'How The Poor Die' is one of his most memorable pieces of realistic reporting—but for anybody wanting to know what non-Communist literary radicals thought and hoped during those years *Now* must be an indispensable document, as *Horizon*, for example, is not.

Now ended in 1947, when the emotional and practical burdens of running it proved too great. By this time George had turned from poetry to prose. His railway job had finished with the war. He was writing to make a living, but the subjects he chose were always ones that interested him, and nothing was done simply for cash. Between 1946 and 1949 he produced books about William Godwin, Aphra Behn, Oscar Wilde and Kropotkin, as well as a collection of essays called *The Writer and Politics*. Some of these were written for a small short-lived firm called the Porcupine Press, in which both he and Herbert Read had an editorial interest, and none can have made him much money. Their merits vary, but the scholarly level of the biographical-critical works is remarkably high. *The Anarchist Prince*, the book about Kropotkin written in collaboration with Ivan Avakumovic, and the trail-blazing book about Godwin's life and ideas, are still necessary reading for anybody interested in the subjects; the studies of Aphra Behn and Wilde have personal and sometimes vivid illuminations to offer; and several of the critical essays are sharply original. Orwell thought the piece about him the best that had been written. George must have worked extraordinarily hard during these years, and his health was not perfect.

I remember an evening at a flat in Highgate, with George stretched on a sofa, pale and obviously in pain, when Inge said they were going to Canada (George had been born there, and possessed a Canadian passport) to build a house for themselves at Sooke on Vancouver Island. It seemed to me a visionary, slightly risible project, and I don't doubt that I made this clear. Roy Fuller, who had edited a selection from Byron for the ill-fated Porcupine, prefaced it by a lively dedicatory poetic letter to George which ended: 'Goodbye, and Godwin bless'. But like me he thought that they would soon be back . . .

The story of how George and Inge failed to build, and then did build, their house on Vancouver Island, doesn't belong to these sketchy personal reminiscences. But how, standing back as one can do after the passage of nearly thirty years since we knew each other well, do I think about George Woodcock?

'I learn by going where I have to go': that line of Theodore Roethke's applies wonderfully well. The forces that pushed George to write poetry in youth are no longer of major importance to him. He has turned into a literary all-rounder, discovering his strengths to be in description and analysis, in the perpetual curiosity he feels about different kinds of social community, in expression of a radical but never dogmatic view of the world. Almost everybody who lives by writing makes compromises of one kind or another, but George has compromised less than most. If he goes to visit the Doukhobors it is because he is interested by their rejection of many things that most of us take for granted, when he studies the history of Canada it is in part at least because he feels there are lessons to be learned from it. His experience of feuds among the Anarchists would have soured many people, but they have done nothing of the kind to George, who retains a belief in the essential truth of Kropotkin's mutual aid, even though he must have seen it contradicted often in practice.

In person he is extraordinarily courteous, something much more than merely polite. Somebody who had corresponded with him remarked to me recently on the patience with which he had answered lengthy enquiries, and the trouble he had taken to be positively helpful. He remains an unswerving individualist, prepared to argue fiercely upon a point of principle, but he would never move from the general to the personal. If one wanted proof positive of his innate courtesy it would be in his readiness to put up with somebody who differs so much, and so vocally, from most of his ideas as me. Most of us change as we grow older, not for the better, but George Woodcock today seems to me wonderfully like the person I knew in the thirties and forties, even in a physical sense. The brown hair has changed to a white silkiness, there are deeper grooves in the face and the mouth has thinned a little, but he remains totally recognizable as the same person. And his concerns and attitudes, the sweetness and serious-ness of his personality, have also survived unchanged. If we were all like George Woodcock, the principle of mutual aid among human beings might be something more than a romantic illusion.

(1977)

A Year in Academe

When, one evening after dinner in London, Bill Pritchard—that is, Professor William H. Pritchard, chairman that year of the English Department at Amherst College in Massachusetts, and a fellow admirer of Wyndham Lewis—asked casually whether I would like to go out for a year as visiting writer, I said with a casualness equal to Bill's own that it sounded a splendid idea. . . .

Eighteen months later I found myself at Amherst. I had been undeterred by the fact that I had never taught, and indeed was unacquainted with academic life. I shivered a little, it is true, at the frequent volleys of memoranda Bill sent across the Atlantic before I arrived, memoranda addressed to his colleagues after meetings. I quote from one of them, about the course in freshman English. We were, it seemed, to begin with the Norton Anthology of Modern Poetry, go on to collections of stories by Hawthorne and Flannery O'Connor, and then:

> Suppose we took a breath and picked up an Arnold essay or two, for the purpose of hearing a Sage speak largely about large matters of Culture, Literature and Society. We don't need to clutch Matt to our bosoms. Just say, now here we are reading a Sage, and what is that like? I do think that 'On the Modern Element in Literature' would be provocative and help to give, at least tentatively, a context for the works to follow.

And what were they? 'Would Thucydides be attemptable? It would then look like this after the Norton Anthology, Hawthorne and O'Connor—Arnold, Thucydides (?), *Aeneid* (?all?), *Julius Caesar*, *Under Western Eyes*, *St Joan*, Orwell's essays, and out by way of some contemporary poems or the new Doctorow.'

Could it possibly be that we were meant to teach all of these books in a fourteen-week term? I disregarded this as a prospect too appalling to contemplate, but it proved to be the case. Thucydides and Doctorow disappeared, and we did only the first six books of the *Aeneid*, but there were replacements for the works omitted. When Bill's wife Marietta came round on the morning before my first class to offer a little reassurance, I felt in need of it. By this time, too, I had

Personal Meetings

become uncomfortably aware that, apart from one or two Professors Emeritus who rarely appeared, I was the oldest person on campus. Somehow, however, what had seemed almost impossible was done. There were eighteen freshmen in my English class, and they were by no means all Easterners. A couple came from the West Coast, half a dozen from the South. Four came from private schools, the rest were state educated. They were without exception polite, pleasant, and eager to learn. The work of perhaps a third among them improved remarkably during the semester, and when they expressed general approval of me at the end of it, I felt momentarily like Mr Chips.

Amherst is a small rich college. The financial problems of its early years, which culminated in 1844 when the unpopular President Humphrey resigned 'before the institution was entirely ruined' as one historian puts it, belong to another world. The college now has a stock portfolio worth over $32 million, and it owns a sizeable part of the town. The students, all male when I was there although it has since become co-educational, numbered around 1,300. The cost of tuition, room and board is around $6,000 a year. The ratio of faculty to students is high, 1 to 9. Among colleges and universities in the east, only Harvard accepted a smaller percentage of applicants this year. Princeton, Dartmouth and Yale are all a little easier to enter than Amherst.

The students might fairly be called a select group. Perhaps it is not surprising that one of the graffiti in the college lavatories says: 'Amherst = social parasitism = training-ground of social uselessness', and that another reads: 'I like Amherst, the rich boys' playground', an observation to which a wit has added: 'I like rich boys'. Yet to a visiting Englishman the suggestion that Amherst gives an easy life to a leisured class doesn't seem persuasive. Distinctions by accent are much harder to make in the United States than in England, and in any case 60 per cent of the students have reached the college through public education, and 30 per cent receive financial support in the form of scholarships and loans. The freshmen from private schools like Choate and Andover were in general more self-assured, but they were not necessarily better informed than the rest.

In fact, a number of my freshmen in this select group were extremely ignorant. Only three out of the eighteen were able to tell me what a sonnet was. In part this was because they were not at this stage specializing in English, but putting a toe in the water to see what it felt like before deciding to major in Economics, Psychology, Political

206

Science—or English. For some of them the discovery of English Literature was more like a cold plunge than the dipped toe they intended. It would be safe to say that a third of them had never read a line of Matthew Arnold, and another third knew only one or two poems. The rest, on the other hand, had already encountered the Sage talking largely, and were quite prepared to talk largely about him themselves.

How did one deal with such a mixed collection? At our weekly departmental meetings the guide-lines laid down—laid down with care, after fairly vivid argument—often seemed to be devised for those who could respond easily rather than those who, to change the watery image, found each successive book part of an increasingly difficult obstacle course. They were designed, I thought, for an ideal student rather than the actual flawed article under our eyes. But perhaps this is inevitable, and perhaps it is a good thing always to aim at the top level of your class. The system finds its justification in the transformation of these raw freshmen into fourth-year seniors with reactions almost invariably both quick and sharp.

Some of my freshmen, however, found the course both indigestible and infuriating, and their very vocal indignation was not lessened by a final examination in which they were given free rein to write about Lenny Bruce. One of the brightest of them used the occasion for a moralistic attack, written with considerable verve, in the form of an 'open letter' to the English Department:

> The examination is intellectually insulting, and representative of the callous, archaic, unthinking, irresponsible, disheveled way that members of the English Department have conducted themselves in relation to freshman English ... All the members of the Department, those hip, free-thinking guys, those models of the open mind, have opened the way to the filth, decay and corruption of today's society. They do not have enough sense to recognize Bruce for what he was, a decrepit junkie, misdirected and potentially dangerous, the Richard Nixon of his time. They salute him, hail him, glorify him ... You, oh you members of this sterling academic community, are responsible for the hypodermic syringes and pornography on 42nd Street, for the collapse of our language, our writing and our art.

I was happy to read his prefatory note: 'Mr Symons, you are an outsider, and so not responsible,' but it seemed a tribute to the free-thinking English Department that he should have been able to write his open letter without worrying about the result. Not that he had any need to worry. I gave him an A grade.

The Visiting Writer (the capital letters are the college's) is concerned also with Advanced Composition, which might elsewhere be called Creative Writing. There was a lot of competition for admission to this course, in which students wrote poems and short stories which were then discussed by the class and by me. One applicant told me that he had married a year or two earlier, out on the West Coast. 'Then my wife was murdered in this really *bizarre* way, and I want to write about it, kind of documentary fiction, it's not a class I want really but personal guidance.'

I turned him down with a shudder, but rashly accepted a student named Manzer, in spite of Bill Pritchard's head-shaking. 'He's a trouble-maker,' Bill warned me, and he was right. Manzer, tall, thin, gingery and inclined to twitch, produced very little work of his own, but criticized everybody else, often in wounding terms. He would wait until other people had finished, and then say, 'Just a few points,' as though he rather than I was conducting the class. To circumvent this I tried to get him to speak first. 'Any comments, Manzer?' He would shake his head, but at the end his hand would go up. 'Just a few points . . .' I got rid of him at the end of the first semester. In a year's teaching I found two poets and one short-story writer who showed green hints of promise. An average sprouting perhaps, but it seemed to me thin.

Most of the poets were concerned only to express themselves, which they did in the most dismal dribbles of 'free' verse. Only a few had ever tried to work within any poetic form. Pressed by me into writing sestinas and villanelles they resisted at first, but ended up enjoying it. A few, however, complained that it was hard work. It is very likely that they had joined in the expectation that Advanced Composition would be a gut course.

And what is a gut course? It is one in which you do practically no written work, and get a good grade at the end on the strength of a single paper. 'You must have a gut,' said one ironical article in the *Amherst Student*. The classic gut of my year was a course called 'Human Sexuality', known colloquially as 'Holes and Poles', which was taken by nearly a quarter of the students. Why do you need a gut? Because in the other courses you are forced to work so hard. That, at least, is the theory. The practice varies considerably.

A Year in Academe

A student at Amherst, as at most American colleges and universities, takes four courses in each semester, thirty-two in his four years of education. To graduate as an English major he must have taken eight English courses in those four years. To work for honours he has to produce a thesis on an approved subject. I was adviser to two honours students. One of them was to write about George Orwell. The thesis of the other, Chris Bogan, was to be his own poems. And who would judge whether his poems deserved honours? Well, in the first instance I would. Later on a number of my English Department colleagues would consider his work. This practice, revolutionary in English eyes, is common in the United States.

I was soon engaged in furious argument with the Orwell student, whose ideas were almost totally opposed to mine. The end of our discussions was that he abandoned the thesis, something about which I felt slightly guilty. Bogan was another matter. When he came into my office, I recognized him as one of four students who had, ever so gently, interrogated me earlier in the year when I had paid a flying visit to inspect and be inspected. Gentleness was, indeed, the key to his character. His voice was quiet, his manner nervous. He talked about his poems, and his doubts of their value, at length but hesitantly, in a way pleasantly different from what I had come to recognize as the bright student's characteristic eager aggression. He was fascinated by English literary life, and by modern English poets. Had I met Philip Larkin? What was he like? What about Roy Fuller? Did they write poems easily, or was it as difficult for them as for him? Did I know of a collection of poetic manuscripts that he could study which gave different versions of the same poem?

At long sessions we went through his work in detail. The first poems he brought me were near-Larkin, then they veered to almost-Frost, and in the end to something that seemed a genuine Bogan voice, a little naive and not grandly eloquent, but expressive and personal. Just before Christmas, when the first snow fell, he produced a short, slight poem that I liked:

> Kindness is not a thing you wear,
> That you put on and off with care
> Never to pull a thread or stretch
> It out of shape. Kindness doesn't stretch
> Or shrink or fade. There's never a need
> To put it in the wash.—Indeed

Personal Meetings

> Kindness is not a thing at all.
> It's something like the first snowfall
> Of the season, the way the snow
> Is gentle in its overthrow
> Of the bare, half-frozen ground,
> The way it falls softly, without a sound.

Before the snow, during the long fall season after our arrival in August, Amherst seemed a lotus land. The changing colours of leaves and bushes, masses of dazzling reds, purples and shades of brown; the undemanding pace of life, an eight-minute walk up College Hill past enormous birds and nearly-tame squirrels to my office in Johnson Chapel or to the splendid Robert Frost Library instead of a half-hour journey to the London Library—it was easy to see this as something nobody but an incorrigible city-dweller like myself would ever want to leave.

My wife and I stayed first for a few days at the Dickinson Homestead on Main Street, where Emily was born and where she lived for her last thirty years. Like much else in South Amherst this formidable red brick mansion, built in 1813, is owned by the college. Visitors are shown round on Tuesdays and Fridays, but there are few relics of Emily, although a child's chair and a kitchen clock in her bedroom-workroom were Dickinson family pieces. Later we moved to a typical white-painted clapboard house, and quickly tuned in to some of the basic facts of American small town life. In Amherst there is no individual butcher or greengrocer, and no public transport within the town. Everything has to be bought at the supermarket, and a car is a necessity. How else are you going to shop? And so a large car park is a necessity too. We discovered the excellence of American shoes, the horror of most American bread (there were sixty varieties in the town supermarket, almost all of them feeling and tasting like sponge rubber), the comparative cheapness of American liquor. We understood why all the houses have mosquito screens. We felt ourselves to be acclimatized.

Not, however, to the snow. The snow changed the landscape, making it more romantically beautiful, and it also changed our feelings about Amherst as lotus land. Snow was there when we ate Christmas dinner with Bill and Marietta, snow had to be ploughed out of the drive after each storm, snow was a reminder that we were a long way from home. The students had gone, the campus was empty.

210

A Year in Academe

Sitting in my study at the Frost Library while I worked on a book about Poe, I looked out on a suitably desolate scene, an endless white landscape under a sky of slate. All this continued for weeks. It seemed, symbolically at least, to end when students began drifting back ahead of time. In the library one day a heavily bearded figure rose to greet me, smiling. It was Bogan, a formidable stranger in this disguise.

The spring semester began, bringing a course on the crime story to replace my freshman English, a mostly new section of Advanced Compositionists, a new editor for the *Amherst Student*. The *Student* appeared twice weekly during term, a paper generally of twelve pages, edited, written and wholly run by the students. The editor changed yearly, and had to do his eight courses a year, with no allowance made for his journalistic work. The paper contained news and opinion about the college, sections on sports and the arts, and its journalistic level was remarkably high. The money to run it was provided by the college, and no visible censorship was imposed. A single issue might contain an article on the 'drug culture', a piece about the ethics of college investments, a study of the curriculum with suggestions for its improvement. The President and the faculty were generally referred to by their surnames, and sometimes attacked. President Ward wrote to rebut one attack, more in anger than in sorrow, but made no attempt to stop it. No paper like the *Student* could exist in Britain, and no other I saw in America was on such a high plane in writing and presentation.

The crime story course began with Poe and Collins, and moved by way of Sherlock Holmes and Father Brown, Christie and Sayers, Hammett and Chandler, le Carré and Deighton, to a book of my own and one by Patricia Highsmith. It was a success, if one can judge by the enthusiasm of the students and the excellence of many papers. Students brought in to me crime memorabilia I had never seen, like a magazine section of a San Francisco newspaper devoted wholly to Hammett. Four of my freshman English students had followed me to this course, including the one so disgusted when asked to write about Lenny Bruce. His feelings, always fervent, fluctuated considerably. Now he was enchanted by Patricia Highsmith's criminal hero Tom Ripley, and wrote a fine essay about him.

March, April, May: examinations, and considerations of theses. Students made an oral defence of their theses, under questioning by

211

two or three members of the Department, with the student's adviser serving as a kind of moderator. I acted as Bogan's adviser, and as questioner in relation to two other theses, one on Oscar Wilde and another on Auden, this last written by a blind student named Adrian Spratt. After the oral defence a recommendation was made that the student should graduate *cum laude*, *magna cum laude* or *summa cum laude*. If a thesis was rejected, the student received the degree Bachelor of Arts, *rite*.

The fates of the students I was concerned with were interestingly varied. The Oscar Wilde thesis was agreed by everybody to be wholly inadequate, and the student graduated *rite*. Then came Bogan, now beardless again. Soon after questioning began it was apparent, to me if not to him, that the examiners liked his poems less than I did. He graduated *magna cum laude*, respectably enough I'd have thought, but he was disappointed.

And last, Adrian Spratt. His thesis was on the movement of Auden's early poems towards sincerity, and its quality seemed a remarkable tribute to the success of a flexible education. What begins for freshmen as something that seems to an outsider almost haphazard, with them being allowed and even encouraged to take in the same term courses in philosophy, classical civilization, Russian literature and twentieth-century European history (these were actually taken in a single semester by Spratt), has become canalized in the final year into an intensive course of study.

How is a blind student to become fully aware of Auden? An immense amount of material not available in braille was taped for him by willing helpers, so that he had a complete view not only of the poems but of the biographical background. He had 'read', and used in his thesis, Isherwood's *Lions and Shadows*, Spender's *World Within World*, my *Thirties*, John Fuller's *Guide to Auden*. His adviser, Richard Cody, spent hours talking to him, arguing, elaborating on difficult points, suggesting necessary footnotes. I spent some time with him myself, and found him a true Auden scholar. At his oral examination, he was completely composed, knew exactly what he had put into the thesis and where it was to be found. He graduated *summa cum laude*.

Commencement—or as we would call it, graduation—day. In gown and mortarboard, borrowed trappings of professordom, I sit outside the Frost Library listening to speeches, looking at the students as they

A Year in Academe

file up to receive degrees. What thoughts stir after a year in American academe?

It must reinforce that sense of openness, warmth, even naïveté, in the American character. This is partly expressed through informality of dress (I could have spent the whole year at Amherst without a suit, quite unembarrassed) and of style. The President doesn't invite you to an informal luncheon in his garden, he asks you to a cook-out in his backyard. But reinforced too is awareness of the bureaucratic and obscure language that creeps through American academies. You don't oppose something, you 'move into an adversary relationship towards' it; you don't ask for support but say 'we would be more than happy to have your input'; you don't talk about sex but 'discuss male-female relationships'. I wasn't surprised when some students said that they couldn't understand the set assignments. I often had trouble with them myself.

And what about Amherst, the Amherst experience as students and faculty tend to call it? I think anybody must come away impressed by a sort of fervour, a sense of dedication to scholarly ideals in the faculty. More than a hint of self-conscious superiority goes with it, and that is often communicated to the students. Amherst men are arrogant, said two girls at nearby Smith College who were in one of my classes. Well, perhaps. 'Amherst encourages idealistic ideas, and then encourages us to be sceptical about those ideas,' Adrian Spratt said in a graduation speech. Perfectly true, but I liked better the comment of another graduating student made (where else?) in the *Amherst Student*. 'When I go back into the world I realize that in a lot of ways this really is Camelot, and you just have to appreciate it for what it is.' That seems just about right. Camelot, given stability and severity by quite a bit of New England high-mindedness. After a year, that seemed a good recipe for a liberal education.

(1976)

213